MORAL PHILOSOPHY:

INCLUDING

THEORETICAL AND PRACTICAL ETHICS.

BY

JOSEPH HAVEN, D. D., L. L. D.,

PROFESSOR IN CHICAGO THEOLOGICAL SEMINARY; LATELY PROFESSOR OF INTELLECTUAL AND MORAL PHILOSOPHY IN AMHERST COLLEGE; AUTHOR OF "MENTAL PHILOSOPHY."

SHELDON & COMPANY,
NEW YORK & CHICAGO.

Dr. Haven's Valuable Series of School and College Text-Books.

MENTAL PHILOSOPHY $2 00

MORAL PHILOSOPHY 1 75

HISTORY OF ANCIENT AND MODERN PHILOSOPHY. (In press).

PREFACE.

THE present volume is the result of the author's studies while Professor of Mental and Moral Philosophy in Amherst College, and was originally prepared as a course of lectures to the senior class in that Institution. It was intended as a sequel to the author's treatise on Mental Philosophy. The favorable reception of that work by the public has induced him to give this also to the press, with the hope that it may be of service to the cause of Education.

Few departments of science have so rich a literature as Moral Philosophy. And yet, by general concession, there are few good text-books of the science. Of the treatises now most generally in use in our schools and colleges, some appear deficient in thorough scientific discussion of the principles and true theory of morals; others, again, in practical detail. In some of them, under the title of Moral Philosophy, topics are discussed which more properly pertain to Psychology, — as, for example, the phenomenon of Conscience, and the problems of the Will, — while the *history* of ethical opinion

— one of the widest and richest fields of investigation — has almost universally been overlooked.

It has been the aim of the author to give, as far as possible, a *science* of morals, and not merely a treatise on moral subjects. With a view to this, the principles which lie at the foundation of the science are first discussed, as concisely as may be, in the opening division of the work; and in the subsequent division these principles are considered in their application to the practical duties and relations of life.

Of the several classes of duties, that class which pertains to the state — or Political Ethics — has received in these pages a fuller discussion than is usually given in works of this kind; yet not fuller, perhaps, than its relative importance demands. It has seemed to the author that the youth of a free country should be carefully instructed in the first principles of civil government, and in the rights and obligations of the citizen. It is the proper province of Moral Philosophy, which treats of the various duties of life, to do this. Yet, strange as it may seem, no branch of moral science has probably received less attention, in this country, than Political Ethics.

J. H.

Chicago, August 1859

CONTENTS.

INTRODUCTION.

Page
NATURE AND PROVINCE OF MORAL PHILOSOPHY, . . 15

DIVISION FIRST.

THEORETICAL ETHICS.

CHAPTER I.

THE NATURE OF RIGHT, ... 21

SECTION I. — RIGHT IN ITSELF CONSIDERED, ... 21
SECTION II. — RIGHT AS DISTINGUISHED FROM OTHER IDEAS OF SIMILAR IMPORT, ... 23

CHAPTER II.

THE GROUND OF RIGHT, ... 27

CHAPTER III.

THE RULE OF RIGHT, ... 50

CHAPTER IV.

Page

THE PROVINCE OF RIGHT, ... 59

SECTION I.—WHAT IS A MORAL ACTION? 59

SECTION II.—IN WHAT CONSISTS THE MORALITY OF ANY GIVEN ACT? 63

CHAPTER V.

FACULTIES OF MIND COGNIZANT OF RIGHT, ... 67

CHAPTER VI.

HISTORIC SKETCH OF OPINIONS RESPECTING THE NATURE AND GROUND OF RIGHT, ... 71

DIVISION SECOND.

PRACTICAL ETHICS.

PRELIMINARY ANALYSIS AND CLASSIFICATION, . . 89

PART I.

DUTIES TO SELF.

CHAPTER I.

SELF-SUPPORT, ... 92

CHAPTER II.

SELF-DEFENCE, ... 95

CHAPTER III.

Page
SELF-CONTROL, ... 100

CHAPTER IV.

SELF-CULTURE, ... 104

PART II.

DUTIES TO SOCIETY.

CHAPTER I.

DUTIES PERTAINING TO LIFE, ... 107

CHAPTER II.

DUTIES PERTAINING TO LIBERTY, ... 116
SECTION I. — SLAVERY DEFINED, ... 118
SECTION II. — SLAVERY, AS THUS DEFINED, A MORAL WRONG, 121
SECTION III. — EFFECT OF SLAVERY ON THE NATIONAL MORALS, AND THE NATIONAL WEALTH, ... 126
SECTION IV. — ARGUMENTS IN FAVOR OF SLAVERY, . . 130

CHAPTER III.

DUTIES PERTAINING TO PROPERTY, ... 142
SECTION I. — FOUNDATION OF THE RIGHT OF PROPERTY, . 142
SECTION II. — ADVANTAGES OF THE INSTITUTION OF PROPERTY, 148
SECTION III. — MODES IN WHICH PROPERTY MAY BE ACQUIRED, 154
SECTION IV. — DIFFERENT KINDS OF PROPERTY, . . . 157
SECTION V. — CRIMES AGAINST PROPERTY, ... 160

CHAPTER IV.

Page

DUTIES PERTAINING TO REPUTATION, ... 167

SECTION I. — SLANDER DEFINED, ... 169
SECTION II. — WHAT THE LAW OF REPUTATION FORBIDS, . 170
SECTION III. — REASONS FOR OBSERVING THE LAW OF REPUTATION, ... 174

CHAPTER V.

DUTIES PERTAINING TO VERACITY, ... 176

SECTION I. — TRUTHFULNESS IN COMMON DISCOURSE, . . 177
SECTION II. — VERACITY AS REGARDS PROMISES, . . . 184
SECTION III. — VERACITY IN RESPECT TO OATHS, . . . 190

PART III.

DUTIES TO THE FAMILY.

CHAPTER I.

DUTIES OF THE MARRIAGE RELATION, ... 198

CHAPTER II.

DUTIES OF THE PARENTAL RELATION, ... 206

SECTION I. — DUTIES OF PARENTS, ... 206
SECTION II. — DUTIES OF CHILDREN, ... 214

PART IV.

DUTIES TO THE STATE.

CHAPTER I.

Page

NATURE AND FOUNDATION OF CIVIL GOVERNMENT, 221

SECTION I. — ORIGIN AND OBJECT OF CIVIL GOVERNMENT, 223
SECTION II. — FOUNDATION OF CIVIL GOVERNMENT, . . . 228
SECTION III. — HISTORIC SKETCH — DIFFERENT OPINIONS AS TO THE NATURE OF CIVIL GOVERNMENT, . 239

CHAPTER II.

VARIOUS FORMS OF CIVIL GOVERNMENT, ... 243

SECTION I. — ANALYSIS OF THE SEVERAL FUNCTIONS AND FORMS OF GOVERNMENT, ... 244
SECTION II. — HISTORICAL SKETCH OF FORMS OF GOVERNMENT, 249

CHAPTER III.

DUTIES OF THE SUBJECT TO THE STATE, ... 271

CHAPTER IV.

DUTIES OF THE STATE TO ITS SUBJECTS, ... 283

CHAPTER V.

DUTIES OF STATE TO STATE, ... 308

SECTION I. — GENERAL RELATIONS AND DUTIES OF STATES TO EACH OTHER, ... 308
SECTION II. — ETHICAL RELATIONS OF REPUBLICAN STATES TO EACH OTHER, ... 322

PART V.

DUTIES TO GOD.

CHAPTER I.

Page

OF THE FEELINGS TOWARDS GOD, ... 326

CHAPTER II.

OF OBEDIENCE, ... 332

CHAPTER III.

OF WORSHIP, ... 337

SECTION I. — OF PRAYER, ... 338

SECTION II. — OF THE SABBATH, ... 346

I. — PRESUMPTION IN FAVOR OF A SABBATH.

II. — INSTITUTION AND AUTHORITY OF THE SABBATH.

CONFLICT OF DUTIES, ... 359

AUTHORITIES, ... 363

MORAL PHILOSOPHY.

INTRODUCTION.

NATURE AND PROVINCE OF MORAL PHILOSOPHY.

Moral Philosophy, what.—Moral Philosophy is the science which treats of morals—the science of right. Natural Philosophy teaches us the laws of external nature; Intellectual Philosophy, the laws of the human mind; Moral Philosophy has to do with the laws of human conduct and duty. As thus defined, it is equivalent to Ethics. It may be termed, also, the science of duties, inasmuch as right and duty are, as regards moral action, one and the same.

Term used in a wider sense.—By the earlier English writers the term *Moral Philosophy* was used in a much more extended sense, to denote in general the science of mind, in distinction from physical science—whatever treats of intellectual in distinction from material things. As thus employed, it includes psychology as well as other sciences; and this use is still, to some extent, prevalent.

Thus many of the works of English and Scotch philosophers on psychology are termed *Moral* Philosophy. By French writers, also, the *morale* is frequently placed in contrast with the *physique.*

Indeed, the dividing line between mental and moral science has not, as yet, been very closely drawn, for the most part, by those who have written upon either. Many of our own most popular works on Moral Philosophy treat of topics which properly pertain to psychology, as, *e. g.*, the nature of Conscience, the Sensibilities, the Will, and other topics of like nature. These are faculties of the mind, and, as such, it pertains to psychology to explain and unfold them. Moral Philosophy, so far as it has occasion to make use of these phenomena, must go to psychology for the facts and the explanations, just as it must go to astronomy for the facts and laws of planetary motion; or to logic for the laws of thought and forms of reasoning. Its proper office is to teach, not logic, nor astronomy, nor psychology, but the science of right — of duty. It has to do neither with the affections, the emotions, nor the will, except so far as these are involved in the investigation and statement of duty.

Intimate connection of Mental with Moral Philosophy. — The connection between the two sciences is indeed very intimate; and for this reason they should be all the more carefully distinguished. The very idea of right is to be sought among the primitive conceptions of the mind. To perceive and judge of the right, is one of the most important offices of the reflective power of the mind. The emotions, affections, desires, furnish a powerful class of motives to human action, whether right or wrong. The will, or the power of voluntary mental action, constitutes the basis of human accountability, and lies, therefore, at the foundation of ethics. Hence, not improperly, the faculties now designated have been termed, by some philosophers, the active and moral powers of man. Dugald Stewart thus designates them.

In regard to the faculties now under consideration, a correct psychology is absolutely essential to a correct science of moral duty.

In another respect, also, is the connection of the two sciences intimate. Duty pertains, first and chiefly, not to the external conduct, but to the responsible, intelligent mind, whose thoughts, feeling, and volitions find their expression in that outward conduct, and determine its moral character. To teach me what are my duties, is to teach me what thoughts and affections I ought to cherish; what purposes and volitions I ought to form and put forth; in a word, what ought to be my entire mental activity, as exerted in the various relations of life. Mental science contents itself with ascertaining what are the varied phenomena of mental action; moral science, while relating chiefly to the same department of observation, — *i. e.*, the human mind, — inquires not so much what *are* the laws and operations of its various faculties, as what they *ought* to be.

General divisions. — The science of morals properly divides itself into two parts — the theoretical and the practical. Before proceeding to discuss the various duties which pertain to the well-ordered conduct of life, it is necessary to inquire first into those general principles on which, as a basis, morality rests, — as, *e. g.*, the nature of right, the ground of right, the rule of right, the province of right, — and in what consists the moral quality of actions. This inquiry into, and discussion of, the general principles which lie at the foundation of morals, may be termed the *theoretical* part of the science. The way will thus be prepared to take up and discuss, in their order, the several duties that devolve on man in the various relations of life; and this may be termed the *practical* part of the science.

DIVISION FIRST.

THEORETICAL ETHICS.

THEORETICAL ETHICS

CHAPTER I.

THE NATURE OF RIGHT.

§ 1.—Right in Itself Considered.

Essential Attributes. — The term *right* expresses a simple and ultimate idea; it is, therefore, incapable of analysis and definition; nor does it, like many other ideas, stand in need of definition in order to be understood. It expresses an eternal and immutable distinction, inherent in the nature of things, not the creation of arbitrary power, whether of man or God. Wherever there is voluntary action of any intelligent rational being, there is always, and always must be, a right and a wrong; and all moral action is, of necessity, either the one or the other. The distinction is one universally recognized. The idea of right lies among the simplest furniture and first principles of the human mind. It manifests itself with the dawn of reason and intelligence. It is not an idea of the schools, a distinction known only or chiefly to metaphysicians; but is the property alike of the learned and the simple, of the child and the philosopher. Opinions may vary widely as to what is, and what is not, right action; what one system or one age pronounces to be right, another system or another age may decide to be wrong; but, as to the essential difference between the right and the wrong, as ideas, or principles of action, no age or system was ever at a loss — no mind, however feeble, was ever confused.

This Idea, whence derived. — It is a question of some importance how we come by the idea of right. Some have attributed it to fashion and education, as did Locke and his followers; others to the laws, human or divine, which forbid or sanction certain actions; others regard it as the product of a special sense, whose office it is to take cognizance of moral distinctions, as the eye perceives color, and the ear sound. Others again regard the idea of right as a simple and ultimate one, and as such underived, a primary original conception of the human mind, not innate, but connate, an elementary dictum of reason.

The universality of the idea, — its early manifestation in childhood, prior to education, and the influence of example, — as well as the clearness and strength with which it manifests itself, in all conditions of society, and under all the varying circumstances of life, — these things go to show that the idea of right is founded in the constitution of the mind, and not derived from any source external and adventitious. Nor can those who take the opposite view give any satisfactory account of the origin of this idea; since, to attribute it to education, leaves the question still open, where did the first man, the first educator, derive his idea of it; while to ascribe it to law, human or divine, is still wider of the mark, inasmuch as law always presupposes the right, as the foundation on which it rests. To attribute, then, the origin or the idea of right to law, is to place the foundation upon the building, instead of the building upon the foundation. And as to the theory of a special sense, whose office it is to take cognizance of the right, it is sufficient to say, that there is no evidence of any such special faculty of the mind, nor is any such needed.

For the further investigation of this topic, the reader is referred to the author's treatise on Mental Philosophy, in which the question, and its several theories, are more fully discussed.

§ 2.—Right, as distinguished from other Ideas of similar import.

Right and Duty.—Right and duty are not precisely synonymous terms, yet are nearly equivalent. We are always under obligation to do that which is right—it is our duty. The right in morals once ascertained, the doing of it is, under all circumstances, a duty. Right is the *foundation* of obligation, and *coëxtensive* with it. It is the rightness of the thing that creates its binding force, and makes it obligatory upon us. There can be no moral obligation to do what is not in itself a right thing to be done.

Still, right and duty, though coëxtensive, are not of precisely the same import. Right is the abstract, in itself considered. Duty is right, considered in relation to us as personal agents—as doers; obligation is the binding power of the right over us, which makes this or that a duty.

Another View.—Some writers make a further distinction between obligation and duty than that which I have now indicated—making obligation more comprehensive than duty. Thus a man may be obliged, by force of circumstances, or by the laws of the land, to do what is not right. Such is the view taken by Whewell, in his Elements of Morality. That which is here called obligation, however, is not really such, but rather compulsion, or necessity. No combination of circumstances, and no power of law, can create moral obligation. In morals, that, and that only, conveys obligation which bears the high seal and impress of right. Whatever goes beyond this, or violates this,—whatever power and pressure of circumstances it may draw around it, whatever sanction and authority of law,—can never bind the conscience, or impose on the spiritual nature of man the restraints of a moral obligation. Law may come in, with its sanctions and penalties, to secure the performance of the right; it may cast the heavy sword of power into the scale that hangs in doubtful balance; or it may require and enforce the wrong; but in neither case can it create a moral obligation which did not previously exist. Had there been no law, it would still have been my duty to do the right. It is still my duty, even though the law forbid. Obligation and duty are coëxtensive.

Right and Rights.—The term *right* varies in significance, according to its use, as an adjective, or as a noun; or, more properly, according to its use in the singular, or in the plural. *Right* is the principle that should regulate my conduct towards others; my *rights* are what I may justly expect and require from others, in their intercourse with me—what they ought to do as respects me. That which is my right, is another's duty; and that which is my duty, is another's right. Every right, then, has its corresponding duty. It is my duty, for example, to obey God; and that obedience he has a right to require. It is my duty to obey the state in all its just and proper requirements—in all things not inconsistent with higher obligations; and this obedience the state has the right to demand of me. In like manner, all my rights look to the corresponding duties of others; and all my duties, to the rights of others.

There would be no *rights*, were there not in the first

place such a thing as *right.* From this, obligation results, duty results, and so *rights* exist.

View of Whewell and others. — If, with Whewell and others, we make rights to depend for their existence on the laws, it follows that there are no rights except those which society recognizes and creates through the medium of law; and were there, for any reason, no longer any law, no man would any longer have any rights; — which is by no means the case. Law may define and prescribe my rights; it may enforce them, see that they are respected and observed; but it does not, and cannot, create them. They are founded in the principles of natural justice, and of universal and immutable right. Were there no laws — were the institutions of society swept away — there would still be rights, so long as there were intelligent and rational beings in existence sustaining certain relations to each other. Suppose, for example, two persons cast ashore upon a desert island, where, beside themselves, is no human being — where, of course, is no state and no law. Each of these persons has still, by the law of nature, certain rights, inalienable from him; as, *e. g.*, the right to his own person, his own labor, his own property; and were the other to wrest these from him, he would be guilty of a manifest wrong — of palpable injustice.

Those who take this view, moreover, go upon the supposition that the laws are based upon right and justice — as unquestionably they should be, but unfortunately are not always. There may be, in the course of human affairs, iniquitous, unjust laws; such things have been, and will be again. Such laws, according to the view in question, however, create rights and impose duties. In such a case I have, according to this theory, *the right* to demand of others what it is not *right* for me to demand of them;

while, on the other hand, it is my *duty* to do what it is not *right* for me to do.

If it be replied, that in this case the rights supposed are merely *legal* rights, and not moral ones, I answer, that, according to the theory, all rights are legal ones, and must be first legal before they can be moral. It is the law that creates rights, moral or other. The morality presupposes and depends upon the legality, as the quality presupposes the substance. To distinguish in this manner between a right which is merely legal, and one which, in addition to that, is also moral, is to step back from the theory that it is law which creates rights.

The truth is, neither right nor rights are dependent on law for their existence. There are rights which are not defined by law — which, possibly, are forbidden by law. All rights exist before they are thus defined. Both my duties and my rights depend for their existence on *right;* and this again depends, not on society, nor law, but is founded in the eternal and immutable nature of things.

The rights, so called, which are established by law, may or may not coincide with moral rights. However this may be, Moral Philosophy has to do, not at all with legal rights, as such, but only with moral. With jurisprudence, as distinct from morals, it has no more to do than with constitutional law, or the science of government.

CHAPTER II.

GROUND OF RIGHT.

Principle of Obligation.—Duty implies obligation. To say that it is my duty to do a given thing, is to say that I ought to do it. Were there no such thing as obligation, there would be no such thing as duty. It is evident then, at a glance, that the principle of obligation is an essential element in morals: it meets us at the threshold, it lies at the foundation of the science on which we are entering.

Such is the constitution of the human mind, that no sooner do we perceive a given course to be right, than we recognize also a certain obligation resting on us to pursue that course. It is a conviction of the mind inseparable from the perception of the right. Given the one, and we cannot escape the other.

Ground of Moral Obligation.—The question arises here, *What is the ground of this ought?*—what *constitutes* it? What is that, in any given action, that imposes on me the obligation to do the same? I ought to do this and that: *Why* ought?

Whatever answer we may give to this question, we must come back ultimately to the simple position—we ought, *because it is right.* The rightness constitutes the obligation. The question, then, virtually resolves itself into this—What constitutes right?

This is a question of no little moment. It has received, at different times, and by different authors, widely different answers, and these various answers constitute so many different theories of morals. They lead us over an interesting and most important field of inquiry, involving one of the deepest problems in the whole range of philosophical thought.

In the preceding chapter, I had occasion to refer to the source of our idea of right, and also to the question, What constitutes our rights? The question now before us is quite distinct from each of these. We are now to inquire, not whence comes the *idea* of right, but what is *right itself?* — not what makes *rights*, but what makes *right?*

Principal Theories. — The principal theories of morals, or grounds of obligation, proposed by different writers, may be reduced, perhaps, to these four: 1. Utility; 2. Law; 3. The nature and character of God; 4. The eternal and immutable nature of things. Each of these has been regarded as the true ground on which to place the distinction of right and wrong, and the consequent moral obligation. The two former of these, again, have each a twofold aspect: Utility, as the ground of right, may denote either the *happiness*, the pleasure accruing from a given course (which is itself a species of utility), or the more direct *advantage* resulting from it. Or, if we place the matter on the ground of legal enactment, the law which makes the right and the wrong, may be *man's* law, or it may be *God's*.

We have, then, these divergent paths opening before us, each proposing to conduct to the true solution of our problem, each trodden by many a mighty man in the domain of thought: the *utilitarian* theory, with its twofold aspect, the pleasure and the advantage of the thing; the *legal* theory, twofold also, as of human or Divine authority; the theory which makes the *Divine character* the foundation of right; and, finally, that which bases it on the *immutable and eternal nature of things.*

Let us, then, examine these several theories in their order:

I. *The Utilitarian.*—*Utility as denoting Pleasure.* Understanding by this term, in the first place, *pleasure*, rather than advantage, the doctrine is this:—the reason why we pronounce one thing right, rather than another, is, that we find the one act to be attended, uniformly, with pleasure to the doer; the other, with pain. One contributes to his happiness, the other detracts from it. Now, the pursuit of happiness, it is contended, is the grand motive and spring of all human action; and if it be once established that the actions which we call right are such, invariably, as to promote our happiness, no other reason need be assigned why we thus regard them. And this, it is contended, is the case. If we select any instance of what we call right action, we find it to be an action which is accompanied with pleasurable emotion. And this is the ground of our approval, the reason why we pronounce the action right.

Now, it is not to be denied, that to do right brings with it a present satisfaction and true happiness. Such is the constitution of our nature. The question is, whether this tendency to produce happiness is what *makes* a given act right. Is the thing right *because* it produces happiness? or does it promote our happiness *because it is right?* Which is the true statement? When I pronounce some past act of my life to be right, and approve it as virtuous, is it because I remember that it gave me great pleasure?—and when I cherish the feeling of self-reproach and remorse, in view of past conduct, is it on the ground that the given action was accompanied with unpleasant and painful sensations?

The Theory not satisfactory.—The simple statement of the question would seem sufficient. We feel instinctively that our decision and approval rest on far other and higher grounds. Virtue and happiness are by no means identical. We have different terms for them, and mean different things by them. The one cannot be resolved into the other. If it be true that all right things are pleasant, it does not follow that all pleasant things are right, much less that their pleasantness makes them right. Many are the propensities of a corrupt nature, the indulgence of which is attended with present gratification, which still are evil and only evil; and in their pleasantness consists the very strength of the temptation they present. The man who yields to the force of such temptations, however, by no means approves the course that he pursues. He goes to the commission of the wrong, not with a conviction that he is doing right, but under a protest from his conscience, and with a feeling of self-reproach and self-condemnation. This ought not to be, according to the theory now under consideration. He ought rather to approve his conduct, on the ground that he was seeking therein his own happiness; and his self-approval ought to rise and increase in proportion to the pleasure he receives.

As denoting Happiness of the Community.—Nor is the case materially altered by substituting the happiness of others, in place of personal happiness, as the ground of right. No doubt right action contributes to the happiness of the community, and swells the sum total of the world's enjoyment; but is it this that constitutes the rightness of the act? Is the noble consciousness of doing right, with all its power to sustain the spirit of a man under the pressure of the heaviest calamities and the gloom of the darkest hour, merely this—the conviction that somehow, in consequence of what he has done, men will, on the whole, enjoy themselves better? Independent, and irrespective of all such considerations, is there not a far nobler satisfaction in having done that which was right, in itself considered, and for its own sake?

The view now considered was the distinctive tenet of the ancient Epicurean philosophy; and has been held, in later times, by Hume and Shaftesbury in England, and by their followers generally.

As denoting Advantage. — Considering, now, utility as denoting *advantage* or *expediency*, we come upon somewhat different ground, — capable, however, of attack and defence by essentially the same arguments. In fact, the former view may be regarded as a modification of the latter; the one specific, the other generic, in its form; — pleasure being itself a species of advantage, at least in the opinion of those who make it the rule of right. Hence, very generally, the advocates of the former view are advocates also of the latter. Still the latter is, of the two, the broader and higher ground.

Self-love, according to this view, is the grand motive of human action. Men do what they think for their advantage. Now, it is found by experience that a certain course of conduct is for the advantage, and the opposite for the disadvantage, of the doer. Hence they come to regard the one course as right, and to be pursued, — the other as wrong, and to be avoided. In a word, it is the utility or expediency of the thing that constitutes the ground and reason of its rightness. Such is the doctrine of Bentham and his followers.

And here it is admitted on all sides that virtuous action does contribute to the advantage, in many ways, of the doer. The question is, whether this is what *makes* it virtuous — whether this constitutes its rightness. Is it right because expedient, or expedient because right?

Consequences of this Theory.—Let us see what follows from this theory. (1) If expediency is the ground of right, then *interest* and *duty* are identical in idea—synonymes for the same thought. To prove a given action right, all that is necessary is to show that it is advantageous to the doer. The same act performed from the same motives, with the same spirit and intentions, is right to one man, and wrong to another; nay, is right to one and the same man, at one time, and wrong at another, according as it turns out for his advantage or not. We can never be sure that we are acting virtuously, until we know how the action is to affect our personal interests. Men have acted from the highest and purest principles, yet have been in reality far from virtuous, because what they did proved not for their own interests. They ought, therefore, to cherish feelings of self-reproach and remorse in view of their conduct.

(2) It follows from this theory that there is no such thing as *intentional* wrong-doing. Men always act, it is said, from the principle of self-love. They do what they think is for their own advantage. Finding by experience that certain actions tend to their advantage, they come to regard such actions as right, and the opposite, for the same reason, as wrong. What have we here for a syllogism?

Man acts always with reference to his own good. To act with reference to one's own good, is to act right; therefore, man invariably acts right! He may mistake, and do what is in the end disadvantageous; but it was a mistake, an error of judgment, and not an *intentional* wrong. This is on the whole a very favorable view of things, and may serve to relieve somewhat the sombre aspect in which the world and poor erring human nature present themselves to a certain class of minds. Men are not so bad, after all. They do as well as they know how. They *mean* to be selfish, and to consult their own interests; and if they sometimes come short of duty in this respect, it is an error of the head and not of the heart.

(3) It follows, also, that there is no such thing as *disinterested virtue.* Utility is the ground of rectitude, the foundation of obligation. We ought, therefore, to give a man credit for his conduct, just in proportion as we perceive him to have been governed throughout by a regard to his own personal advantage. To act thus is to act right, and to comply with the claims of duty. There can be no virtue which springs not from this source. The more fully a man promotes his own interests, and seeks his own personal advantage, in all he does, provided only there be no direct violation of the rights of others, the higher esteem ought we to cherish for that man in our hearts. On the other hand, where an action is of such a nature that we are not quite sure whether the man *was really seeking his own* advantage, or that of *others*, in what he did, we ought to withhold our approbation.

But, strange to say, selfish as the world is, it does not so decide. It does sensibly diminish our moral approbation of any act, to see, or suspect even, that self-interest was the leading motive of conduct; it heightens our admiration and esteem, to perceive that the act was performed without the least regard to that, but from entirely different motives.

Contradicts Consciousness. — And this leads us to remark, in general, that the theory under consideration *contradicts the facts of consciousness.* If utility were the ground of moral obligation, the foundation of right, then, whenever we recognize such obligation, we should be *conscious* of this element as the basis of it — should be conscious of perceiving the tendency of the given act to promote the personal happiness or the personal advantage of the doer, and that our conviction of obligation in the case arose from that circumstance; whereas, in fact, we are conscious of no such thing, but in many cases of directly the reverse. The sense of obligation exists, not only irrespective of the idea of happiness or of advantage to be derived from the given act, but often in opposition to it; the desire of happiness, or of personal advantage, drawing us in one direction, the sense of obligation in another. It is not true that duty and interest are identical. We have different names for them, we mean different things by them. We are conscious of acting, now from one, now from the other, of these principles. It is not true that men never intentionally do what they know to be wrong. This was the capital defect in the ethical system of Socrates, and also of Plato, who make virtue a matter of science, and sin to be merely ignorance. Whose consciousness does not testify the opposite of this? Who will not say, with Ovid,

"Video meliora, proboque, deteriora sequor;"

or, with Euripides, "I know that what I am about to do is evil, but desire is stronger than my deliberations." Surely the poets, in this case, are more nearly right than the philosophers. Who has not reason to say, with Paul, "That which I do, I allow not."

Neither is it true that we act always from personal and selfish considerations. We are conscious of the opposite — conscious of doing that which is right, *because* it is right, and not for the sake of personal advantage. Nor in such cases is the verdict of conscience against us; but, on the contrary, it is precisely such actions that draw forth the testimony of her warmest approbation; so far from reproaching us for not acting with more direct and uniform reference to our own advantage, conscience more frequently condemns us for having acted from no higher principle.

We cannot but regard the facts of consciousness, then, as altogether at variance with the theory under consideration.

Utility as denoting Good of the greatest number. — Suppose, now, we give the term utility a still wider extension, meaning by it, not the advantage of the *individual* merely, but the good of the *greatest number* — does it become in this sense the foundation of right and of moral obligation? There are still insuperable objections.

In the first place, how can it always be known what *will* promote the interests of the greatest number? The tendencies and results of actions are often hidden from human perspicacity. We do not know how they will affect the interests of any considerable number of persons. A laborious calculation of consequences would in most cases be necessary, in order to such a conclusion; and even then we could never arrive at certainty — never be sure that our reasonings and conclusions were correct. We should be in suspense, therefore, as to the morality of actions, unable to decide whether they are right or wrong, until we could first know their ultimate bearing on the general welfare. Such a calculation of consequences is quite beyond the capacity of the mass; only the more enlightened and far-seeing are competent to form such judgments, and even they not with any certainty. Only the few, therefore, are competent to form ideas of right or wrong, and apply them to human conduct, while the vast multitude are left without any such faculty to guide them.

At variance with Facts. — Furthermore, it may be justly objected to this theory, in the form in which it is now stated, that it is directly at variance with the facts in the case. As a matter of fact, we *do not* always calculate the consequences of an action before we pronounce it, in our minds, right or wrong. We are conscious of no such procedure. We do not stop to know what bearing it is likely to have on the public welfare. We do not raise the question at all. We neither know nor care. Instinctively we decide as to the propriety and rightness of the given act; we approve and condemn without reference to consequences, and on other grounds than that of expediency.

It is fatal to this theory of utility, in whatever form it is stated, whether as referring to the happiness of the individual, or the happiness of the community — to the advantage of the individual, or the advantage of all, that, so far from being conscious ordinarily of any such considerations, in our estimate of the morality of actions, we are conscious of quite the opposite. Our moral decisions are often pronounced under circumstances which preclude the *possibility* of all such prudential considerations. Narrate to a child, just old enough to understand you, some story of flagrant injustice and wrong — the flush of indignation, the glow of resentment are visible at once on that cheek; the decision of that moral nature, its verdict of disapproval and condemnation, is to be read at once in that eye, that brow, that clenched hand — the whole mien and aspect of the miniature man. Has it been calculating the expediency and utility of the thing — the consequences to society of what its outraged nature condemns?

Utility presupposes Obligation. — But there is a further objection to making utility, in any of its significations, the ground of moral obligation. It is that all these principles as thus applied, virtually *presuppose* the existence of moral obligation, and therefore cannot be the ground of it. I perceive such a course to be conducive to happiness; therefore, says the advocate of this view, I am under obligation to pursue that course. But why *therefore?* Why *ought?* Suppose I choose to do that which is *not*, on the whole, for my happiness, — what then? Whose business is it but my own? Either there is no manner of obligation in that case, or else it lies out of and back of the principle now supposed. The same may be said of utility in the sense of advantage. It presupposes an obligation to do what is seen to be useful and advantageous; and the question still remains, What is the *ground* of that obligation which the doctrine of utility presupposes?

II. *Theory of Legal Enactment.* — Let us look, now, at the theory which places the foundation of moral obligation on the ground of *positive enactment.* Laws have been made, human and divine, requiring, forbidding, etc. Hence our approval and condemnation of actions, and our conviction of obligation. The just and the unjust, the right and the wrong, in human conduct, are simply its conformity, or want of conformity, to law.

Of those who take this ground, some look no higher than to *human* enactment as the ground of rectitude and the foundation of moral obligation. The laws of man make the right and wrong of things, and are the sufficient and ultimate standard of morals. There is no higher law. No other reason need be given why I should do, or not do, a given thing, than that the laws of my country require it.

Such, among the ancients, was the doctrine of the Sophists. Plato, in the "De Legibus," and Aristotle, in his "Ethics," make mention of the doctrine as maintained by some in their day.

Among the moderns, Gassendi and Hobbes are almost the only writers of distinction who have had the boldness to avow, and the consistency to maintain, a doctrine at once so shameless, so obnoxious to the common sense and common honesty of mankind, and so destructive of the first principles of morality. Occasionally, indeed, the spectacle is presented of some one, more patriotic than discreet, who, in his zeal to defend the constitution and laws of his country, so far forgets himself, in the pressure of the exigency, as to take the general position that the laws of the land are to us the final court of appeal, and that we are to look no higher for authority. Even such persons, it is to be presumed, are not fully aware of the true nature and legitimate consequences of this doctrine, nor of the company they keep in maintaining such a position.

They would shrink, it is to be hoped, from the doctrine, reduced to its simple elements, and affirmed, as a principle in ethics, that *might makes right,* — a sentiment that even a German rationalist has pronounced *infernal,* — and from the atheism that discards the Deity, and overlooks the moral nature of man, while proclaiming human law as the standard of morals and the foundation of right.

Objection to this View. — If it were of any use to reason against a doctrine so little deserving the name of philosophy, or the notice of a calm reply, it were sufficient, perhaps, to ask how it is possible, on this principle, since law is itself the source and foundation of right, to compare one law or code with another, — those of Draco, *e. g.*, with those of Solon or Lycurgus; the edicts of Nero with those of Constantine; and because one system is mild and humane, another barbarous and inhuman, pronounce one to be more right and just than the other? If law is its own authority; if it makes right; if back of it there is no appeal, no ultimate standard of rectitude, — then, of course, everything which is once enacted, and obtains the sanction of established law, is right and binding, no matter what it may be, — one equally so with another, — and it is absurd to make a distinction between them. The commands of the veriest despot are as just and right, as obligatory on the conscience, as those of the wisest and mildest ruler. Law is law, and that ends the matter. A law morally wrong is an impossibility, an absurdity. Inasmuch as laws vary, moreover, in different lands, what is right in one country is wrong when you cross a river or a mountain; what is a virtue in Holland is a sin in Belgium.

Divine Law as the ground of Right. — Much more reasonable and philosophical is the view of those who regard the *divine* will and law as the foundation of moral rectitude. This view was maintained by Occam, among the scholastics — by Paley, and many others, among the moderns. Yet even to this view insuperable obstacles arise.

Objections to this View. — 1. If this view be correct, then we have only to suppose the will of Deity to change, and what is now wrong becomes instantly right, — the good and the bad, the virtuous and the vicious, change characters at once. We have only to suppose him other than he is, and to have commanded other than he has, to have reversed the decalogue; and the things now commanded would then have been wrong, and the things now forbidden would have been right. Murder, adultery, false witness, theft, covetousness, would have been virtues, commendable and obligatory; while to honor our parents, and to love our neighbor as ourselves, would have been morally wrong. In other words, there is no difference, in respect of moral character, between these actions in themselves considered; the difference lies wholly in the fact that one is commanded, and the other forbidden; they are right or wrong only as they are, or are not, the will of Deity.

It is no answer to this to say that God is holy, and therefore will not command that which is evil; nor, that he is immutable, and therefore will not change. The question is not as to the *matter of fact*, but as to what *would* be true, in case he and his law were not what they are. If it were possible for God to throw around sin the sanction of his law, would it, because of that sanction, *cease* to be sin, and become holiness? Does the rightness of an act consist wholly and simply in its being lawful?

2. It follows, also, that, had there been no divine law to establish the character of actions, human conduct had been neither virtuous nor vicious, neither good nor bad; but all actions would have been alike indifferent. To hate our neighbor, to take his property, his good name, or his life, would have been not only allowable, but equally as commendable and meritorious as the opposite. Nothing would have been unjust, nothing wrong.

3. There is no propriety or sense in speaking of God's law as just and good; in affirming that his statutes are right, his commandments holy, etc.; for moral approbation is wholly misplaced and uncalled for. It is without meaning. For, if there is no standard of right, and no ground of obligation but the law itself, how can its requirements be any other than right and binding, whatever they may be? To say that his statutes are just and right, is to say, simply, that his statutes are his statutes. More than this: when we speak of the law as holy, just, etc., do we not attribute a moral character to the law itself? But how can this be? If the law creates moral distinctions, how can law itself possess a moral character? — how can it be either right or wrong? This is to suppose right created, and yet to have existed before it was created.

4. Further, for the same reason, we are shut out, on this principle, from attributing to Deity himself any moral character. Law is the foundation of right, and law is from God. Back of his will there is no law, and, of course, no ground of rectitude. God has himself, therefore, aside from his own law, no moral character, no virtue; for, be-

yond his own will and pleasure, there is no *law* imposing obligation, and constituting for him the right and the wrong. One thing is as right as another for him; everything is equally right; and, strictly speaking, nothing is, for him, either right or wrong. It is language without meaning when we say, with one of old, "Holy, holy, holy Lord God, just and true are thy ways." Before he enacted the first law, there was no such thing as right. It depended entirely on his pleasure whether to enact that law. There was no obligation to enact it; for no law, as yet, existed to create obligation. Suppose he had not done it?—right would not have existed, and, of course, in that case, could not have pertained to the divine character. Not until he creates the right by making law, can he by any possibility possess a moral character; and even then, it is a moral character which he himself creates, and imposes upon himself by arbitrary enactment. Had he made a law precisely the reverse of the actual one, it would have been equally right and binding, and himself equally as holy. But it is difficult to see how the thing made can put the maker himself under obligation; how from his own work he can derive the foundation of a character which he had not in himself prior to the work. It is difficult to estimate the intrinsic excellence of that holiness which owes its origin to a purely arbitrary enactment; which might just as well never have been made, or have been entirely other than, and the reverse of, what it is;—a holiness which, when strictly viewed, amounts merely to this,—that the being who possesses it *does what he does.*

Law as the Basis of Obligation.—It may be supposed, perhaps, by some, that the divine law, while it may not absolutely create the distinction of right and wrong, does nevertheless create the *obligation* on our part to do, or not to do, the things required; that it is to me the sufficient

4*

reason why I ought to do thus and thus. This is a view entitled to a careful consideration. I must do thus, *because* such is the will of Deity. The question is now as to this word *because*. Granting that the will of Deity is as affirmed, what has that to do with my conduct? — wherein and how does that place me under obligation to do what the Deity wills? Where lies the binding power of the law itself? Manifestly not *in itself, as* law, but in something else. There must be something to make the law binding, or it can bring with it no obligation to obedience on my part. And in saying this, we really *abandon the position, that law is itself the basis of obligation.*

This something we may find in one of three things. It may be in the *character* of the law given, — a holy, just, and good law, and one which we ought therefore to obey. But this is to place the ground of obligation, not in the law itself, but in something else, viz., moral rectitude. I am bound to obey, not because there is a law, but because there is a *holy* and *just* law.

Or we may trace the binding power of the law to the *relation* which the Deity sustains to us. He is our creator, preserver, benefactor; and as such, has the right, it is said, to control and govern us. But does this, we reply, give him the right to govern and control, *irrespective* of *moral distinctions?* If it does, then right and wrong are the mere arbitrary creations of his will, — a view which we have already considered and rejected. If it does not, then the ultimate ground of obligation is to be found in the *rectitude* of the divine requirements. In either case, it is not the law itself that constitutes the obligation.

Does, then, that which constitutes the binding force of the divine law consist in this: that the Deity is in himself such a being as he is, the greatest, the wisest, the best; and therefore his will is obligatory on other beings? This again is to recognize moral distinctions as lying back of the law itself, and as giving to that law its character and its force. When you say that God is good, just, holy, the best of beings, and, on that account, ought to be obeyed, you abandon the position, that law itself creates moral distinctions, and that it contains in itself the ground of obligation. His being and nature are prior to his law, and the foundation of it; and if his being and nature are themselves good, then certainly it is not his law that makes them so; and if it is from them that our obligation to obedience springs, then certainly not from the law itself.

Whatever view we take, then, of this matter, we are compelled to give up the position that the divine law is the ground of moral obligation. An action is right, not *because* God wills it; on the contrary, *he wills it because it is right.*

View of Dr. Chalmers.—The distinction between the rightness and the lawfulness of an act, is admitted by some, who still place obligation on the ground of law. This is the case with Chalmers. In general, it may be remarked, that no writer breathes throughout a higher moral tone and purpose, or utters truth with more eloquence and earnestness than he. His style is an avalanche broken loose, a sea of expression, rolling, sentence after sentence, wave upon wave, with a loftiness and force quite irresistible. It is the style of the orator, however, rather than of the philosopher; indicating fervor and strength of feeling, rather than precision and clearness of thought. There is a certain nobleness of sentiment that wins our admiration. We feel sure that some leviathan is ploughing up those waters, and making them to boil; but it is a leviathan not willing to be caught and classified for purposes of science. In the present case, Dr. Chalmers, if we understand him, derives *obligation* from the divine law, but *right* from the divine character; thus separating the two. While he rejects the view of Paley, that makes the divine command the foundation of right, he still makes that command the foundation of our *obligation to do* the right. Not until Deity interposes with his authority in its behalf, does the right become obligatory.

Objection to this View. — It is difficult to perceive the justness of this distinction. In the first place, it limits the term *obligation* to a strictly *forensic* use, a sense to which it is by no means restricted. A wider sense belongs to it. We are under obligation, ethically speaking, to do many things not specifically required by law. But, more than this, it seems to *divorce* obligation from right, as if right did not carry in itself a corresponding obligation, but was dependent on law to come in and give it authority; or as if, on the other hand, obligation might sometimes, or might at least be supposed to, run counter to right.

Right and Obligation, how related. — We cannot think such a distinction either necessary or allowable. On the contrary, we regard right and obligation as coëxtensive, and on a common basis. The foundation and origin of the one, is also the source and foundation of the other. Given, the right, and there is given along with it the obligation to do the right. We cannot conceive them separate; the former without the latter; a right thing which we are under no obligation to do, or a wrong thing which we are under no obligation to avoid. This obligation is universal, absolute. complete. Law cannot add to it, or make it more perfect than it already is. Law may indicate and enforce, but cannot create moral obligation. Show me t' at a thing is *right*, and you show me a reason, and the besι of all reasons, why I *ought* to do it. The moment I perceive the rightness, I perceive also the obligation. If the one is founded in law, so is the other; if the divine character is the foundation of the one, it is the ground of the other also.

Matters of an Indifferent Nature. — It is admitted that, in respect to matters in themselves indifferent, as, for instance, the ceremonies of a ritual observance, law may impose an obligation not previously existing. But such is not the case now under consideration. We are concerned, in this discussion, only with such matters as come under the cognizance of the moral faculty, as being in themselves right or wrong; and the question is, What *constitutes* the obligation to do, not a thing indifferent, but a thing which we perceive and know to be right? Our answer is: The very *rightness* constitutes the obligation. The question returns then, On what does the *rightness* depend? Not on utility, not on law. An action is right, not because expedient; but expedient, because right. It is right, not *because* God wills it; on the contrary, *he wills it because it is right.* What, then, constitutes rightness?

III. *The Divine Nature the Source of Right.* — It may be said that right and wrong lie not in any of these things, — not in the pursuit of happiness or of personal advantage; not in law, human or divine, — but in the *nature and character of God himself.* This, as we have already stated, is the view of Chalmers. It is the view, also, of many others. We have discussed so fully the previous theories, that there is no need of dwelling long upon this. The same objections that lie against the theory of divine law, as the source of obligation and the ground of right, apply with equal force to this view. God's law is but the expression of his will; and his will is but the expression and transcript of his character. It is his nature in action. To say that his law constitutes right, then, is virtually saying, in another form, that his nature and character are the ground of right; and whatever objections lie against the one view, are, in reality, equally objections to the other.

Objection to this View.—If right or wrong depend, ultimately, on the character of God, then we have only to suppose God to change, or to have been originally other than he is, and our duties and obligations change at once;—that which was a virtue, becomes a crime; that which is a crime, is transformed into a virtue. Had he been precisely the reverse of what he is, he had still been, as now, the source of right, and his own character would have been as truly good, and just, and right, as it is now. This is, virtually, to rob him of all moral character. We may still say that he is holy, and that his ways are right; but we mean by it only this, when we come to explain,—that he is what he is, and does what he does. The holiness of his acts consists, not at all in the essential character of the acts themselves, but only in the circumstance that they are *his* acts.

It does not meet this objection to say that God *is* holy,—holy by a necessity of his nature,—and that he can never be otherwise: that is not the question; but simply, whether his being what he is is the ground of all rectitude and of all obligation; whether that which he does is right *because it conforms to his character*, or whether his character is holy *because it conforms to the right.* This is a very important distinction.

We have this objection, then, to the view which resolves virtue into the divine character, and makes right inherent originally in the divine nature: that while it seeks to honor God by making him the source of all excellence, it really takes away from his character the highest excellence and glory that can pertain to it—that of conforming to the right.

IV. *The Eternal Nature of Things as the Ground of*

Right. — We seem to be driven, then, to the only remaining conclusion, that *right and wrong are distinctions immutable and inherent in the nature of things.* They are not the creations of expediency, nor of law; nor yet do they originate in the divine character. They have *no* origin; they are eternal as the throne of Deity; they are immutable as God himself. Nay, were God himself to change, these distinctions would change not. Omnipotence has no power over them, whether to create or to destroy. Law does not make them, but they make law. They are the source and spring of all law and all obligation. Reason points out these distinctions; the moral nature recognizes and approves them. God's law, and will, and nature, are in conformity to these distinctions; else that law were not just and right, nor that nature holy. Our moral nature is in conformity to these distinctions; hence we approve and disapprove, as we do, the various actions of men. The deeds are right, not *because* we approve them; on the contrary, we approve them *because they are right.* They are right, not *because* they are commanded; but they are commanded *because they are right.*

Even Deity subject to the Law of Right. — There is a sense in which Deity himself is subject to this eternal and immutable law of right. There are things which it would not be right for even Deity to do. So fully does his moral nature approve the right and abhor the wrong, that the Scriptures declare it impossible for him to do evil. There is no purity like his; no approval of the right, no condemnation and abhorrence of the wrong, so strong and intense as his, in the whole universe. This, his moral nature, is to him a law, the highest possible and conceivable, placing him under obligation, not indeed to another, but to himself, to adhere ever to the eternal principles of right, and truth, and justice.

This View honors God.—In their anxiety to honor and exalt the Divine Being, some have shrunk from the idea that there is any law or obligation resting on the Deity to do one thing rather than another,—that there is, or can be, anything which it would be wrong for him to do. But, which most honors and exalts God—to resolve the distinction of right and wrong into the arbitrary decisions of his will, thus leaving him without moral character, or to regard that distinction as immutable and eternal, extending even to the throne and will of him who layeth the beams of his chambers in the waters, and hangeth the earth upon nothing? Which most honors him—to make his nature and his will the foundation of right, or the eternal principles of right and justice the foundation of his character and his law? Which gives the noblest and most exalted conception of the Divine Being? Which of these two views imparts the loftier significance to that sublime anthem of the angels, that goes up unceasingly before his throne, and shall yet go up from the entire universe: "HOLY, HOLY, HOLY Lord God Almighty, which was, and is, and is to come?" and to that song of the redeemed that stand upon the sea of glass: "*Just* and *true* are thy ways, thou king of saints. Who shall not fear thee, O Lord! and glorify thy name?"

Objection stated and answered.—It may be said, perhaps, that to make right and wrong inherent in the nature of things, is virtually to place their foundation and origin in God; since the nature of things depends, after all, on him. He who made all things, is the author of their nature also.

This objection derives its force from the somewhat indefinite expression, "nature of *things*,"—a phrase used with great latitude of meaning. As used to denote material objects and their qualities, it is true that both *things* and the nature of things are the work of God; as used to denote finite intelligences, the same is true, — they are the work of the Divine Intelligence, they and their original nature. But when we speak of things and the nature of things, as applicable to this discussion, we do not, of course, refer to material objects, nor yet to spiritual intelligences, but to the actions and moral conduct of intelligent beings, created or uncreated, finite or infinite. We mean to say, that such and such acts, of an intelligent, voluntary agent, whoever he may be, are, in *their very nature*, right or wrong. Now, God does not create the actions of intelligent, free agents; and, of course, does not create the nature of those actions. To say that the moral character of an act is created by Deity, is simply to beg the question in dispute.

The Theory asserts what. — When we say that right and wrong are inherent, then, in the very nature of things, we simply assert that certain courses of conduct are, in their very nature and essence, wrong — certain others, right; that they are so, quite independent and irrespective of the consequences that result from them, or of the sanctions and authority with which they may be invested; that they are so, not because of the laws, either human or divine, that give them force; that they would be so, were there no law, or were it the opposite of what it is; that even the actions of Deity himself fall within the range of this universal principle; and that it does not depend on his will, or even his nature, much less on his power as Creator, to establish or abolish this immutable distinction.

We say it is in the very nature of things that the whole is greater than a part; that a straight line is the shortest distance between two points; that two straight lines cannot enclose a space. We cannot conceive the opposite to be true. It does not depend on the will of Deity whether these things shall be so or not. He does not create these relations. They are eternal and necessary truths. In like manner, there are certain truths pertaining to the conduct of all rational and intelligent beings, — certain moral distinctions, which we regard as immutable and eternal, — inherent in the very nature of things. And on this firm, eternal basis rests the foundation of our moral obligation.

CHAPTER III.

THE RULE OF RIGHT.

Question stated. — What *makes* a thing right is one question, and how do we *know* it to be right, is quite another. The former was discussed in the preceding chapter; the latter is now before us. What rule have we by which to judge of the moral quality of actions? — what standard? — what means of information? The decision of the former question is not necessarily the decision also of this. That which is the ground of right, and the basis of moral obligation, is not, of necessity, the source of our knowledge respecting the right, and the rule of our duty.

The Answer. — It is a sufficient answer to the question before us, to say, in general, that *the will of God* must be regarded as the rule of right and the standard of duty to man. The divine will, while it is not the source and ground of *right* — as already shown — is nevertheless the source of our *knowledge* of right, the rule of duty to us. It does not *create* right, but *reveals* it, makes it known. That will itself reposes upon the right, and is conformed to it. That will is our law. Such is the character of the Divine Being, and such, also, our relation to him, as Creator, Governor, Benefactor, as to make his will binding upon us, and that law, which is holy, just, and good, our rightful and only proper rule of action.

That Will, how revealed. — This rule is made known to us in various ways. It is given, first of all, in the moral nature of man himself, who is endowed with the faculty of distinguishing between right and wrong, and is so constituted that, by the law of his nature, he approves the right and disapproves the wrong, whenever perceived. It is given also in the constitution of nature, in the ordering and arrangement of things about us; which constitution and arrangement are such as to indicate clearly the will of the Deity as to the course which we should pursue. It is given yet more fully and clearly in that revelation which he has made of his will in the sacred Scriptures.

I. *In the Moral Nature of Man.* — Such is the constitution of the mind as to fit it for taking cognizance of moral distinctions, and, what is more, for approving the right whenever perceived, and condemning the wrong. And this moral nature and constitution of the human mind is from God, and is in itself an indication of his will. It may not, of itself, point out with clearness and definiteness, in all cases, what actions are right, and what are wrong; this may be, to some extent, a matter of opinion and judgment — a matter of belief rather than of positive knowledge; yet, within certain limits, the moral nature of man decides without hesitation as to the character of given actions, and approves or condemns accordingly. It is seldom at a loss as to the great dividing lines which separate the kingdoms of right and wrong, of crime and duty. An instance of flagrant injustice or ingratitude, related in the hearing of a child, or of a savage, unbiassed by education and the restraints of civilization and society, calls forth at once his disapproval, and awakens his indignation at the wrong. It is the voice of nature, essentially the same in all climes and ages of the world, approving the right, condemning the wrong. It is the voice of God, speaking through the moral nature and constitution which he has bestowed upon his creatures. Thus it is, that they which have not the law, "are a law unto themselves."

II. *In the Constitution of Nature.* — The will of the Creator is further revealed in the constitution and nature of things about us. It is impossible for one of ordinary intelligence and habits of observation not to perceive a fixed connection between virtue and happiness, vice and misery, in the world. Certain courses of conduct are uniformly attended with certain results. It is the natural tendency of a certain manner of life to produce misery and evil consequences; it is the tendency of an opposite course to produce opposite results. And from this alone might be inferred, with sufficient clearness and certainty, what is the will of the Creator, as to the course which his creatures shall pursue. These results are intended, not accidental; and they are intended as an indication of the divine will.

A Case supposed. — Let us suppose, for example, the question to arise in the mind of an intelligent heathen, having no other than the light of nature to guide him, whether a life of sensual gratification — the indulgence, without restraint, of the merely animal appetites — were agreeable to the divine will. He finds such indulgence to be attended with momentary gratification, followed by subsequent misery; that it results in injury to the powers of body and of mind; that its tendency is to suffering, poverty, vice, crime. He observes these facts. He perceives them to be the legitimate and inevitable results of the constitution of nature, a part of the system of things;

and if he acknowledges the system itself to have had an intelligent originator and designer, can he be at a loss as to the intention and will of that Creator in the case supposed?

It is in this way that we may learn from the constitution of nature what is the will of our Creator. All nature has its laws. Man, as a part of the great system of nature, is no exception to the rule. Both his physical and his spiritual being have their laws. These laws are to be learned, in either case, by observing the results and tendencies of different actions; and the laws of our moral nature, thus ascertained, constitute what we may call a system of natural religion.

Whether this is really Law.—And here the question may arise, whether that which we call law in such cases—as in the expression, *laws of our moral nature*—is really, after all, of the nature of law, properly so called; or whether it is merely advice or admonition. Certain courses of conduct, it is admitted, tend to produce misery and ruin, while other courses promote the happiness of all concerned. This is to be construed, however, it may be said, not as a law prohibiting and commanding, but as simply an indication, or admonition, as to the course which it is wisest and best for us to pursue. The suffering which follows wrong-doing is not a punishment of the wrong, but simply a warning against its future commission.

I reply: it is of no consequence to the present argument whether it be the one or the other—whether punishment or merely warning—whether law, or merely advice. In either case, it is a sufficient indication of the will of the Creator respecting the course which his creatures should pursue. It shows plainly enough what his wishes and instructions are—what he meant by constituting us as he did.

Not mere Advice.—As a matter of fact, however, the indications to which I refer are not merely advisory, but, in many cases at least, prohibitory; not mere warning, but punishment. The suffering comes after, and often long after, the wrong has been done, as in the case of those youthful follies which produce their results in subsequent years, when the evil is accomplished, and the constitution already hopelessly impaired. The consequences, in such a case, are not fully known until it is already too late to remedy the evil. Nay, the man may already have reformed, and his life may be one of active and noble usefulness; yet, nevertheless, the punishment, long delayed and slow of approach, but sure as the established laws of the universe, shall by-and-by overtake him. The fires which youthful folly and vice have kindled are not always extinguished by the tears of subsequent repentance, but burn on, slowly consuming, until the whole structure lies in ruins. There is a point, moreover, beyond which even reformation becomes hopeless, not to say impossible. All further warning and admonition, in such a case, are useless; yet the suffering, which is the inevitable result of wrong-doing, is none the less inflicted.

Now, in these cases, the misery which is consequent upon vice cannot be intended as warning or admonition, for it comes too late; the evil is done. It is not advice, but law; not warning, but penalty. If it be said the suffering is intended as a warning to others, I reply, so is *all* punishment; but is none the less punishment on that account.

III. *In Revelation.*—The will of God is further made known in that revelation which he has given us in the sacred Scriptures. The sources of information already considered are at the best imperfect and defective. There was need of another, a more direct, a more complete and explicit declaration of the divine will. In the Scriptures we have this needed revelation. They supply the defects of the previous sources of information — make known to man what he most needs to know respecting himself, his Maker, and the uncertain future, and bring to bear upon him motives to obedience and a right life, such as could be drawn from no other source. It cannot be denied that man's moral nature teaches him much; much also the constitution of things around him; and it may be fairly conceded that an honest, sincere inquirer after truth, having no other means of information than the light thus derived, but disposed to make the best use of the instruction thus obtained, would not be likely to go far astray in his views of what constitutes a right course of life.

Yet, in both the sources of information already considered, there are, it must be confessed, serious deficiencies, such as render a further and better revelation of the divine will an absolute necessity of the race.

Man's Moral Nature Defective. — As to the moral faculty, while it enables us to comprehend the right and the wrong as made known to us, — while it causes us to perceive and feel our obligation to do the right and to avoid the wrong, — it does not of itself point out to us precisely what our duties and obligations are, — precisely what is, and what is not, the right thing — the thing to be done. This we are left to learn, for the most part, in other ways. Conscience is not itself, strictly speaking, a *revelation.* Given, the right, or the supposed right, and conscience holds us to it, presses upon us the obligation, approves our obedience, chastises our disobedience with its scorpion lash. In regard to the question, What is duty? — what, to-day, and for me, under present circumstances, is the right thing to be done? — it has no special revelation to make, other than to form a judgment, the best it can, in view of all the circumstances of the case, aided by the light of reason and experience.

Conscience, psychologically viewed, is in fact simply the judgment, or reflective faculty of the mind, exercised upon moral themes. As thus employed, it has no advantage of infallibility, or absolute correctness, more than as employed on other matters. Hence, as in all our judgments, so in these, we are liable to err, we do err; we mistake the path of duty, not seldom, even where we seek to go right. Now, it is just here that additional light is needed — some clearer, more explicit revelation of duty and the will of God. Conscience is satisfied if only we do what we suppose to be right; but how are we to know with any certainty what *is* right?

A Case supposed. — I can conceive, for example, an intelligent and right-minded heathen, convinced of his obligations to the Supreme Power, and disposed to yield that homage and worship which are due from the creature to the Creator, yet at a loss to know what worship would be acceptable to Deity. I can readily suppose him to be satisfied of the guilt incurred by a life of sin, and of the necessity of making some expiation for that guilt, but ignorant of the way in which the anger of a just God against the evil-doer may be appeased. I can conceive him interrogating conscience in vain to know what, in these circumstances, he is to do. Conscience has nothing to say, except to accuse him of violated obligation, and of ever-accumulating guilt. What shall he do? Shall he offer the most costly sacrifice? — shall he cast his child into the Ganges, or himself into the flames? The man needs some other instruction, some other light than nature, and reason, or his own moral sense, afford, in order to discover the path of life.

System of Nature also Insufficient. — As respects natural

religion, or the constitution and nature of things about us, that, too, must be confessed, in some respects, an insufficient guide, of itself, to the right course of life; and such we find it has always proved in the history of the world. It has never fully met and answered the wants of the human mind. Much may be learned from it, but not all that man wishes to know. It is invaluable and yet insufficient. It teaches only by *experience;* and that experience often comes too late, — comes when the evil is done, and there is no remedy, — as in the case of the youth who squanders in idleness and profligacy the best years of his life, and finds out too late the loss he has incurred. That experience, moreover, is drawn wholly from the *present world*, the state of things in which we find ourselves here placed; it knows nothing, teaches nothing, with respect to the *future*, except by inference; it gives no certain knowledge with regard to anything beyond the present life, or whether, indeed, there is anything beyond. I may *infer*, from what I observe of the connection between virtue and happiness, sin and misery, in the present life, that if there be a future state of existence, the same law will hold there; but I cannot *know* this, much less that there is a future existence. Nor can I learn, from anything in the constitution of nature, the true remedy; or whether there is any remedy for the evils of sin, any escape from its guilt. These are matters which, most of all, I wish to know; yet on these points nature is silent.

Now, the force of sinful passion, and an evil nature in man, strengthened, as that nature and those passions are, by indulgence and habit, must ever prove too strong for the restraints of such a system as this. It will keep no nation, no age, effectually in check. And such proves to be the case. Both the religious and the ethical systems of the pagan world — systems which flourished in the palmiest days of the most cultivated and refined nations of antiquity — show conclusively that natural religion is not enough. Neither in the one nor the other do we find clear and adequate conceptions of the Supreme Being, of the future state, of the way of pardon to the erring and the lost; neither in the one nor the other do we find any restraining power, effective and sufficient to keep a people or an age from the grossest corruptions and sins. Under all these systems, ethical and religious, the tendency of the nations was from bad to worse.

The Deficiency Remedied. — Something other and better was needed, — some more explicit revelation of the divine will and of human duty, some influence more powerful to restrain men from known sin, was needed, and was given. In the sacred Scriptures we have that which we seek in vain among the philosophies and the mythologies of the world, — that knowledge which neither natural religion nor the unaided reason and moral sense of man can furnish. It is not the province of Moral Philosophy to unfold and state in their order the great truths made known in revelation, much less to present the arguments by which such a revelation is established. It is the business of Theology to do this. It is sufficient to our present purpose to say, that the Bible reveals God and his attributes more perfectly than they could otherwise be known to man; that it fully and explicitly and positively makes known his will, that law which is to us the true rule of duty; that it reveals in all its grandeur and power the doctrine of the future, — a life beyond the narrow confines of the present, in which men shall be rewarded or punished, according to the deeds done and the character formed in the present life; above all, that it reveals to sinful man the way of escape from guilt and ruin, through HIM who is the way, the truth, and the life.

CHAPTER IV.

PROVINCE OF RIGHT.

Two Questions.—In further discussing the science of right, two questions present themselves. 1. *What is a moral action;* or, in other words, what sort of actions are properly so called? 2. *In what consists the morality of any given act?* Where lies the virtue or the guilt of it? These questions comprise a topic which has not been discussed in the preceding chapters, viz., the *province* of right. We will take them in their order, as now stated.

§ 1.—What is a Moral Action?

Not all Action Moral.—What class of actions are properly called *moral?* Not all human actions. Some actions have no moral quality. I start at the accidental falling of a window, or discharge of a musket. A person unconsciously talks in his sleep, or in delirium, or, it may be, rises and walks about, performs certain actions, takes the property, or perhaps the life of another, or puts an end to his own life. These are not properly moral actions. They are involuntary, as in the instances first mentioned,—or irrational, as in the cases last specified,—and in neither case do we attach praise or blame to the act. It has no moral quality.

Morality pertains to what.—Morality, the quality of virtue or guilt, of praise or blame, pertains only to the actions of *intelligent* and *rational* beings, and only to the *voluntary* actions of such beings. By action, I mean to include, of course, the various forms of mental activity, and not merely the putting forth of physical power. It is not merely when I move my limbs, raise my hand, or bring into use some one of the bodily organs, that I act; when I think, when I cherish an emotion, affection, or desire; when I put forth a volition, even though the external act should for any reason not follow that volition — in all these cases I act. All these are so many forms of mental activity; and when we speak of moral action, it is to the activity of the mind, primarily and chiefly, that we refer. An external bodily act is moral only so far as it involves and proceeds from some activity of the mind. Otherwise it has no more morality, no more desert of praise or blame, than the movement of an axe, or hammer, or any other mere passive instrument. The body is the instrument of the mind.

Implies Intelligence. — A moral act is always an *intelligent* act. The being who performs it must be capable of comprehending himself, and his own activity; must know what he is about; must understand the bearing of what he does; must act with reference to some end, and having in view the means necessary to secure that end. Mere brute instinct differs from this, lacks this; works blindly; comprehends not itself, nor what it does; works from impulse, not from intelligence. The brute is incapable of moral action.

Implies Reason. — A moral act is always a rational act. A mind destitute of reason may still act intelligently, may act with reference to a given end, and adopt the means best fitted to secure that end. The insane man does this, and often displays no little sagacity and wisdom in the accomplishment of his purposes. He knows what he is doing, and why he takes this or that means to accomplish his purpose. He acts intelligently, but not rationally. His mind is disordered in its action. And so far as this is the case, he is not responsible for his actions. They are not properly moral acts. It may be, and often is, extremely difficult to decide in such cases whether, and in what degree, the mind really is insane, and therefore irresponsible; under cover of this doubt and difficulty, many a crime doubtless goes unpunished; but where it is evident that reason no longer keeps her throne, by common consent the actions of such a mind are regarded as having no moral character.

Implies Volition. — A moral act is always, I suppose, a *voluntary* act. If any act is strictly involuntary, not proceeding from any choice or intention of the doer, mere accident, or mere instinct, or muscular reäction, — as the springing when a window falls, or the closing of the eye when a blow is suddenly aimed at it — actions which are not only without intention and volition, but which no purpose or effort of will could wholly prevent, — such an act, surely, has no moral character. It falls not within the province of right. That only is a moral act which is voluntary, freely put forth of choice and purpose — which we could have refrained from doing, had we chosen.

On the same principle, so far as our thoughts and emotions are strictly involuntary, not within our own control, they cannot properly be classed among our moral acts. It is a principle of the plainest justice, that a man is to be held responsible only for such actions as lie within his power to do or not to do. No law can place me under obligation to perform an act which it is wholly out of my power to perform, — as, *e. g.*, the lifting of a mountain; nor yet to refrain from doing what I cannot possibly, by any effort or volition of mine, avoid doing. To such acts neither virtue nor guilt attaches — neither praise nor blame. Whatever mental activity is of this sort, strictly involuntary and beyond our control, is to be classed in the same category with involuntary muscular movements or contractions.

To a great extent, however, both thought and feeling are moral acts, since *indirectly*, if not *directly*, it is in our power to shape and control them. I cannot, indeed, by a direct act of will, call up or prevent any thought or feeling; but still it is in my power to determine the general course and direction of both. I cannot, perhaps, avoid certain emotions, in view of certain objects presented to the senses or to the thoughts; but I can avoid the perception of those objects; can shut the eye and the ear upon them; can fix the thoughts upon other things, and thus avoid the emotions which they are fitted to awaken. In so far as I fail to exert this control over my own mental activity, in so far I am responsible; in so far the act is of a moral character.

Implies a Moral Faculty.—If I mistake not, there is still another element involved in all moral action—viz., a capacity for perceiving moral distinctions, a power of distinguishing between right and wrong. This we may call the moral faculty. Where this is entirely wanting, I cannot conceive of praise or blame, virtue or guilt, as properly attaching to the conduct. Such a being is certainly not a proper object of law, nor of reward and punishment. This is the case with the brute, and it is the crowning difference between the brute and man. The former has no conception of right or wrong in conduct—no idea of obligation—no feeling of self-approval, nor yet of regret, and remorse, for anything it has done. The brute has no conscience, and, for that reason, is not a moral being. If the human mind is ever reduced to such a condition, whether in the state of idiocy, or in certain forms of insanity, as no longer to possess the power of recognizing and feeling moral distinctions, its acts, in such a case, could not be called moral acts: they have no moral character.

§ II. — In what consists the Morality of any given Act?

Question stated. — When any act is perceived to have a moral character, whether right or wrong, the question may still arise, In what consists, or where lies, the moral quality — the virtue or the guilt — of that act? Wherein does the virtuous act, for example, differ from any other?

This is quite a distinct question from the one discussed in the preceding section, and deserves special consideration.

Does the morality pertain to the *external* act, the physical movement which performs what the will intends; or does it lie in the *volition*, the simple act of will which immediately precedes the external act? Or is it in the resolution, previously formed, to put forth such a volition when the proper time shall come? Or in the thought of the mind which lay back of all this, and which led to the resolution, and so to the deed? Or, if not in any of these, then is it to be found in the *intention*, or *design*, with which the act is performed?

Not in the External Act. — Evidently not in the external, physical act does the morality lie. That, in itself considered, has no moral character. The bodily organism is merely the instrument of the intelligence, which animates and controls its movements; and those movements, in themselves, have no more moral character than the movements of a saw, or any other merely passive instrument. Accordingly, the same external act, as performed by different actors and under different circumstances, may vary exceedingly in its moral character; and that variation may run through the whole scale of morality, from the deepest degree of guilt to the highest degree of virtue.

Let us suppose a case — the taking of human life, for example. It is done in malice, or for gain. That is murder. It is done by the executioner, in obedience to law. That is a simple act of justice. It is done to save life. That is self-defence. It is done by accident, without design. That is no crime. Yet in all these cases the external act may be the same, the instrument the same, the effect produced the same.

Evidently the moral quality lies not in the external act.

Not in the Executive Volition.—Nor yet does the morality pertain to those mental states which immediately precede, and give rise to, the external act; since these are, necessarily, the same, whatever the moral character of the act. The volition which immediately precedes and produces the movement of the arm by which a blow is struck, is one and the same thing, whether that blow results in murder, or in the execution of justice, or in accidental homicide, or in self-defence. In any case, it is simply a volition to strike a blow by the movement of the arm. And so, also, of the resolution which precedes the direct volition, or effort of the will. Whatever imparts moral character to the act, taken as a whole, imparts it also to these constituent elements of the act; but in themselves, neither the external movement, nor the direct volition to move, nor the resolution or purpose to put forth such a volition, have any distinctive moral character. There is something else always to be taken into the account before we can determine the moral character of any of those elements which are involved in a moral act.

Consists in the Intention. — That which gives character to the act, and which alone determines its moral quality, is the intention or design with which the act is performed.

In the case supposed, it was the intention of one man to commit murder; he struck the blow for that purpose, with that design; and this intention constitutes his guilt. Hence he would have been really guilty of murder, in the sight of Him who knows the secrets of the heart, even had the blow failed to accomplish its purpose. The intention, the design was — murder. The intention of another man was the simple discharge of his duty as an officer of justice — a right intention, and so a right act. The design of another was to defend himself, or others, from lawless violence; and if we are satisfied that this was really his purpose, and that the act was necessary to that end, or even that he believed it to be so, we justify him at once from the imputation of crime. Still another man intended by the blow merely a certain mechanical effect; but the instrument which he wielded for that purpose, glancing from its intended course, struck down a bystander. The result was accidental. He who struck the fatal blow had no such design, and this being once ascertained, there is no longer the charge of guilt.

We act upon this Rule. — In estimating the character of actions, we always proceed upon this principle. We look at the *intention*, the design of the doer; we seek to know what the person *meant;* and if we are satisfied that no wrong was intended, we exculpate him from blame; otherwise we hold him guilty. It is not so much the actual result as the intention that we look at. So, in respect to our own conduct, it is not so much what was actually accomplished, for good or ill, as what was designed and attempted, that forms the standard by which we estimate our own guilt or innocence — our good or ill desert. The good man, sacrificing and toiling much for some worthy end, but all to little purpose, consoles himself by the reflection that his actions are to be weighed, not by their success, but their design; that he deserves well who meant and endeavored well.

Where we are satisfied, on the other hand, that an act, however desirable in itself, is prompted by no good intention, we hesitate to assign it the rank of a virtue. A ruler requires the loyalty, love, and obedience of his subjects. That obedience they may render, however, not from loyalty or love, but from fear, or the desire of gain. With such obedience he is not satisfied. It is an obedience rendered, not for the sake of honoring or serving the ruler, but with a purely selfish design. There is no virtue in such obedience. The case is the same with respect to the parent and his children, and with respect to man in his relations to the Supreme Ruler. God looks at the heart, scans the purposes of man; and as is the meaning and intention of the man, so, in his sight, is the man himself.

Virtue what.—On the principle now established, we may define morality or virtue to be *the doing right, intentionally, and because it is right.* That alone is strictly a virtuous act which is done voluntarily—done as right, and because it is believed to be right; in other words, which is done from a sense of duty. Whatever neglects, overlooks, or violates this rule, whatever other character it may possess, is not of the nature of true virtue. "That is a virtuous action," says Chalmers, "which a man voluntarily does on the simple ground that he *ought* to do it."

CHAPTER V.

FACULTIES OF THE MIND COGNIZANT OF RIGHT.

To explain in detail the operations of the several mental faculties, is the province of Psychology. To this it pertains to treat explicitly of the moral faculty, the power of the mind by which it perceives and recognizes moral truth, and also of the emotions awakened in view of such truth. So intimately, however, are these themes related to the Philosophy of Morals, that it seems necessary to consider them briefly in this connection. For a more full discussion of the nature and power of Conscience, the reader is referred to the sections which treat of these topics in my work on Mental Philosophy.

Analysis of Conscience. — When any moral act — our own, or that of another — is presented to our thoughts as an object of distinct consideration, the process through which the mind passes is somewhat peculiar, and will be found, if I mistake not, to comprise several distinct steps or elements, essentially the same in all cases. There is, in the first place, an impression, or perception, more or less clear and decided, that the act in view is a *right* or a wrong act — whichever it may be — a recognition of it as such. This is an exercise of judgment, an intellectual operation. The proposition, or affirmation of the mind, in view of the case, is "*That is right,*" or "*That is not right.*" This decision is more or less clear and positive, in proportion as the act contemplated is more or less strongly marked in its features and general character. In some cases we hesitate, and form a doubtful opinion; in others, the decision is instantaneous and positive.

No sooner is this decision reached, than there follows another mental state, — the conviction or perception of obligation in respect to the act contemplated. The proposition now is, "*I ought,*" or "*I ought not.*" This, too, is an intellectual process, a conviction, a judgment; not unaccompanied, however, with feeling, which is the case indeed with most of our intellectual operations. That which awakens intellectual activity, awakens also some degree of feeling. Hence, we speak of feeling the truth of a proposition, or the force of an argument; of feeling our obligation to do this and that. A careful analysis, however, will show that the feeling, in this case, is distinct from the intellectual perception; that it succeeds, and is based upon such perception, and derives from it whatever character and strength it possesses.

This idea of obligation, it may be further observed, relates to the past, as well as to the future. I ought to have done, or I ought not to have done, this or that, — an act, the scene of which lies among the years that are long past, and in lands, it may be, remote. It extends also to the actions of others. We form our opinions, and pass our judgment, on the character and conduct of those about whom we read or hear. These persons ought, or ought not, to have done thus and thus.

Further Analysis. — When the obligation to a given course is perceived, there follows yet another state of mind, — the approbation or disapproval of the conduct, according as it conforms to, or violates that obligation. This approving or condemning verdict is also an act of conscience, or the moral faculty — one of its specific and appropriate functions. Like the preceding, it is strictly, in the first instance, an intellectual act, an exercise of judgment, a verdict given in view of the case as presented to the understanding; followed, however, immediately, in many cases, with the strongest emotion. It is a verdict on which depends much — often, everything that is of value in life. Herein lies the power of an approving or accusing conscience. The proposition now stands, "I have done well" — "I have done ill;" and in that simple verdict, calmly rendered, but seldom reversed, lies a sustaining or condemning power, greater than that of thrones and armies — a power that can look danger and death in the face, and defy a world in arms — a power that can make the guilty man tremble, though surrounded by all that wealth, and station, and princely dignity can confer.

Summary. — These several momenta comprise the essential elements of what is usually termed conscience, or the moral faculty. As thus analyzed, conscience is simply the intellect perceiving and judging of moral truth, together with a corresponding excitement of the sensibilities, in view of the objects thus contemplated. The term is used, however, to denote not merely, or so much, the act itself, the process of mind now analyzed, as the *power* of thus perceiving and judging. Nor is it a power, a capability merely, which can be exercised or withheld at the pleasure of the possessor. It is more than that — a constitution of the mind in virtue of which it *shall*, under ordinary circumstances, perceive, and feel, and act thus — shall recognize such distinctions and obligations, and shall, in view of the same, pronounce such verdicts.

Psychologically viewed, it is not so much a distinct faculty of the mind, coördinate with perception, memory, imagination, etc., as a distinct exercise, or department of action, of the general faculty of judgment, and of the power of feeling, as employed with reference to one particular class of truth, viz., moral. The mind is so constituted, that in view of such truth, it shall act as now stated, recognizing the right and the wrong of human conduct, measuring its actions and those of others by this standard, and approving or condemning accordingly. This power we call the moral faculty.

Authority of Conscience. — With regard to the authority of this faculty, it is evident that, with the view now given of the nature of conscience, it is impossible to consider it as in any sense an infallible guide. It is a moral judgment, accompanied by a moral feeling, and, like all other judgments and feelings, is liable to err. It is, in this respect, on the same footing with all the other powers of the human mind. Not one of them is infallible. A man may act conscientiously, and still be in the wrong. His judgments are not sure to be right. At the best, he is liable to err; and the fact that he goes according to the dictates of his conscience, does not free him from this liability. He must, indeed, abide by the decisions of conscience, and govern his conduct accordingly; but he must see to it that those decisions are intelligently formed. He must bow to the authority of conscience; but he must also take heed that his conscience is not a blind guide, but one on whose eye and on whose path falls the clear light of nature and of reason, and the still purer light of God's word.

CHAPTER VI.

HISTORIC SKETCH OF OPINIONS RESPECTING THE NATURE AND GROUND OF RIGHT.

It is often of the highest service, in our investigation of truth, to know the opinions which have been held by others, and the results at which other minds have arrived, as regards the matters in question. Especially is this the case with regard to the questions which have occupied us in the preceding chapters. A brief outline of the various opinions which have been held by writers of different periods, both ancient and modern, as to the nature and foundation of right, may give us a clearer view of the matter discussed, and serve to fix in our minds the principles advanced in the preceding chapters. We begin with the philosophy of the ancients.

Doctrine of Socrates. — Socrates may be regarded as the first of the ancient philosophers who gave special attention to the nature of virtue. His teachings lay the foundation of scientific ethics; but only the foundation. His doctrine of right is a peculiar one. Virtue is nearly synonymous with *knowledge*, in the Socratic system. The *doing*, is consequent upon the *knowing*, of what is good, and best to be done. Nothing is virtuous in conduct, which is done without discernment. Hence, no man is voluntarily vicious. He does as well as he knows.

As to the question what things are right, and what are wrong, the teachings of Socrates do not furnish an explicit answer. He refers us to the laws of the land in which we may happen to live, for the establishment of specific ethical rules; and while he does not expressly teach that the *foundation* and *ground* of right is its *utility*, still he has much to say of the utility of virtue.

Disciples of Socrates. — 1. THE CYNICS. — Virtue, according to the Cynics, consists in a life according to nature; a complete independence of all arbitrary and conventional laws and usages; the absence of, and entire freedom from all *wants* and all *desires;* complete superiority to all these things. To such an extent did they carry this doctrine, as to render both themselves and their philosophy objects of general aversion and contempt.

2. THE CYRENAICS. — With the Cyrenaics, on the contrary, *pleasure* is the chief good, and virtue is to be commended and pursued, as conducing to this result — the means to this end. Socrates had given prominence in his teachings to the happiness which virtue affords. Aristippus, looking solely at this, makes happiness the chief end of man, and recommends moderation, self-control, self-culture, as the most direct means to the attainment of this end.

Doctrine of Plato. — Plato holds fast the Socratic notion of virtue as science — a thing to be learned. In respect to the highest good, he takes a middle ground, between the conflicting schools just mentioned — neither admitting, with the Cyrenaics, that pleasure is the chief good of life, nor, with the Cynics, rejecting it entirely, as unworthy of regard.

The *idea* of the good and the evil, according to Plato, is not derived immediately from sense, as are our perceptions of external objects, but constitutes, along with kindred ideas, as of the beautiful, etc., a distinct and peculiar province of knowledge, an *a priori* faculty of the mind. As back of the senses, and their perceptions, there lies a power that can compare and contrast these perceptions one with another, — a power of the soul superior to sense, and independent of it, — so, in like manner, the soul, by its own inherent activity, conceives and distinguishes the beautiful and the odious, the good and the evil. This fac ulty is what, in the different schools of modern philosophy, passes under the name of original, or intuitive conception, original suggestion, the reason, etc.

In one point, the ethical philosophy of Plato seems to us defective. The conception of *duty* — the *right*, as such, in distinction from the merely good — is nowhere distinctly and prominently brought out, but lies quite in the background. This is a defect, however, which pertains equally to the Socratic ethics.

Doctrine of Aristotle. — The great mistake which, from Socrates onward, has prevailed respecting the nature of virtue, that it is one and the same with knowledge, is, in the philosophy of Aristotle, for the first time, distinctly set right. Virtue is with him not so much an intellectual element and process, as a moral one; it is not a knowing, but a doing. The doing, according to Socrates and Plato, is consequent upon the knowing; if a man knows the good he will do it. With Aristotle, on the contrary, the knowing is consequent upon the doing; the more a man does, and seeks to do the right, the better he will know the right. To make virtue a merely intellectual affair, overlooks, according to Aristotle, an essential element of our nature, — *i. e.*, the moral element, the natural instinct of the soul, which demands and strives for the good, and which approves and is satisfied with that only which is right in human conduct and endeavor. Virtue is not so much, then, a thing to be learned, as a thing to be done or practised, in the following out this natural craving and instinct of the soul. It is by the practice of virtue that we become virtuous. Virtue is the *habit* of doing right. Nature lays the foundation in so constituting the mind that it craves and approves the good; reason and intelligence build on this foundation; habit confirms and binds together the whole. Our good and evil dispositions are originally in our own power; but when once formed, by habit, to virtue or to vice, they are no longer under control.

The highest good, the chief end and motive of human endeavor, Aristotle concedes to be happiness in some form. But, then, what is happiness? Not the gratification of the senses, surely; for, in this respect, man is in no way superior to the brute. The true happiness for man is the highest activity of his intelligent nature, the unrestrained energy of well-being and of well-doing, which satisfies all the conditions of his mental and moral nature. It is the perfect activity of a perfect life.

In practical matters, virtue lies in pursuing the right mean between opposite extremes. Thus justice is the moral mean between doing wrong and suffering wrong. This mean varies with circumstances and individuals.

Doctrine of the Stoics. — The Stoics make much account of law and order in the universe. Everything must conform to the order of nature. The highest law of human action, the highest end of life, is to shape our conduct according to the universal law of nature, and live in harmony therewith. Live according to thy rational nature, is the practical maxim, or rule of life, of the Stoics.

But pleasure is not a good — has no moral worth — is to be disregarded and despised. It is no end of nature, but something accidental. It is not an activity, but a passive state of the soul, a limitation of that activity which alone the true blessedness. External good of every kind is morally indifferent; virtue alone is real good. Actions, of course, are to be regarded as good or evil, not according as they result in advantage or disadvantage to the doer, not according to their tendencies and consequences, but in themselves. A certain course of conduct is to be approved and pursued, not because it conduces to health and happiness, but for its own sake. Health, wealth, happiness, are indifferent and worthless — to be preferred, perhaps, to sickness, poverty, and the like, but not to be considered as good in themselves.

The good man is he who governs himself according to reason; the bad man is he in whom reason is not awakened, but instinct has the mastery. And, inasmuch as every man is under the dominion of one or the other, the good man is wholly good, and the bad man wholly bad. Nor are there any *degrees* of virtue, — all good acts are equally good, and all bad acts equally bad.

The system of the Stoics was, it must be confessed, rigorous and severe. As compared with the ethical philosophy of Aristotle, it strikes one as ideal, and impracticable.

Doctrine of the Epicureans. — Quite the reverse of this was the ethical system of the Epicurean school. In common with most of the preceding schools, they make the highest good consist in *happiness;* but then, the chief element of happiness is *pleasure,* — so that this may be regarded as the highest good. By pleasure, however, they do not mean merely the gratification of the present moment, but that which will ensure the happiness of the whole life. Even pain, if it will lead to a greater pleasure, is to be welcomed. The pleasures of the soul, accordingly, are of greater account than those of the body merely, since the former are lasting, and the latter momentary. And, what is more, pleasure is inseparable from a *virtuous* life. There can be no true and lasting happiness without virtue. As thus defined, the system of the Epicureans is equally removed from that of the Cyrenaics on the one hand, who regard pleasure as the chief good, but mean thereby chiefly the pleasures of sense, and from that of the Cynics and the Stoics on the other, who regard all pleasure as a thing to be despised.

Ethical Philosophy of the Moderns.—Thus far our attention has been directed to the ethical doctrines of the ancients. Turning now to more recent times, we shall find the same great questions arising for discussion, which we have found agitating and dividing the ancient schools,—*e. g.*, the nature of virtue, and the ground of right—whether right and wrong are independent principles, or whether they are to be estimated according to the results, the advantages and disadvantages to which they lead. In tracing these doctrines, I can refer only to the views of the more prominent authors and schools of philosophy.

Early English Moralists.—Since the prevalence of Christianity, and the purer views of morality which it could not fail to introduce, the idea of *right* as an independent principle of action—the idea of *duty*, in distinction from the merely good—has been brought more prominently to view in the systems of morality. The same is true, also, of the principle of *conscience*. The nature and authority of conscience have been much in dispute; but by general agreement it has been regarded as the foundation of moral science. A great part, in fact, of the ethics of the seventeenth century consists of the discussion of cases of conscience. The Reformation, doubtless, led the way to this, by teaching that the conscience cannot be safely entrusted to the keeping of the church and the clergy, or subject to any human authority; but that every man is individually responsible for his own belief, and his own actions. As early as the twelfth century, indeed, we find *Abelard* teaching that the fundamental rule of duty is the divine will, as revealed in conscience and in Scripture.

The early English moralists take essentially the same ground. *Jeremy Taylor*, in his *Rule of Conscience*, makes the authority of conscience the basis of his system of morals, and quotes with approbation the saying of St. Bernard: "Conscience is the brightness of the eternal light, the spotless mirror of the divine majesty, and the image of the goodness of God." The doctrine of Taylor is, that as God is present, governing the world by his providence, so he is present in our hearts by his laws, governing us by conscience, which is his substitute, or representative. This gives to conscience not merely a place as the foundation of morals, but clothes it, in a sense, with a divine commission and authority. This view of conscience as, conjointly with Scripture, the ground and acknowledged basis of morality, seems to have been very generally entertained by the leading minds of the seventeenth century in England.

Theory of Hobbes.— This view was not without antagonism. A powerful opponent arose, at once subtle and bold, in the person of Thomas Hobbes, the philosopher of Malmesbury, who held that Law, or the State, is the origin of all rights and duties. In the state of nature, every man is at war with every man, and in such a state there are no rights or duties,—"The notions of Right and Wrong, Justice and Injustice, have there no place." From this state of nature man emerges into society, and the civil body, or the State, is, as a matter of self-defence, constructed. This it is which gives law,—and thus arises duty and the nature of right. The doctrine "*that every private man is judge of good and evil actions*," he pronounces a poisonous and seditious doctrine, dangerous to the State; "whereas it is manifest that the measure of good and evil actions is the *Civil Law*." To him who lives in civil society "the Law is the public Conscience by which he hath already undertaken to be guided." This annihilates at a blow man's moral nature, and resolves morality and duty into the power of the civil arm. Might makes right.

These principles were received with very little favor, and called forth many replies. As Whewell very justly remarks, however, these tenets, so startling and offensive, were very far from being new. "The whole of this controversy had agitated the schools of philosophy many ages earlier." It was in substance the same question which comes up for discussion so frequently in the dialogues of Plato and of Cicero, whether right and wrong are independent qualities of actions, or whether they are merely terms to denote the advantages or disadvantages that result from certain courses of behavior. This question, discussed, as we have seen, by Cynic and Cyrenaic, by Stoic and Epicurean, runs through the whole history of morals.

Cudworth. — One of the principal opponents of this scheme of Hobbes was Ralph Cudworth, who, in his *Treatise concerning Eternal and Immutable Morality*, takes the ground that our perception of right and wrong is an ultimate fact in our nature, that these ideas are simple and incapable of analysis, and that the mind is able to form them antecedently to positive institutions. He shows that the doctrines of Hobbes were but the revived dogmas and sophistries of earlier schools — essentially the very dogmas against which Plato argued in condemning the doctrine of Protagoras, that all our knowledge is derived from sense. With Plato, he maintains that some of our ideas proceed not from sensible objects, but from the mind's own activity; among these the idea of right and wrong; and that these ideas, though existing only in the mind, are not creations of the mind, but realities eternal and immutable.

Doctrine of Locke. — The doctrines of Locke have been the occasion of much dispute. It is by no means easy to assign to this distinguished man his true position in philosophy and morals. It seems clear, however, that whatever may have been his own personal views and feelings, the tendency of his philosophy was quite in the opposite direction to the system of Cudworth and the independent moralists. Deriving all our simple ideas from sensation and reflection, or the observation of things without, and of our own mental operations, he seems to leave no place, according to this account of the matter, for the ideas of right and wrong. These, consequently, are not simple and original ideas, but *derived* — the result of education.

Accordingly, moral good and evil are not, in this philosophy, independent principles. "Good or evil are nothing but pleasure or pain, or that which occasions or procures pleasure or pain to us. Moral good and evil, thus, is only the conformity or disagreement of our voluntary actions to some law whereby good or evil is drawn on us by the will and power of the law-maker; which good and evil, pleasure or pain, attending our observance or breach of the law, by the decree of the law-maker, is that we call reward and punishment." — (Book II., ch. 28, § 5.) This manifestly places Locke in the lower school of moralists, in distinction from the higher ground of Plato and Cudworth. The morality of his system is that of *consequences* rather than of eternal and immutable distinctions. The tendency of his philosophy, it may be remarked, was much further and stronger in this direction than he himself was probably aware. Like most great minds, he seems to have held views inconsistent with his own system. His philosophy led to results which he would by no means have adopted.

Clarke and Price.—In opposition to the views of Locke, and in accordance with the system of Cudworth, Dr. Samuel Clarke maintains the eternal nature and independent character of moral distinctions. These eternal differences and relations of things determine the essential fitness and reasonableness of certain courses of conduct, and the unfitness and unreasonableness of the opposite courses. With reference to this fitness, the will of God always chooses; and creatures ought also to choose with reference to the same. Duty, obligation result from this source, independent even of the divine will, and of all prospect of reward or gain.

Dr. Price, also, in opposition to Locke, ascribes the origin of our ideas of right and wrong to the *understanding*, or the *reason*, which terms are used to denote the general faculty of intelligence, and which is affirmed to be "itself a source of new ideas." We reach these ideas by means of an intuitive perception, or intuitive judgment. They express qualities of actions, and not mere impressions and sensations, pleasurable or painful, of our own minds; realities, eternal and immutable.

Shaftesbury, *Hutcheson*, *Hume.*—With the writers now named, there comes into use a new mode of expressing and accounting for our moral ideas and perceptions. It was now asserted that there is a peculiar faculty of the mind whose office it is to perceive these distinctions, and to this faculty the name of *the moral sense* was given. *Shaftesbury*, himself an advocate of the independent and original nature of moral distinctions, introduced this use of terms. He speaks of the *sense* of right and of wrong, and calls it the *moral* sense. He likens it to the natural sense of the sublime and the beautiful. Hutcheson gives greater prominence to this view, and makes it the basis of his system. We have a natural sense or instinct for the right, as we have for the beauty of color or sound — as we have instincts and affections for other specific objects. *Hume*, adopting this view, and carrying it to its extreme results, makes virtue and vice, as well as beauty and deformity, matters of mere taste or sentiment. Right and wrong do not denote any independent quality in the *object* thus designated, but only an effect or sensation produced in our own minds; just as sweet and bitter, the pleasant and the painful, are merely our own sensations, and not properly qualities of objects. Referring to the doctrine — supposed to be fully proved in modern times — "that tastes and colors, and all other sensible qualities, lie not in the bodies, but merely in the senses," he adds: "The case is the same with beauty and deformity, virtue and vice." — (Essays, Part I. Essay XVIII.) Thus we are brought back again, in the revolving cycle of opinion, to the old doctrine of Protagoras, that nothing is true or false, any more than sweet or sour, in itself, but only with reference to the perceiving mind. Whatever anything *seems* to be, to any mind, that, and that only, it is.

Butler. — The writings of Butler have justly placed him in the front rank of English moralists. He asserts, more clearly, perhaps, than any preceding writer had done, the existence of a moral faculty, while he nowhere closely or sharply analyzes the precise nature of this faculty. His principles are those of the independent school of moralists, that right and wrong are something in themselves, and not merely in their consequences. Still, these principles are nowhere very distinctly announced or systematically defended. He seems purposely to have avoided technical or philosophical terms, and to have expressed himself in common and popular language, in treating of this class of subjects, — a language not always sufficiently definite for philosophical purposes. He is classed among the unsystematic moralists by Whewell. Notwithstanding some vagueness of expression, however, Butler clearly maintains the independent nature of moral distinctions. There is a difference, he holds, among our faculties, not of degree, merely, but of kind, — some are superior to others, of higher authority; and the faculty to which belongs an authority and supremacy over all the rest is conscience.

Warburton. — Dissatisfied with the doctrines of Cudworth, Clarke, Price, and Butler, on the one hand, as placing the ground of morals in the eternal fitness of things, and also with the moral sense of Shaftesbury, Hutcheson, and their disciples, as reducing morality to a mere sentiment or taste, a class of moralists arose who maintained that the *will of God* is the basis of morality and source of obligation. We need look no further than this. To know that the divine will requires a given thing, is of itself sufficient to put us under obligation to do that thing. There is no morality without law, no other basis of obligation than the divine command. Such was the view of Warburton. He lays it down as an axiom that "Obligation necessarily implies an obliger." The action is thus regarded not as right or wrong in itself, and obligatory *because* right, but only as *commanded.* This view became, for a time, the prevalent mode of thought, and gave character to the moral teaching, especially of the university of Cambridge. It is the view maintained essentially by *Law*, Professor of Moral Philosophy in the university, and still more fully by *Waterland*, Master of Magdalen College.

Paley and his followers. — This view received still further development and modification at the hands of a writer more vigorous and popular in his style, and far more widely known, than either of those just mentioned. I refer to the celebrated Dr. Paley. To resolve all obligation into the mere command of God, might seem somewhat arbitrary. Is there not a *reason why* God commands what he does? Seeks he not always the happiness of his creatures? Is not this, then, the real and ultimate criterion of duty? Paley was not the first to combine these two principles. Mr. *Gay*, Fellow of Sidney College, Cambridge, author of the dissertation on the Nature of Virtue prefixed to King's Origin of Evil, had already advanced this view. "Thus the will of God is the criterion of virtue, and the happiness of mankind the criterion of the will of God; and therefore the happiness of mankind may be said to be the criterion of virtue but *once* removed." Gay, accordingly, defines virtue to be "conformity to a rule of life, directing the actions of all rational creatures with respect to each other's happiness; to which conformity every one, in all cases, is obliged." The same doctrine is also advanced by *Tucker*, author of the "Light of Nature Pursued," a work frequently referred to by Paley. This author regards the *highest good* "to be none other than pleasure, or satisfaction;" and speaks of it as absurd to talk of things as being *right in themselves*, without regard to consequences, inasmuch as "things are rendered right by their tendency to some end." We are now fairly and fully again upon the morality of consequences, of utility, and expediency,— no new doctrine, as we have seen, in the history of morals. It is evident, likewise, that Paley is by no means original in advancing this system at the time when he wrote. The writings of *Law*, and especially of *Gay*, and *Tucker*, and *Rutherforth*, had fully prepared the way for it.

Paley defines virtue to be "the doing good to mankind, in obedience to the will of God, and for the sake of everlasting happiness." It has been frequently and very justly objected to this scheme, that it recognizes only *one class* of duties — those to mankind; and also that it seems to make it essential to a virtuous act that it should be done *for the sake* of future reward. In carrying out this philosophy, Paley loses sight of the idea of *right*, and of duty as based on the right, and resolves all obligation into mere command, without reference to the question what we *ought* to do. In this he follows Warburton and the Cambridge moralists; but goes further than they had done, inasmuch as he makes moral obligation the result, not from the will of God alone, but from any command or will of another which we cannot well resist. The sum and substance of duty is to act with regard to the highest expediency.

Priestley and Bentham.—The philosophy thus introduced anew to public notice, became immensely popular. It was at once adopted in the university of Cambridge, where, as we have seen, the same doctrine had for sometime previously been taught. Among those who, about this period, take substantially the same ground, must be reckoned two distinguished writers on Political Science, —Priestley and Bentham,—neither of whom, however, is to be regarded as properly a follower of Paley. Indeed, Priestley had, in his Essay on Government, published some seventeen years before the appearance of Paley's works, distinctly announced "*the greatest happiness of the greatest number*" as the true and only proper object of government. Bentham founds his system of political morality expressly on this principle—*utility;* by which he means, as above, the greatest happiness of the greatest number. There is no essential difference between this doctrine and that of Paley.

Stewart.—In opposition to these views, Dugald Stewart, in his Philosophy of the Active and Moral Powers, takes decidedly the ground of the earlier English moralists, and holds moral distinctions to be eternal and immutable. The words right and wrong express *qualities* of actions, and not *consequences* merely. When we say, of an act of justice, that it is right, we do not mean, with Shaftesbury and Hutcheson and Hume, simply that it excites pleasure in the mind, as a particular color pleases the eye; nor, with Hobbes, that society and the strong arm of the state require it; nor, with Warburton and the Cambridge men, that the will of God makes it imperative, and that is the end of the matter; nor yet, with the school of Paley and Bentham, that it is *expedient*, *useful*, for the *highest happiness* of all; but, on the contrary, to say that such a thing is right, is to assert that respecting it which is quite independent of our constitution; as much so "as the equality of the three angles of a triangle and two right angles."—"For my own part," he says, "I can as easily conceive a rational being so formed as to believe the three angles of a triangle to be equal to *one* right angle, as to believe that, if he had it in his power, it would be *right* to sacrifice the happiness of other men to the gratification of his own animal appetites."

Hall. — There were not wanting among the theological and popular writers of England, many to raise their voice against the dangerous tenets of the school of Paley. Robert Hall, among the more modern writers, thus indignantly rebukes this false philosophy: "How is it, that on a subject on which men have thought deeply, from the moment they began to think, and where, consequently, whatever is entirely and fundamentally new must be fundamentally false — how is it, that in contempt of the experience of past ages, and of all precedents, human and divine, we have ventured into a perilous path, which no eye has explored, no foot has trod; and have undertaken, after the lapse of six thousand years, to manufacture a morality of our own — to decide by a cold calculation of interest, by a ledger-book of profit and loss, the preference of truth to falsehood, of piety to blasphemy, and of humanity and justice to treachery and blood?"

American Moralists. — In the preceding sketch, I have confined myself thus far to the opinions of English writers. Of the French and German philosophers, in so far as they have discussed the particular topics now before us, the limits of the present chapter do not allow me to speak. In our own country, the two great systems — that of *independent* morality, and the morality of *consequences* — have each had their adherents. *Edwards*, the distinguished theologian, in his dissertation on the Nature of Virtue, regards virtue as "the *beauty* of those qualities and acts of the mind that are of a moral nature," and defines it as consisting essentially in "*benevolence to Being in general*," and more particularly in love to God, as the greatest and best of beings. This benevolence he regards as a higher principle than that moral sense, or conscience, that is natural to mankind.

Dr. Wayland. — Dr. Wayland regards the ultimate rule, the basis of morals, as consisting in, and arising out of, the essential *relations* of things; as, *e. g.*, the relation of parent and child, of state and citizen, of creator and creature. These relations once known, certain *obligations* and *duties* also become manifest.

Dr. Hickok. — According to this eminent moralist and philosopher, the highest good, the ultimate rule and test of action, the basis of moral obligation, is *worthiness of spiritual approbation*, conformity to the *spirit's own intrinsic excellency.* This ultimate right is simple, immutable, and universal.

DIVISION SECOND.

PRACTICAL ETHICS

PRACTICAL ETHICS.

PRELIMINARY ANALYSIS AND CLASSIFICATION.

Our attention has hitherto been directed to those principles which lie at the foundation of ethical science — principles, a correct understanding of which is of the highest importance, if not indeed indispensable to our progress, as we enter upon the second of the two great departments into which moral science was divided at the outset.

Before proceeding to the consideration of the several duties of which this part of our science is to treat, it seems necessary to fix upon some convenient classification of these duties; to this end, a general survey of the field we are about to investigate, and some analysis of the several branches of duty, become desirable.

General Division. — As we cast our eye over the various lines of conduct which constitute the practical duties of life, a general division strikes us at once. Some of these duties seem to have more direct reference to ourselves, others to our fellow-men, others still to our Maker. These would seem to be the natural divisions into which this department of the science falls.

And yet, such is the nature of duty, that a wrong done

to one's self, is also a wrong done to society and to God; and so of all the other departments of duty. It is impossible to neglect or violate a duty to society, or to God, without injury to self,—so closely interlinked is the whole circle of duties, and of interests, each with the other. Only in a general sense, then, and merely for the sake of convenience, can any such division be made as that now proposed. In like manner, we may regard the bodily organism as composed of different members, or parts,—the head—the trunk—the limbs,—while at the same time the system of bones, of veins, of nerves, pervades the whole; and to injure one of the members, or parts, is to injure the whole system.

Further Analysis.—Adopting the general division already indicated, we have, I. The duties which relate more directly to SELF. Of these the principal are, 1. The duty of *Self-support.* 2. Of *Self-defence.* 3. Of *Self-control.* 4. Of *Self-culture.*

II. The duties which relate more directly to OUR FELLOW-MEN. Of these, some are *general*, relating to man as such, or to society at large. Of this class are the duties respecting *Life*, *Liberty*, *Property*, *Reputation*, *Veracity.* Others, again, arise from the *particular institutions* of society, and the relations that thus spring up between the different portions of the community, as thus united. Of this class are the duties arising from the *Family Relation*, as those of Husband and Wife, Parent and Child; and also the duties pertaining to *the State*, as those of the *Citizen* or *Subject*, of the *Government*, and of *States among themselves.*

III. The duties which more directly relate to THE SUPREME BEING. Of these, the principal are the duty of *Reverence*, of *Love*, of *Obedience*, of *Worship.*

Summary of Classes. — Omitting now the more general divisions, the following principal classes or departments of duty present themselves for investigation, in their order:

I. DUTIES TO SELF.
II. DUTIES TO SOCIETY.
III. DUTIES TO THE FAMILY.
IV. DUTIES TO THE STATE.
V. DUTIES TO GOD.

These will constitute the several parts of the second division of our science, *i. e.*, of Practical Ethics.

PART I.

DUTIES TO SELF.

It is necessary, as we proceed, to bear in mind the remarks already made, that no duty is to be regarded as exclusively a duty to ourselves, nor yet to society, nor to the state. The duties which we owe to ourselves are also, in a sense, duties which we owe to the family, to society, to the state, and to our Maker. These all receive injury by any neglect or injury of ourselves; and these all have an interest, accordingly, in the faithful observance of the duties due to self. At the same time, there are certain duties which relate more specifically and directly to ourselves. Of these the chief are, *Self-support*, *Self-defence*, *Self-control*, and *Self-culture*. These will be considered in successive chapters.

CHAPTER I.

SELF-SUPPORT.

General Statement. — There are certain things which every one must do for himself, which others either cannot, or, under ordinary circumstances, will not do for him. Among these is the duty of providing for his own physical wants — the duty of self-support. Every one owes it to himself to make such provision for his own wants as not to be dependent on the charity of others.

Nature intends this, and makes provision for it by conferring upon us those powers and faculties which are requisite to the various pursuits of industry, and by attaching to honest labor the reward of success, to idleness the penalty of inevitable suffering and want. These are the laws and conditions of our being, established by the Creator, fixed and immutable. He that will not work, neither shall he eat, is the universal law of the race. Labor is requisite in order to the production of the fruits of the earth. The food that sustains us, the fabrics that clothe us, the dwellings that shelter us from the inclemency of the seasons, — whatever contributes to the comfort and supplies the varied and innumerable wants of man, — is the product of labor. Now, this labor, that is universally requisite to supply the wants and gratify the desires of men, is something which every one is bound to perform for himself. No one has a right to require another to labor for him unrequited. I may exchange labor for labor, — I may give money, which is simply the representative of labor already performed, for the labor of others which I wish to procure. Lacking this, I must earn my bread by my own toil. I have no right to compel another to labor for me without reward. Nor has another any right to require this of me.

Exceptions to the Rule. — The only exceptions, I suppose, to this law of self-support, are those cases in which there is a real inability to labor. When, in consequence of sickness, casualty, or constitutional deformity, there is lacking, either wholly or in part, the power to provide for one's own subsistence, to that extent is the person thus incapacitated freed from the duty of self-support, on the obvious principle that it is unjust to require of any man what he cannot possibly perform. Hence the duty of others who are able to labor, or who possess in abundance the means of life, to provide for the necessary wants of the sick and suffering; but not to support in idleness those who are able to labor.

Conditions essential to Self-support. — In order to make suitable provision for one's personal wants, certain conditions are absolutely essential. *Industry* is necessary — the diligent, faithful pursuit of some honest calling; but not industry alone. To acquire is merely one part of the business. If we expend our acquisitions as fast as we make them, there is no provision for the future. *Frugality* is necessary, as well as industry. No man has a moral right to expend all that he earns, if by so doing he leaves himself, or those dependent on him, without adequate provision for future support. Industry and frugality become virtues when directed to this end; and the want of them becomes a sin against God and man. It is the duty of every man, not absolutely incapable of the thing, to take care that neither himself nor those dependent on him shall become a tax upon the industry and toil of others. Hence the duty both of industry and frugality on his part. It was a wise remark of an ancient Greek philosopher, that wealth consists not so much in great possessions as in *small wants.* It is not the man that acquires the least who is the poorest, nor is he the richest and most prosperous who gains the most.

CHAPTER II.

SELF-DEFENCE.

Reasonable.—The same rule that makes it a duty to provide for the further subsistence of the body, in order to the preservation of life, justifies and requires its defence from lawless aggression and violence, for the same end. If it is duty to preserve life by supplying the bodily wants, it is a duty to preserve it by guarding against needless injury and destruction. If it is incumbent on us to take precautions against disease and accident, it is equally our duty to ward off the attacks of sudden violence, whether of man or beast; and if, in order to this, a resort to extreme measures becomes necessary, then we are justified in resorting to such measures.

The reasonableness of this view will appear, if we reflect that every man is by the constitution of nature, in an important sense, his own guardian. He is to look after his own interests, and attend to his own wants. No one else can do this for him. His own life and safety are of vastly more consequence to him than they are to any one else. If he is too negligent, or indolent, or cowardly, to protect his own life and person against lawless aggression, he is false to himself.

Hence, it is the instinct of nature, as well as the dictate of reason, to defend ourselves when in danger. It has been called, not improperly, Nature's first law. It is a constitutional impulse, and he who implanted it in the human mind had a design to be accomplished by it. In yielding to this impulse, within due bounds, we are simply carrying out this design.

Due not to Ourselves alone.—Nor is this a matter merely allowable—a thing to be justified, merely. It rises to the rank of a duty, and that not to ourselves only. It is not a matter in which we only are concerned. Others have an interest in it. Our lives are of value to many beside ourselves. If we fall under the blows of the assassin, we leave others, unprotected and helpless, it may be, dependent on the charities of the world, to struggle with misfortune and want. This calamity we have no right to entail upon them.

We owe it, also, to many who are not directly dependent on us. Were it understood that, whether from lack of right or lack of courage, men would not defend themselves when attacked, acts of violence would be much more numerous than they are. Every instance of resolute self-defence acts as a preventive of similar crime. The safety of the entire community is in a measure entrusted, in such cases, to our keeping.

Objection.—But do not the Scriptures forbid self-defence? Did not Christ command us, when smitten on one cheek, to turn the other also? I reply, it was not the intention of our Saviour, in those words, to forbid self-defence in cases of real danger, but only the exercise of a revengeful and quarrelsome spirit. Better even to suffer a repetition of the wrong and abuse, than on slight and needless grounds to engage in controversy. That Christ did not mean to forbid self-defence in cases of serious danger, is evident from his permitting his disciples to arm themselves, on at least one occasion. "He that hath no sword, let him sell his garment and buy one."—"And they said, Lord, behold here are two swords."—"And he said unto them, it is enough." One of these swords was actually used in defence of his Master, by one of the disciples, but a short time after these words were spoken. Now, although the purpose of Christ required that he should be given up at this time to his enemies, and therefore defence was not necessary, and so not allowed, still, our Saviour would not have spoken in this manner, much less have permitted his disciples actually to arm themselves, and even to draw and use the sword in the instance referred to, had he regarded all self-defence in such cases as sinful, and therefore to be condemned.

Further Objection. — But it may be said, why not leave the defence of person and property to the law, which is the properly constituted guardian of the rights of the community? I reply, in all cases where a resort to the law is possible, this should be done. We are entitled, as citizens, to the protection of the civil arm; and where the case admits of appeal to that protection, it is undoubtedly the proper mode of defence. But in many cases, such an appeal is out of the question. When attacked by the midnight robber and assassin, the protection of my life or property is, by the very circumstances of the case, committed to my own hands. I must resolutely and instantly defend, or tamely surrender them. Now, when it comes to this, as it often does, which of the two shall die, — the assailer or the assailed, — no reason can be shown why I should prefer the life of the aggressor to my own. He deserves to die. The very act of violence which he is perpetrating forfeits his claim to life. I have the right to live, and to defend myself that I may live.

Limitations of the Rule. — Within what limits, it may be asked, and on what occasions, is the resort to extreme measures justifiable in self-defence? The case already supposed suggests, I think, the true limit. I am author ized to take the matter of protecting my person and property into my own hands only when there is no other apparent and probable mode of defence; and I am at liberty to resort to extreme measures in the case only when milder measures will not answer the purpose. If a simple warning, or the mere presentation of a weapon, is sufficient to deter the aggressor from his purpose, I am not justified in doing more, since self-defence in that case does not require it. But if I can preserve my own life only by taking his, or if I have reason to *believe* that this is the only alternative, the measure is justifiable.

It is to be observed, moreover, that it is only from *lawless violence* that life is to be preserved at the expense of life. Suppose, when attacked, I act upon the principle of self-defence. The assailant becomes himself assailed, and it may be that his life, in turn, is in danger. Is it for him now to proceed upon the principle above stated, and preserve his own life by taking mine? Would he be justified in so doing? Manifestly not. The violence from which I defend myself is *lawless;* that from which *he* defends himself is *lawful.* He had no right to put my life in danger; I have the right, in self-defence, to endanger his.

On the same principle, the prisoner under sentence of law, or under arrest, is not at liberty to set himself free by an attack upon his keeper. The right of self-defence does not belong to him under those circumstances.

Further Limitation.—It may admit of serious question, whether, for the defence of property alone, where life is not also at stake, it is right to take human life. A robber assails me on the highway. He demands my property merely, and promises that my life and person shall be unharmed, in case I surrender my purse. He has no right to make that demand, much less a right to threaten my life, in case of refusal. I can protect my property only by taking the life of the aggressor. Have I a right to do so? In the eye of the law, I should be guilty of no crime, in the case now supposed, were I to do this. But have I a moral right? Where my life is in peril, and can be preserved only by the death of my assailant, I am at liberty to defend myself to the last extremity, *since my life is, at least, of equal value with his.* But is it certain that my *property* is of equal value with the life of the assailant? This is not so clear. There may be cases in which the protection of property may be justifiable, even at the expense of life. But, where any doubt remains, it were certainly better to part with any amount of property, rather than to incur the guilt of unlawfully shedding human blood.

Defence of the Rights of Others.—I would by no means be understood as limiting the right of defence to those cases in which our own life, person, or property is in danger. The same principle extends to the rights of others. The lives, the safety, the property of others, may be committed to our care, and dependent on us; in that case, the same reasons that render the defence of our own lives or property justifiable, require us to defend theirs. Every man owes it both to himself and to his family, to defend from danger those who look to him as their natural guardian and protector.

A Questionable Case.—It may sometimes happen, in other cases besides those of lawless aggression, that our own lives, or property, can be protected only at the expense of the life and property of another. My neighbor's house and my own are both in danger of destruction, by fire, at one and the same moment. There are means of preserving one of them, but not both. Which shall it be? Does duty to myself require me to protect my own property at the expense of his? A plank, floating on the water, comes within my reach as I am struggling for life. It is sufficient to bear up one alone. At my side is another person, also struggling for life. Does the law of self-protection apply in such a case? It is difficult to lay down any rule that shall apply to all such cases. They must be determined according to circumstances. As a general principle, it is better to suffer harm ourselves, than to protect ourselves at the risk of injustice to others; better always to suffer wrong, than to do wrong; and where there is danger of wronging another, in the act of protecting self, it would be the impulse of a true and generous heart to forego the claims of self-protection. There can be no doubt on which side we shall be most liable, in such cases, to err. The danger is, that selfishness will prevail over a due consideration of the rights of others, and that the instinct of self-preservation will prove stronger than all our scruples.

CHAPTER III.

SELF-CONTROL.

PROMINENT among the duties which we owe to ourselves, is that of self-control. This relates to the government of the temper, and of all those appetites, propensities, and passions, which, while having their foundation in the constitution of our nature, require to be kept under restraint, subject to the dictates of reason and discretion.

As relates to the Temper. — Every man owes it to himself to maintain perfect control over his own temper. I refer more particularly to those feelings of indignation and resentment which naturally arise in view of injury received, and which is properly called anger. These feelings require to be held in check with a firm and steady hand. Unrestrained, they trample on all that is sacred, and subject reason, judgment, principle, the man himself, to their petty tyranny. They destroy character and influence, and shorten life itself.

The man who has no control over himself in this matter, — whose anger breaks forth, lawless and ungovernable, on every provocation, — is wholly at the mercy of events. He is not his own master. He is like one afflicted with the St. Vitus' dance, who has no control over his own movements, but must go when the fit takes him, wherever he may be. Nay, worse; it is in the power of his enemies to bring the fit of anger upon him, and make themselves merry at his expense.

These feelings are capable of control. By due care and self-discipline, they may be brought into subjection to reason and the will. But to do this, requires effort, resolution, vigilance. It is the work of time. There is, however, no nobler conquest for any man to make than the conquest of himself; none, perhaps, more difficult; must I add, none more seldom made. It is easier to subdue kingdoms, and lead armies captive, than to subdue and lead captive one's own rebellious passions. Hence it is, that "He that is slow to anger, is better than the mighty; and he that ruleth his spirit, than he that taketh a city." For want of this control, many of the greatest men in the world's history, most distinguished for valor and brilliant achievement, have been really among the weakest of men — objects of compassion rather than of envy to every sensible mind. The hero who wept that there were no more worlds to conquer, seems never to have learned that within his own bosom lay a restless and turbulent kingdom, over which, with all his armies and all his power and valor, he had as yet attained no dominion.

As relates to other Passions and Propensities. — But self-control relates not to the temper alone; it implies the due restraint of all our passions, appetites, and propensities. It includes what we mean by temperance, in its widest sense — abstinence from all those excesses and vices which injure the health, impair the strength and activity of body and mind, weaken the character and influence, cut short the life. To yield to the passions and appetites of the animal nature, without restraint, involves these consequences. They may be remote, and slow of approach, but they are sure. The eternal and immutable laws of nature have established this connection, and decreed these results. They are not to be avoided. Hence, it is one of the plainest dictates of prudence, one of the first and most imperative duties which we owe to ourselves, to keep these appetites and propensities of the animal nature under strict control. If to defend the person from the violent assault of robber or assassin, be a duty, much more to defend the mind and moral nature from injury and ruin. Sensuality ruins both body and soul. He who yields to this foe is lost.

It may be difficult, in many cases, to assign the precise limit within which indulgence of the appetites is allowable, and beyond which it becomes a crime. Such limits there are; and it is for each one, by careful observation, to determine for himself where they lie. One thing is certain, that he who finds the demands of appetite increasing upon him beyond his power of successful resistance, has already passed that limit.

Objection. — It may be urged by some, that, inasmuch as the passions and propensities of our nature are a part of our original constitution, and, in a sense, the gift of the Creator, it is therefore right to indulge the same, without other limit than that which nature itself imposes; in other words, without restraint. This is the practical philosophy according to which too many, doubtless, are disposed to govern their conduct. It is a philosophy, however, as false as it is shallow — at war not more with reason and revelation than with the common sense of mankind. The fact that a given propensity or passion is founded in the nature with which the Creator has endowed us, is surely no warrant for the indulgence of that propensity or passion beyond the limits which the Creator has himself assigned. He who indulges his passions without restraint, transgresses these limits, and, in reality, does violence to his own nature. Self-control, firm and habitual, is not less the dictate of reason than the command of God.

Necessary to Self-respect, and the Respect of Others. — The exercise of a due self-control, both in regard to the temper and the various animal propensities of our nature, is necessary to all true self-respect. No man who is under the dominion of his baser appetites and passions, can truly respect himself. He knows his own weakness and degradation ; knows and feels that he is a slave, that the sceptre has departed from him, that the crown of his integrity and honor is in the dust. The effect of this is most disastrous upon the character. He who has lost his self-respect, has lost that which no gold can buy. His courage and his moral strength are gone ; nor can virtue long maintain its ascendency in the absence of this principle.

Self-control is necessary also in order to the respect of others. No man can for any length of time receive the real homage and respect of others, who lacks the mastery of himself. Station, power, wealth, may do something for him; native talent and genius, still more; but not even these can ultimately keep back from merited contempt the helpless slave of his own miserable passions. Sad indeed is the spectacle, of one born to high honors, and endowed by nature with princely gifts, from whose hand is stricken the sceptre of dominion over his own spirit.

CHAPTER IV.

SELF-CULTURE.

Statement. — To abstain from those things which injure us, to avoid those excesses and undue indulgences of the natural appetites and propensities which work mischief and ruin, is a duty, but not the whole duty which every intelligent rational being owes to himself. There are things to be attained, as well as things to be avoided; positive, as well as negative duties. Self-culture, not less than self-control, becomes imperative. I have no right to neglect my own highest welfare and advancement. My duty is only in part performed when I refrain from that which positively injures and degrades my mental or bodily powers. It is my duty to develop and cultivate those powers to the highest degree of which they are, under the circumstances, susceptible, — to make the most of the faculties with which nature has endowed me. This is the duty of every man — a duty which he owes first of all to himself, but not to himself alone. The family, the state, society at large, the Creator — all have an interest in this matter, and are concerned in its performance or neglect. The highest wrong is done not to self alone, but to others, by every instance of such neglect.

Extends to what. — The duty of self-culture includes in its proper province the entire range of our natural faculties, whether of body or mind. It includes physical culture not less than mental. A healthy and well-developed physical organism is one of the very choicest goods of life; and, in so far as it is a result to be attained by careful training and culture, it is a duty imperative on every man to make that attainment, and to put forth the effort necessary to it. A sound mind in a sound body, is a maxim true in philosophy and true in morals. The history of the Greeks shows what may be done in this branch of education. In modern times, and more especially among our own countrymen, this department of education has fallen into disrepute, and been very generally overlooked. The theory with us is to discipline and develop the mind, and let the physical powers take care of themselves. Our institutions of learning, our whole educational system, look chiefly to this. It admits of serious question, whether in this we are not committing a radical mistake. So intimate is the connection between the physical and the mental state, that the highest condition and most favorable development of the latter can hardly be secured without due attention to the training and discipline of the former.

Includes also Mental Discipline. — Self-culture extends also to the improvement of the intellectual and moral powers. No man is at liberty to neglect his own mental discipline and culture. Not even are the claims of business paramount to this. No pressure of professional or business engagements can justify the neglect of mental discipline. No man in this busy world has a right so to involve himself in the pursuits and cares of active life, that it shall be out of his power to give both time and care to the improvement of his own mind. Nature never intended this. He who made the mind, and endowed it with its wondrous faculties, had no such intention.

Nor is the culture of the mind to be made subordinate to success in the various employments of life, and to be pursued merely as a means to that end. A means to that end it unquestionably is. But that is not the whole or the chief reason why it should receive attention. The improvement of the mind is, *in itself*, a good of inestimable worth, aside from all the gain that comes of it in the more successful pursuits of life. A well-cultivated mind, richly stored with the best acquisitions, is itself a treasure with which no material wealth can compare. "For wisdom is better than rubies; and all the things that may be desired are not to be compared to it."

Not limited to the Intellect. — Nor is the duty of which I speak limited to the culture of the *intellect* alone. Memory, imagination, judgment, the reasoning powers, taste, conscience — all are to be educated and strengthened; but the *sensibilities* also claim regard, and likewise the *will.* These great departments of the mind's activity are not to be overlooked in the process of mental training. The heart requires education and discipline, as well as the head; the feelings, no less than the intellectual powers. He only is the symmetrical, fully developed, well-educated man, with whom all these faculties of his higher and spiritual nature have received due care and training. He who fails of this, fails in one of the first duties which he owes to himself.

Encouragements to this work. — Very great are the inducements, very pressing the motives, to the faithful performance of this duty. Other acquisitions are external, and of precarious tenure; these, a part of the soul itself — so much of real value added to the man. Other riches may take wings; this is the true wealth that remains, while the mind itself has any being, its inalienable inheritance.

Nor does success in this work depend wholly on early advantages. In the absence of these, amid the pressing cares of active life, much may be done by judicious method, industry, and perseverance, to repair the deficiences of early training. Many of the brightest names in literature and science attest the truth of this.

PART II.

DUTIES TO SOCIETY.

CHAPTER I.

DUTIES PERTAINING TO LIFE.

Value of Life. — Of the duties which we owe to our fellow-men in general, one of the most imperative is the regard which is due to human life. Life is one of the greatest goods, one of the first and chief rights of nature. In comparison with it all other natural goods and possessions are of little account; since, when life itself is at an end, all those possessions and enjoyments which pertain to and depend upon it are also ended. "All that a man hath will he give for his life." Hence, to take human life, has been regarded in all ages as a great crime. It is to rob a man of all his possessions and enjoyments at a stroke, to cut him off from all his plans of business, or of pleasure — from all the pursuits and all the friendships of life, and to usher him, without warning or preparation, into the scenes of a new and untried existence.

The injury thus done is irreparable. Property taken by fraud or violence, may be restored; reputation unjustly assailed, may be made good; health may be regained; but life itself destroyed, it is not in the power of man to make good the loss. Hence a peculiar sacredness attaches to human life. It is the gift of Deity. Man cannot impart it; and what he cannot bestow, he has no right to take away. Only he who gave it can authorize its destruction.

Distinctions Recognized. — The laws of the state make certain distinctions in the crime of taking human life; as murder, manslaughter, etc. It is sufficient, in morals, to draw the broad distinction between the premeditated and intentional, and the merely accidental taking of life. The former incurs the highest guilt; the latter may be innocent. It is not a violation of the moral code, provided it is not the result of carelessness which might and should have been avoided. If, by reckless driving through the streets of a crowded city, life is sacrificed, the doer of the mischief is responsible for his carelessness, though not guilty of murder. If, by the recklessness of an engineer, the vessel, or the car, with its freight of life, is driven to destruction, the author of the calamity, though not justly chargeable with intentional murder, is by no means free from the guilt of taking human life. In such cases, the laws of most nations arraign him for *manslaughter*, making the distinction between that and the premeditated and intentional taking of life, which is denominated *murder*.

When the crime is not only premeditated, but secret in its execution, the agent not exposing his own life by giving the victim an opportunity of self-defence, there is added to the guilt which otherwise and necessarily pertains to the act, the meanness of cowardice. The murderer under such circumstances becomes the *assassin.*

When an unlawful assault is committed, such as from its nature must be more or less dangerous to life, should such assault ultimately result in death, although such result may not have been strictly intended by the assailant, still, as the act was itself unlawful, a crime, and not an accident, the author of the violence is not free from responsibility for the fatal consequences. He is guilty of manslaughter.

In general, with respect to injuries inflicted upon the person, malicious intention is inferred from the act itself; and whatever consequences result, are presumed in law to have been intended, unless there are some mitigating circumstances to excuse the act, and to show that it was unintentional.

When one person kills another in the heat of passion, in a sudden quarrel, arising from provocation, and without previous intention to take life, it is also, in English and American law, termed manslaughter; but if the passions have had time to cool, and the person provoked afterwards kills the other, it is regarded as murder.

The term *homicide* is usually, in law, applied to denote, in general, the taking of human life, whether by design or unintentionally, including murder and manslaughter, etc. When the act is purely unintentional and accidental, it is termed *excusable homicide.* The Jewish law, even in such cases, gave no protection to the slayer, unless he took refuge in certain cities specially designated as places of refuge. The English law imposes a fine on the person who has committed excusable homicide, — a fine which, however, in practice, is remitted, — and also makes him forfeit the instrument with which the offence was committed. This is termed a *deodand,* and the law exacting it is still in force.

Homicide Justifiable in what Cases. — There is a distinction in law between *justifiable* and *excusable* homicide. The cases just referred to, where the slaying is simply accidental, are instances of *excusable* homicide, though not perhaps justifiable. Homicide in an unpremeditated affray, though strictly in self-defence, is in English law also regarded as *excusable* rather than justifiable. This is termed *chance-medley*. When death occurs as the result of any game which is likely to end in blood, — as of boxing, sword-playing, etc., — or as the consequence of any dangerous and unlawful act, — as shooting, or casting stones in a town, — the homicide is not in law justifiable: it may or may not be excusable. By the public laws of Athens and Rome, he who killed another in the public games authorized by the state, was not held guilty of homicide; so by the English law, death resulting from the exercise of any sports and games authorized by the king, is regarded as *excusable* homicide.

By the old Jewish and Roman laws, as well as by the laws of England and of our own country, homicide is justifiable when committed in self-defence from any unlawful and violent assault, or for the prevention of any atrocious crime. If any one attempts robbery or murder, and is killed in the attempt, the killing is justifiable. The Jewish law justifies the slaying of the robber only in the act of breaking open a house, and that only in the *night time:* "If the sun be risen upon him, there shall be blood shed for him." The Roman law was similar, with this difference, that a thief detected by day might be slain, should he defend himself with a weapon, provided the slayer first make outcry for help. Roman law allowed any one to slay a person assaulting him with a weapon, whether the assailant were a robber or not, provided the assailed was in fear of his life, and could in no other way effectually protect himself. English law allows the same.

The laws of Solon make the same distinction as the Jewish and Roman law between the slaying of the robber by night and by day. The ground of this distinction is evidently this: that in case of night attack, greater danger to life may fairly be presumed on the part of the person assailed, inasmuch as he cannot so fully know the precise extent of his danger, and cannot so readily obtain help. He may therefore be justified to the extent of his supposed danger. By day there are other means of redress.

Execution of Law.—There are cases in which human life becomes forfeited by crime, and the laws of the land and the voice of universal justice demand the payment of the forfeit. In such cases, not justice to the criminal alone, but justice to the whole community, and the safety of the whole, require the death of the criminal. The very *sacredness* of human life demands this protection from the hand of violence, and makes it an imperative necessity that "Whoso sheddeth man's blood, by man shall his blood be shed." In no other way can the proper protection be thrown about the innocent and defenceless, than by making the life of the murderer the penalty of his crime. When an officer of justice, in pursuance of the sentence of law, takes human life, under such circumstances, he is of course not guilty of a crime, but, on the contrary, is discharging a high and solemn duty.

In other cases,—as where an officer, in the discharge of his official duties, is violently resisted and assailed; as, for example, by a prisoner seeking to make his escape, or resisting the process of arrest and imprisonment,—a necessity may exist for the resort to extreme measures; and, in such a case, should the person thus resisting be killed by the officer, in the attempt to discharge his duty, the act must be pronounced justifiable.

Palliating Circumstances.—The instances to which I have referred may be regarded as cases of justifiable homicide. They all fall under the law of self-protection, or the protection of society. There are many cases, however, which do not properly fall under that rule, yet where the circumstances are such as, while they do not justify, at least palliate, in some measure, the guilt of homicide. Some offence, perhaps, has been committed, which the law either takes no cognizance of, or which is beyond the power of law adequately to redress. The provocation is great, the injury deeply felt, the course of justice slow and uncertain, and even at the best, the punishment of the offender, provided, by some defect of evidence or some quibble of the law, he do not ultimately escape conviction altogether, is likely to be small in comparison with the injury committed. The temptation, in such a case, is great for the injured man to take the law into his own hands.

There may be cases in which circumstances shall seem to palliate, in a measure, the wrong of such a procedure; but no circumstances, however they may excuse, can justify the taking of life by way of revenge, or redress for wrong committed, whether the injury be to the person or to the character and reputation of the injured party. Whatever be the loss, whatever the dishonor, the person injured has no right to be himself the judge or the executioner of justice. He has no right to touch the life of his enemy. The law alone has that right; and if not man, yet God is just, and will avenge the injured and the innocent. Were every man, when wronged, to take the law into his own hands, and become his own avenger, the consequences to society would be disastrous in the extreme.

The Duel. — There is a form of homicide, or attempted homicide, which differs from any other form of assault with intent to kill, chiefly in the fact that it is made with the knowledge and coöperation of the party assailed, the attempt being mutual. This may be done with more or less of previous formality. When the challenge to such an encounter is previously given and accepted, and the combat is conducted in accordance with certain rules acknowledged in such cases, it is termed a duel, or an affair of honor; when without such ceremony, it is simply termed a hostile encounter, and differs little from chance-medley, a sudden affray, except that it is premeditated by one or both the parties, and not unfrequently anticipated by the other. In either case, it is an assault with the avowed intent to kill, with more or less of premeditation and mutual consent.

The history of the duel is not to be overlooked in estimating its character. It is, beyond doubt, a very ancient custom. It seems to have originated in the earlier stages of civilization, among rude and barbarous nations, of war like habits. It was virtually an appeal to the Supreme Ruler of men and events, to decide the uncertain question of right or wrong, innocence or guilt, between the contending parties. It is closely analogous, in this view, to the trial by ordeal, and the judicial combat. Whatever apology for this custom may have been found in those earlier and ruder times, when law was a less efficient protector of the right and of human life, and when every man was under the necessity, in a measure, of taking his defence into his own hands, no such apology or excuse can ordinarily be urged at the present day. It is a relic of barbarism, utterly unworthy of the civilization of the nineteenth century. As a means of justice, it is utterly senseless and absurd. At the best, it is an equal chance which party shall prevail, the guilty or the innocent. Skill in the use of weapons must usually decide this; and the skill and the strength that shall give advantage in the combat are quite as likely to be on the side of the wrong as of the right. To speak of obtaining satisfaction by submitting a dispute to any such process, is simply and purely ridiculous.

In one respect, the duel is certainly more honorable than secret assassination, or some other forms of homicide, inasmuch as it gives the assailed party warning, and an opportunity for defence. Still it is, when not a mere farce, intentional murder, and is accordingly so regarded and treated by the laws of nearly all civilized nations. No man has a right to take human life in order to avenge any real or supposed personal insult or injury; nor has any one a right to expose his own life, in this manner, to the murderous assault of a foe.

Suicide. — The same reasons that forbid one to take the life of his fellow-man forbid him to take his own. He has no more right to cut short his own life than that of another. Life is sacred — the gift of the Creator — a treasure which it is not allowed us to trifle with, which we cannot confer, and therefore have no right to take away. Nor is it a wrong done to himself alone, when, with rash hand, a man cuts short his own life. Society is wronged. Society has a claim on him for life, and labor, and valuable service. There are those dependent, it may be, on his care and toil, who have a still higher claim upon him. He has no right to desert them — no right to betray his trust, and leave those who are dependent on him to struggle alone with misfortune and want. It is his duty, rather, to stand up like a true man under the heavy pressure of whatever trials and calamities may befall him, manfully bearing the lot of life, and by his presence and example, not less than his toil, helping others to sustain the heavy load.

It is a striking instance of the insufficiency of the light of nature as a guide to duty, that among the ancients suicide was regarded as not merely allowable, but, in certain cases, commendable; and was resorted to by some among the wisest and the best of the truly great men of that time, as an escape from the calamities and burdens of life.

It is a melancholy spectacle of the imperfection of human reason and the human conscience. It was for Christianity to reveal the true philosophy of human life, — to make known the sacredness of life, as such,— to teach the far loftier courage and heroism of patient endurance,— to direct the eye of the desponding sufferer to that "far more exceeding and eternal weight of glory" for which the present sorrows were intended to prepare him, and to which they are the necessary avenue of approach. It bade him run with patience the race set before him, fixing his eye upon Him, the great heroic sufferer, "who endured such contradiction of sinners against himself;" and "who, for the joy that was set before him, endured the cross, despising the shame, and is set down at the right hand of the Majesty on High."

It may be added, that the reasons already urged against suicide apply equally to any course of conduct by which life is shortened, or its energies weakened. No man has a right to shorten his days, or impair his vital energies, by any course of vicious indulgence or excess. This is only an indirect form of suicide. Too frequently is this fatal error committed by those who, in the heat of passion or the ardor of youth, yield to the impulses of the sensitive nature, regardless of consequences. And not alone by those who yield to the dominion of the lower appetites is this guilt incurred. In the pressure of business, or the ardor of intellectual pursuits, the body and the mind may be, and too frequently are, overtasked, resulting in the premature decay of the vital powers, and an early grave. It is not by direct and intentional acts alone that life is destroyed, and the guilt of suicide incurred.

I would not be understood, in what has been said, to imply that life, however sacred, is to be preserved at all hazards. There are other interests higher and dearer than life itself — interests which we may not sacrifice for the sake of preserving even life. Rather than betray the cause of truth and right, rather than desert the principles of justice and honor, and prove recreant to duty and to faith, a man may well die. In defence of the innocent and helpless, in defence of the right, in defence of his family and his country, in defence of his religious belief, he may well lay down his life, if need be. As a martyr, as a patriot, as a lover of truth and justice, there may be occasion to die. Life is not the highest duty nor the most sacred treasure of man.

CHAPTER II.

DUTIES PERTAINING TO LIBERTY.

Liberty a Natural Right. — One of the first and plainest natural rights of man is the right to himself, — that is, to liberty, — a right to the disposal of his own time and industry and personal movements as he sees fit, within such limits as the rights and safety of others allow. That this is the intention of nature, is evident from the constitution of man. He desires liberty, and is never happy when deprived of it. He pines for it, dreams of it, toils for it, risks everything to obtain it. To deprive him of this right, without due cause, is to inflict upon him one of the greatest wrongs. There is nothing, next to life itself, with which a man will not sooner part than his liberty.

Modes in which one may be deprived of it. — Of this right man may be deprived in various ways. Sometimes it is justly forfeited by his own conduct; and in that case, society has the right to take it from him. Sometimes he is unjustly deprived of it by the violence and cupidity of his fellow-man.

Imprisonment for Crime. — 1. *Society* may justly deprive a man of liberty by *imprisonment for crime.* This the law has a right to do. The protection and safety of the community require it. He who violates the rights of others, forfeits his own; and the principles upon which society is constituted require it, as a measure of self-defence, to restrain the liberty of him who abuses his liberty to the detriment of others. It may justly imprison him for trial; and after trial and conviction, it may justly imprison him for punishment. It may justly require of him, while thus in confinement as a convict, such amount of personal labor as shall at least be sufficient for his support. The extent and mode of such imprisonment is to be determined by law. When it is protracted beyond due limit, or is attended with unnecessary severity, — when the term of trial is needlessly delayed, or when a degree or mode of punishment is inflicted beyond what the nature of the offence strictly demands, — the coercion thus exercised become unjust, and society is in turn the aggressor.

Confinement of the Insane. — 2. For the reasons already mentioned, it is the right of society to place insane persons in confinement, provided the safety of their families and friends, or even their own safety, requires such restraint. It is a measure of self-defence, and even of benevolence; nor is any wrong inflicted upon the sufferer in such a case, provided the deprivation of liberty be not attended with any unnecessary severity, or any real unkindness.

Captivity in War. — 3. Another mode in which one may be deprived of liberty, is by *captivity in war.* If war itself is justifiable, under any circumstances, then it is allowable for the victorious party to make such disposal of its captives taken in war as shall prevent them from taking further part in hostilities against itself. This can be effectually done, perhaps, only by imprisonment; and this imprisonment may continue until the close of hostilities, unless previously terminated by the exchange of an equal number of prisoners taken by the other party. Formerly, all captives taken in war were reduced to slavery. This was the great source of supply of slave labor, not only in Greece and Rome, but in the powerful empires of earlier origin. Homer, and the Greek tragedians, represent the lot of those conquered in war, and also of their wives and children, as one of servile and hopeless bondage. Among civilized nations, this mode of conducting war is by universal consent abandoned.

Involuntary Servitude. — 4. Still another mode in which liberty may be taken away, is that form of involuntary servitude known as slavery. As this is a matter of much importance, and one upon the morality of which conflicting views are entertained to some extent, especially in our own country, it seems to require a more full and careful consideration. It will, therefore, constitute the principal topic of the present chapter. It will be to the purpose, in the first place, to *define* slavery; the way will then be prepared to inquire whether slavery, as thus defined, is a *moral wrong;* what its effects are upon the nation, both as respects morals, and financial prosperity; and, finally, what arguments may be adduced in favor of it. These topics, in their order, as now stated, will be discussed in the following sections.

§ I. — Slavery Defined.

When the right of personal ownership and personal control, that properly belong to a man, are taken from him, for no fault and by no consent of his own, and vested in another, giving to the latter control over the person and industry of the former, the man thus subjected becomes a slave, and the one to whom he is subjected is termed the master. I say for no fault, and by no consent of his own, — for imprisonment for crime, of which I have already spoken, is not slavery, though it may be accompanied with some degree of involuntary service; there is *control*, but not *ownership*; — nor are we at present concerned with *voluntary* servitude, in any of its forms. Slavery, as now understood, — that is, as an actually existing institution, — always implies *ownership* on the part of the master, and *involuntary servitude* on the part of the slave.

This ownership is complete, and, to a great extent, irresponsible. The slave is in the same category with any other property or possession — as truly the property of the master as the horses or dogs that belong to the same plantation. The control of the master over the one is as complete, unlimited, and irresponsible, as his control over the other. His time, his labor, his acquisitions, his person, his children, are not his own, but his master's. He is to be bought, and sold, and worked, and whipped, at the master's pleasure. He has *no rights of his own.*

Slave Laws accord with this Definition. — This is the character of complete slavery, as recognized by the laws of other nations, as well as our own. "Slaves," says Gaius, the distinguished Roman jurist, "are in the power of the masters. Which power, indeed, is one recognized by the laws of nations; for among all nations, it is to be observed, that the power of the master over the slave has been the power of life and death, and whatever is acquired by the slave, is acquired by the master." This we know to have been not only Roman law, but Roman custom. The slave had neither security of life, nor property in any thing he might acquire. He belonged to another, and not to himself.

The institution of modern slavery is based on the same principles. The slave is the property of the master, and has no right to himself. The laws of different states vary, but the principles of the system are essentially the same in all. According to the code of Louisiana, "The slave is in the power of the master to whom he belongs. The master may sell him, dispose of his person, his industry, his labor; he can do nothing, possess nothing, nor acquire anything, but which must belong to his master." According to the laws of South Carolina, "Slaves shall be deemed, taken, reported, and adjudged to be chattels personal in the hands of their masters, and possessions to all intents and purposes whatever."

These, then, I take to be the essential elements of slavery — viz., ownership, property, absolute control. Where these exist, there is slavery.

Limitations of Power. — Certain limitations of the power of the master, may or may not exist in the different states, according as the slave code may be more or less strict. In some cases, the master is forbidden to put his slave to death, or treat him with unnecessary cruelty. Practically, such a limitation amounts to little, when it is remembered that the testimony of the slave is not admitted on evidence in the courts of law, and also that it is for the interest of the masters to sustain each other in the exercise of discipline and authority over the slaves. It must in the nature of the case be extremely difficult, if not impossible, under such circumstances, to obtain clear and satisfactory evidence of cruelty on the part of the master, and equally difficult to secure the impartial administration of justice, even in cases of notorious violation of the law in question, where the interests of both judge and jury so clearly identify them with the offending party, and where the safety and permanent existence of the system is seen to depend on firmly sustaining the power and authority of the master over his slaves.

But, even if such limitations could be, as they cannot be, practically carried out and enforced, they do not change the essential character of slavery, as already defined. They do not make the master less an owner, or the slave less property or a chattel. They do not invest him with any *rights*. They are merely a concession to the natural feelings of humanity. They are of the same nature, as Whewell well remarks, with "the English laws against cruelty to animals. It is now penal in this country to torture a horse or a dog; but a horse or a dog are still only objects of possession, without any rights, or any acknowledged moral nature."

§ II. — Slavery, as thus Defined, a Moral Wrong.

It can hardly admit of serious question that slavery, as thus defined, involves a moral wrong. In the strong language of Whewell, it is "contrary to the fundamental principles of morality." It is a wrong, inasmuch as, 1. *It violates the natural rights of man.* It reduces him from a *person* to a *thing* — than which no greater wrong can be inflicted on humanity. The victim of this injustice is no longer, in the eye of the law, a *man;* he has become a mere thing, has no rights, and, consequently, can suffer no wrong. He stands on a level with the brute. He has his pleasures and his pains; so has the brute. He has his natural impulses and desires; the brute also has his. The strong affections, the tumultuous passions of our nature, that agitate the bosoms of other men, stir also in his; they have their counterpart, also, to some extent, in the affections and passions of the brute. Nor, in the eye of the state, are these feelings of any more value and consequence in the one case than in the other. With all their natural instincts, thoughts, feelings, passions, affections, they are both, the man and the brute, and the one *equally* with the other, the property of the master.

Yet this creature, this thing, has that which the brute has not — *a rational and moral nature;* and no man, no society of men, nor any human legislation, has the right to deprive him of it. The law that does this, or attempts to do it, is a *law without a right.* To treat a rational, moral being as if he were an irrational and irresponsible creature, — a man as if he were a brute, — is to inflict the highest indignity and injustice which human nature is capable of receiving.

So palpable is this, that even the Roman jurists admit that no man is a slave by nature.

Another Element of Injustice. — 2. Slavery is a wrong, inasmuch as it not only deprives the slave of his natural right of self-disposal and control, but *subjects him to the lawless will of a master.* Irresponsible power is a dangerous thing. It is never safe to trust any man with it, however humane and well-disposed. There is in the human bosom, implanted among its native elements, a love of power — power over whatever lies about us — power over our fellow-men especially, as being the most difficult of control, and affording therefore, when brought under subjection, a higher sense of pleasure, amounting to a sort of triumph. The man who can command his fellow-man, feels his own superiority much more than he who can exercise his authority only over the lower orders of creation. Now, whenever this power becomes complete and unlimited; when its word is law, and must be obeyed; when it becomes the power of absolute ownership; when the being who is subject to it has no will nor voice of his own, no mode of redress, no *rights;* when he is the mere property of another; when he and all that is his—the body with all its organs and powers, the mind with all its faculties of action and capacities for enjoyment and suffering, the friends that may gather around him, the wife and children that may cling to him as their natural protector — all, all are entirely at the disposal of another, in the power of a master, and that power, for the most part, and to all practical purposes, unlimited and irresponsible to any earthly tribunal, — who will say that such power as this can safely be confided to any man over his fellow-man? Who will say there is no risk in all this — no danger that a power so far-reaching and absolute and fearful may be abused?

The True Question. — Now, it is precisely this risk, this danger of abuse, this almost certainty that, in many cases at least, the power in question *will* be abused, that constitutes in no small degree the guilt of the entire system. It is no answer to say, that in many cases the power is not abused. Undoubtedly this is true. Unquestionably many masters are kind and humane. That is not the point. Even if it could be shown that the great majority are so, — that kindness is the rule, and cruelty the exception, — it would not in the least affect the present argument. It is precisely these exceptions, liable at any moment and anywhere to occur, impossible of prevention — it is this liability to abuse that constitutes one of the most appalling features of the system. Is there no wrong in subjecting a man endowed by the Creator with all the rights and privileges of humanity, possessing a rational, spiritual nature that places him, however degraded he may be, at an infinite remove from the beasts that perish — is there no wrong in subjecting this rational and accountable being to a servitude worse even than that of the brutes by so much as his nature is superior to theirs? Is there no wrong in subjecting him to a power which *may be* at any moment and to any degree abused, and against the abuse of which he has no safeguard, no protection, no mode of redress?

A Third Element. — 3. Slavery is a wrong, inasmuch as *it deprives the slave of that intellectual, moral, and religious culture which is his right.* It is essential to slavery, as a system, that the slave be kept in ignorance. Any considerable amount of instruction would prove fatal to the perpetuity of the system. If the slave were once to know what are his rights, and in what manner it would be possible to regain them, it is obvious that he would no longer rest passive under the weight that is crushing him to the earth. He must not have access, then, to the thoughts that are stirring the mind and heart of the race to which he belongs. He must be shut up in a night of deepest intellectual and moral darkness. It were not safe even that he should know so much as to be able to read and write. To some extent, oral religious instruction might perhaps be safely imparted; but even this must be kept fully within the control of the master. It would be inconvenient, for example, should the conscience of the slave, by reason of religious training, interpose itself as a barrier to the absolute will and caprice of the master. Nor would it be by any means expedient to place the Bible, without note or comment, in the hands of a slave capable of reading and understanding its pages. That book which has proved the great instrument of freedom, civil and religious, in the history of the world, — the *magna charta* of human rights, — might teach him truths which, as a slave, it were better he should not know; might teach him that God has made of one blood all the nations of the earth; that to one and the same God master and slave stand alike responsible for the things done in the flesh, and that this God is no respecter of persons.

Actual Policy of the System. — We find, accordingly, that the actual policy of the system is to keep the slave as much as possible in ignorance. To teach him to read or write is made, in many of the slave states, an offence punishable with fine and imprisonment; while to place in his hands any document containing information calculated to make him discontented with his servitude, is thought worthy of the most severe and summary punishment.

Need it be said that this is a moral wrong? Is not mental and moral culture the *right* of every human being endowed by nature with an intelligent and rational soul — of every being made in the image of his God, made moral and accountable? Is not the revealed will of God the birthright of every child of Adam — of every fallen, ruined being for whom Christ has died? Have I any right, for purposes of my own convenience or profit, to deprive him of this? Does the system into whose very foundation such a prohibition enters, and which could not exist for a day without it, involve no moral wrong?

Essential, as distinguished from Incidental Wrongs. — In discussing the moral character of this institution, I have spoken only of those evils which seem inseparable from any system of complete slavery. Of those wrongs which are *incidental* to the system, as it exists in this or in other countries, and which constitute the worst features, in many respects, of such a system, — as, *e. g.*, the separation of families by sale, the disregard of the marriage tie, the nameless and shocking barbarities which are of too frequent occurrence wherever slavery exists, — I purposely forbear to speak in this connection. I can conceive of a system of servitude that should dispense with the shame and guilt of these peculiar features, that should be free from the odium of such vices and barbarities; but I cannot conceive of any form or system of complete slavery that shall be free from the wrongs which have been discussed in the present section. Wherever there is ownership and property in man, and that entire control and disposal of his person, faculties, and services, which such ownership implies, there are, and must be, and always will be, as the legitimate and inevitable consequence, the wrongs of which I have spoken, viz., the violation of the natural rights of man, by reducing him from the condition of a person to the condition of a thing; by subjecting him to the irresponsible, lawless will of a master, with the imminent danger that that power will be abused, and with no protection against such abuse, nor redress from any wrong or outrage that may be inflicted; and, finally, by shutting him up in more or less complete ignorance and darkness — depriving him of that mental and moral culture which is his right. And, in view of these necessary and essential features of any and all systems of complete slavery, I cannot but pronounce any and every such system a grievous wrong in morals.

§ III. — Effect of Slavery on the National Morals and the National Wealth.

In order to a fair and just appreciation of the real character of any system, we must observe its effects, its practical working, and the consequences that actually flow from it. It is not enough to reason *a priori* as to what the moral character of slavery must be. It is necessary to verify such reasonings by actual observation. If the effects are disastrous, the system itself cannot be right. The tree must be judged by its fruits. There are two points of view from which the system now under consideration may well be regarded in its actual working, viz., its effect on the morals, and on the financial prosperity, of the state.

I. *On Morals.* — There can be little doubt that the arrangement which places one man, or a considerable number of men, at the entire disposal and control of another, subject to his absolute and irresponsible will and power, is a system of things not the most favorable to moral excellence, whether of the master or the servant. The exercise of such authority must, in the nature of the case, tend to foster a spirit of pride and arrogance — to make a man overbearing and haughty in temper, quick and irascible, impatient of restraint and contradiction. The passions of our nature, the animal propensities, ever ready to assume the mastery, and requiring to be kept in check with firm hand, finding now no barriers to their indulgence but those which are self-imposed, will be likely to break over those feeble barriers, and acquire unrestrained course and dominion. The tendency of the system to these results in morals, so far as the master is concerned, is inevitable. Many and honorable exceptions there will be; but the *tendency* is still the same. It must be so while human nature is what it is. The temptation to abuse of power over those who cannot or dare not resist, — to undue severity of punishment, where the passions of the master are roused, and there is none to say what doest thou, — to the gratification of the baser appetites in their various forms, — must be too great for ordinary and unaided human virtue. The tendency of such a system must ever be, not to progressive refinement and moral culture, but to barbarism. We should expect to find in connection with such a civil polity, a state of society and of morals somewhat peculiar, — acts of violence and barbarity not infrequent, the street affray, the duel, the murderous assault, the unrestrained indulgence of the animal appetites. This it would be reasonable to expect; and this, unless all history is false, we do find, the world over, to be the general state and tendency of things where the system of slavery prevails.

Effect on the Slave. — Nor is the effect on the morals of the slave more favorable; on the contrary, it is even more disastrous. In proportion as the feeling of self-respect and self-dependence is taken away, and a man is taught to look upon himself as merely the tool in the hands of another, the instrument of another's will and pleasure, without responsibility of his own, just in that proportion the foundation of moral character is undermined. Nothing can be more demoralizing in its effect upon the character. Strip a man of all that constitutes manhood, — of all self-reliance and self-respect, of all the rights which nature has conferred upon him, and all the faculties with which the Creator has endowed him; take away from him all control and disposal of himself, all ownership of himself, — and all that can stimulate to activity, and incite to noble attainment and excellence, is gone at once. He sinks down to the level of the brute. What inducement is there for him to hope or strive for anything other or better than his present lot, and the enjoyment which the moment may bring with it? He becomes, as a matter of course, improvident and reckless, content with the gratification, so far as may be, of his merely animal appetites; indolent — for why should he be otherwise? deceptive and dishonest — for what motive has he to honesty? governed only by fear of the lash, with little thought of anything future, with little knowledge of that hereafter whence are derived the most powerful motives to present virtue. His mind shrouded in ignorance, his moral nature almost wholly uncultivated, his condition is little above that of the beast with whom he toils, and with whom he perishes.

Exceptions there may be, many and remarkable, to this general law. As in the case of the master, so in the case of the slave; some will rise above the influences that surround and drag them down, and, in spite of all these depressing and demoralizing influences, will maintain their integrity. But such is not the rule, such is not the tendency of the system. No one who has either reflected on the matter, or observed the actual working of the system, can honestly suppose that it is. It is a notorious fact, that, as a general rule, wherever this system exists, the slave is indolent, deceitful, dishonest, improvident,—not to be trusted away from the eye of his master. Can that be a right system which produces such effects on those whom it most directly concerns?

II. *Effect on the National Wealth.* — It can hardly admit of question that slavery tends greatly to impoverish a country. It exhausts the resources of the most fertile soil, and seeks ever new and unexhausted territories on which to plant itself. From these, again, it must in turn migrate, if it would thrive. We have only to compare the slave and the free state, lying side by side, in our own country, alike in climate, soil, and productions, — the same mountains and rivers and skies common to both, — the same constitution encircling, and the same flag floating over them; — we have but to mark the thrift and enterprise and accumulating capital of the one, and the comparative stagnation and poverty of the other, — the crowded streets, the busy industry, the numerous population of the one, the sparsely settled condition and neglected aspect of the other, — to be satisfied on which side of the dividing line that separates freedom from servitude the sources of prosperity lie.

Nor is it difficult to perceive why it should be so. In the states where servitude is the established institution and order of things, labor becomes disgraceful; in the free state, industry and honest toil are honored and rewarded; and all classes of citizens labor, each in his own way and at his own employment. The difference is that which always holds, by the laws of nature, between idleness and industry, — viz., poverty and wealth. It is an essential principle, moreover, in political economy, that in order to the most efficient and productive labor, a man must have some personal interest in that on which he labors, else the highest incentive to effort will be wanting. This is precisely what is and must be ever wanting in any system of involuntary servitude. He who labors not for himself, but for another, and whose chief motive to effort is the fear of the lash rather than any hope of reward, is not likely to be the most industrious or profitable of servants. The system which depends on such labor, violates the fundamental laws of nature, and cannot prosper.

§ IV. — Arguments in Favor of Slavery.

It is not enough, in the consideration of a matter so important as the present, in its bearings on the happiness and welfare of the race, to look merely at one side of the question, without inquiring what may be said on the other. The result of our inquiries thus far has been adverse to the system in question: it is no more than fair to consider the arguments in favor of the system.

Defended on the ground of Family Government. — Some writers place the matter on the ground of family government, and defend it on that ground as right and to be justified, when the authority thus exercised seeks, as in the government of the family, the best good of the governed, and is administered solely with a view to that end.

To this it may be replied, in the first place, that the supposition now made by no means holds good of the system as a whole. It is not true that slavery, as it actually exists in the world, or ever has existed in its true and complete form, is a system the real design and aim of which is the welfare and highest good of the slave. Humane and pious masters there doubtless are, and have been in all periods of the world's history, who have sought to make their power consistent, so far as possible, with the welfare of their slaves. They have not been unmindful of the good of the governed. But that, even in such cases, the welfare of the slave has been the direct aim and end of the institution, the thing *for which* it exists, rather than merely an *incidental* benefit secured in spite of all the opposite tendencies and natural results of the system, no one, I think, can intelligently maintain; much less that such is the real end and object of the system as a whole. Everybody knows that the end aimed at in the institution of slavery is not the good of the slave himself, but the gain of the master; and to assert the contrary is simply absurd. If any one were to assert that the efforts now making, by government, and individuals, to introduce and domesticate the camel in this country, were prompted by a simple and pure regard to the comfort and happiness of that valuable animal, we should esteem him as a person of humane disposition, but somewhat weak in understanding. Were we to cite, in confirmation of this theory, the laws which prohibit cruelty to animals, and the many instances in which camels have been well treated, we should, while gratified to learn these facts, hardly regard them as establishing the point in question. That the system of involuntary servitude, which reduces man from the condition of a person to that of a thing, makes him a mere piece of property, like a horse or a dog, takes away from him all power of self-direction, and makes him subject to the lawless and irresponsible will of a master — that this system, so repugnant to all natural ideas of right and justice, has any claim to be regarded as an *eleemosynary institution*, designed to promote the highest good of the slave, remains to be proved.

Further Reply. — The argument rests, moreover, on the assumption that the slave is not capable of self-government, — which has never been shown to be true, but which, on the contrary, facts seem to contradict, — and that, consequently, inasmuch as he is not capable of owning, directing, and governing himself, the master has the right of owning and governing him, — which by no means follows. Is the slave unfit to be his own master? And, even if he is, does that give me as an individual the right to govern him? How came he into that relation to me, and I to him, that places him in my power, and gives me the authority to govern him? Have I really any right to sustain that relation to any of my fellow-beings? Granted: that this man, left to himself, might not order his affairs so wisely and so well as I could order them for him — what then? Does it follow that I have the right to take out of his hands the ownership and control of himself, and make him my property?

Argument from Inferiority. — The ground on which the defence of the system is more frequently placed, is that the negro is by nature inferior to the white race. His proper position in the scale of being, that for which nature evidently intended him, is the condition of servitude. We are depriving him, therefore, of no right when we subject him to bondage. This argument is invalid in its premises, and false in its conclusion. It is not true that the negro is by *nature* — whatever he may be by the circumstances of his position — essentially inferior to the white race. Facts prove the contrary. Placed under influences equally favorable for mental and moral development, with equal advantages and equal inducements, he has uniformly shown himself capable of equal attainments. He is endowed by nature with the same mental and moral faculties that belong to other men; and those faculties are susceptible of the same culture. He has the same affections and passions with other men; the same sense of right and justice, the same moral nature. The very laws which forbid the teaching of slaves to read and write, are of themselves a sufficient contradiction of the theory of his native inferiority.

But, even if it were as now assumed, could it be shown that the negro is inferior by nature to the Caucasian race, it is by no means a legitimate conclusion that the Caucasian is for that reason entitled to reduce the former to bondage. The very fact of inferiority, if it be a fact, constitutes a reason, not for reducing him to a still deeper and more deplorable degradation, but for elevating him to a higher and better condition. It is a circumstance which calls not for severe measures, and the wresting from him in his feebleness and ignorance what light and what strength he has, but rather for compassion and gentleness; it is a reason, not for making him my property, and depriving him of all ownership and control of himself, not for making him a mere chattel, a thing to be used and abused at my pleasure, but rather for instructing and elevating him to something higher and better than he is.

Besides, the question naturally arises, *How came he to be* thus inferior? Viewed in its present condition, under all the depressing influences of a state of hopeless servitude, the slave population may well be supposed inferior in many respects, both mentally and morally, to the dominant white race. But how came it to be so? Is it cause, or consequence? Does the condition of servitude result from the perceived inferiority, or the perceived inferiority from the condition of servitude? If by force or fraud I succeed in catching a man and putting out his eyes, that surely will not entitle me to make him my slave after that, because he is blind! The question would be asked, What occasioned that blindness?

Argument from Scripture. — The position which the advocates of slavery often assume, and of late more frequently than formerly, is that *the Bible recognizes and sustains slavery.* If this be so, it is certainly a strong presumption in its favor, and will go far to weaken and impair, if not altogether to set aside, many of the arguments already presented. It requires, therefore, a careful and candid consideration.

That slavery is *recognized* in the Scriptures, both of the Old and New Testament, is evident; that it is not expressly and directly *condemned* or prohibited in either, may also be admitted; that it is *justified*, either by the spirit, or precepts, of the sacred writings, is not true; on the contrary, it is emphatically and diametrically opposed to both.

Under the Jewish economy, slavery, in a modified form, existed, and was suffered to exist — was tolerated, not justified. It stood on the same ground with polygamy, and similar kindred vices. Many things were suffered then to exist which a true and strict morality could by no means sanction, and which are nowhere sanctioned, but, on the contrary, condemned by the whole spirit of Christianity. Such, for example, was the ancient Jewish law and custom of divorce for the slightest offences, and even for no offence, but the caprice of the husband. Such the law and custom of polygamy. On the same ground we may also place the institution of slavery, so far as it then existed.

Jewish and Modern Slavery unlike.—It must be remembered, however, that the system of servitude known and practised under the Jewish economy, was in many respects essentially different from the slavery of modern times. It was another and a very different thing. The difference was as great, as that between an absolute, and a constitutional and limited monarchy. The power of the Jewish master over his servant was closely and strictly limited. The servant was not, in the modern sense, a slave — a mere piece of property, a thing. He was still a man. He had his *rights*, and they were carefully guarded and secured by law. The master was not, either in theory, or practically, irresponsible. In purchasing a servant, he purchased not so much the man himself as the right to the labor and services of the man, and even that under certain important restrictions. The purchase was to be made, in the first place, of some foreign nation. If the servant found his situation disagreeable, and effected his escape, he was *not* to be delivered up to his master (Deut. xxiii. 15, 16); nor was the servitude in any case to be perpetual. Every fiftieth year witnessed the release of every servant from bondage throughout the land. Religious rights were especially guaranteed to the servant. He was to have full opportunity for religious instruction and worship. If the master maimed or otherwise abused him, he was to be set free (Ex. xxi. 26, 27); if the slave were killed while under the master's correction, the master was to be punished (Ex. xxi. 20).

Now, it is evident that these are very important restrictions. A system of servitude thus modified and limited, would be a very different institution from any known as modern slavery. When these limitations and restrictions shall have been adopted into the slave-codes of those states where men are now held in bondage; when it shall be *unlawful* to deliver to his master a slave that has escaped; when every fiftieth year shall set free all that are in bondage; when every slave that receives personal injury, to the loss of an eye or a tooth even, by severity of treatment, shall go free for his eye's or tooth's sake; when the death of the slave under the hand of his master shall subject the master to severe and certain punishment; when the full privileges of mental and religious instruction shall be secured to the slave, — then, and not till then, it will be time enough to plead the system of Jewish servitude as a precedent for modern slavery. Such restrictions, it is perfectly obvious, are quite incompatible with the system as it exists among us; they would bring it to a speedy end.

Greek and Roman Slavery. — But the slavery which is recognized in the New Testament, it is said, was much worse than that of the Jewish state. In the Grecian and Roman states the master's power over the slave was unrestricted, amounting even to the power of life and death. It was to slavery in this its severer and more complete form, that the New Testament writers had reference. This is true. But do these writers *justify* such a system, or merely recognize its existence? Is it approved, or merely tolerated? Is it anywhere defended, and placed on the high ground of moral right, or merely recognized as an existing civil institution? These are important questions. It is for those who undertake to defend slavery from the Bible, to show that the sacred writers justify the system of servitude then in vogue; that they recognize not merely its existence, but its moral rightness. This cannot be shown. So far from approving and justifying anything of the kind, the whole tenor of the sacred writings, and especially of the New Testament, is directly opposed to all such systems, laws, and practices.

The spirit of the divine precepts, the sum and substance of that law which is to govern our conduct, is contained in that universal rule, "All things whatsoever ye would that men should do unto you, do ye even so unto them." Our regard for the rights and happiness of others is to be measured by our regard for our own welfare, and our own rights. Is such a rule compatible with the existence of such a system of slavery as prevailed in Greece and Rome, or as still prevails among modern nations? Is it not, on the contrary, utterly subversive of any and every such system? Were this one precept carried out, slavery, in whatever form, and whatever land, would as surely and as speedily terminate, as night ceases when day begins.

Duties of Masters and Servants prescribed.—But, it is said, the New Testament prescribes the duties of master and servant, and so tacitly gives consent to the system. It is true, the gospel enjoins upon the master the duty of forbearance, and kindness, and of rendering to the servant that which was just and due, and upon the servant the duty of obedience to the master. But these duties are enjoined, not on the ground of the *rightfulness* of the relation, but simply as that which, under all the circumstances, was the best course to pursue, and would be most pleasing in the sight of God. Precisely in the same way, and on the same principle, the disciples of the Christian faith were advised to submit to the arbitrary and tyrannical decrees and irresponsible power of tyrants, such an one as Nero even, not because such exercise of tyrannical power was a thing to be justified, a right thing, but because to submit and to suffer wrong was, under all the circumstances, better — better for them, situated as they were — than to resist. "Vengeance is mine, I will repay, saith the Lord." Does this justify Nero? On the same principle, the Christian disciple was bidden to turn the other cheek to the hand that had already smitten, since it was better, on the whole, — better at least for him, as a Christian, — to suffer outrage patiently than to take his defence into his own hands. Does this justify acts of personal assault and violence? They who defend slavery on this ground, must, on the same principle, if they reason consistently, defend any system of civil oppression and tyranny, however arbitrary and unjust, and any personal violence inflicted by lawless and angry men upon the victims of their ferocity.

In the well-expressed language of an able writer and moralist, Dr. Hickok: "This obedience was by no means required on the ground that slavery was righteous, and the master's authority morally valid. It would be more prudent for the slave to obey, and tend most to cultivate his piety. He was required to be obedient 'not only to the good and gentle, but also to the froward;' even obedient where cruelty and wickedness led to the 'buffeting' of the slave 'for doing well.' It was expedient to obey; just as, when you cannot escape from a tiger, it is expedient not to provoke him. It by no means justifies the usurped authority. It was better for the slave to obey; and especially it would serve to augment piety, and recommend the religion of Him, who in his humiliation was smitten and 'opened not his mouth.'"

Why not directly forbidden. — But why, it may be asked, was not the system directly forbidden, or at least declared to be unjust and morally wrong, if such is indeed its true character? I reply, *it is really* forbidden by the spirit and the precepts of Christianity — really, though not directly and explicitly. The rule to do unto others whatsoever we would that they should do unto us, as really forbids that involuntary servitude which exacts of a fellow-being unrequited service, and robs him of all his dearest rights, as if the practice of such a wrong were mentioned by name, and specially prohibited. A reason doubtless existed for not thus designating it in so many words. It was a social evil, incorporated into the whole fabric of civil society and government. To have singled out the evil, and by direct precept to have prohibited it, would have been, perhaps, neither the wisest nor the surest mode of redress. It would have been a direct interference of Christianity with civil government. In the language of Dr. Wayland: "If it had forbidden the evil, instead of subverting the principle, — if it had proclaimed the unlawfulness of slavery, and taught slaves to *resist* the oppression of their masters, — it would instantly have arrayed the two parties in deadly hostility, throughout the civilized world. Its announcement would have been the signal of servile war; and the very name of the Christian religion would have been forgotten amidst the agitations of universal bloodshed. The fact, under these circumstances, that the gospel does not forbid slavery, affords no reason to suppose that it does not mean to prohibit it; much less does it afford ground for belief that Jesus Christ intended to *authorize* it."

The Mode of Redress. — We have been occupied in the preceding pages with the discussion of the moral character of this institution of slavery. It is no part of the business of the moralist, strictly speaking, to point out the best methods of redressing the wrongs and evils of society. This it is for others to do. One thing, however, I may properly say in this connection. Whatever measures are adopted, looking to this end, must necessarily be gradual in their operation, in order wisely and well to accomplish their purpose. The social fabric is not to be rudely shaken, nor its whole structure radically changed in a day. Time is requisite, and the slow growth of principle. Much is to be hoped from the progress of society, and the gradual prevalence of more enlightened views, and of a loftier and purer morality. In proportion as society advances, and Christianity obtains a firmer hold on the mind and heart of the race, this system, so utterly at variance with all just notions of right and duty, and so repugnant to the feelings of common humanity, must and will gradually disappear, as the shadows from the mountain side, and the mists from the bosom of the lake, when the sun mounts the heavens in his strength.

Progress of European Society.— If we look at the social organization of the European nations, we find them, in the course of centuries, passing through a series of changes, from the state of absolute servitude of the laboring classes, to that of more or less perfect equality and freedom. For some two centuries or more after the Norman conquest, the greater portion of the cultivators of the soil in England were serfs, or *villeins*, as they were then termed, bound to the soil, and owing service to the proprietor thereof. The peasant belonged to the soil, and, with all his family and descendants, from generation to generation, was at the disposal of the lord of the manor. These unlimited labor-rents were gradually, during the succeeding centuries, commuted into more definite services, and the peasant acquired legal right, or copyhold, as it was termed, to the lands which he cultivated. It is only about two hundred years since the cultivator of the soil in England ceased to be held in personal thraldom.

In many parts of Germany, serfdom still exists; in others,

the peasant is no longer attached to the soil, but, instead of unlimited service, pays his landlord some definite amount of labor as land-rent; in other cases, this is commuted for rent in grain or money, and the servitude becomes almost nominal.

In Russia, the serf was little better than a slave, except that his service was limited. He was bound to work for the owner of the soil a certain number of days in the week, laboring for the rest of the time, for his own subsistence, on lands allotted for the purpose. Nor was it until the accession of the present government that this system was abolished.

Sentiment of Paley. — Soon after the close of the struggle by which the American Colonies became independent of England, Archdeacon Paley, referring to the system of slavery, and to the part which the English government had taken in upholding it, made use of the following language, in his work on Moral Philosophy: "The great revolution which has taken place in the Western world may probably conduce (and who knows but that it was designed) to accelerate the fall of this abominable tyranny; and now that this contest, and the passions which attended it, are no more, there may succeed perhaps a season for reflecting, whether a legislature which had so long lent its assistance to the support of an institution replete with human misery, was fit to be trusted with an empire the most extensive that ever obtained in any age or quarter of the world." Could this excellent moralist, after the lapse of three quarters of a century, be permitted to look upon this Western world as it now is, and behold the present greatness and prosperity of the country that was then just commencing its career, as he beheld with astonishment this dark blot still upon our escutcheon, would he not, and with justice, repeat, with reference to our own nation, the question then so forcibly put, with reference to the British government, "whether a legislature that had so long lent its assistance to the support of an institution replete with human misery, was fit to be trusted with an empire" so extensive and powerful?

CHAPTER III.

DUTIES PERTAINING TO PROPERTY.

MAN has not only the right to life, and to liberty, but also to *property*, or the possession and enjoyment of whatever he may, by his own industry or good fortune, or the gift of others, have honestly acquired. Prominent among the duties, therefore, which we owe to our fellow-men, — that is, to society, — are the duties which have respect to property. The principal topics to be considered are the right of property, the uses of such an institution, the modes in which it may be acquired, the different kinds of property, crimes against property, and the various limitations of the right of property.

§ I. FOUNDATION OF THE RIGHT OF PROPERTY.

Labor and not Law. — Whatever man produces as the result of his own skill and labor, is properly his, and no one else has the right to take it from him. It is his property by a natural right. There is need of no law, or social organization and compact, in order to this. His title to use, possess, and enjoy what he has himself produced, by virtue of his own powers and his own industry, is just as good before as after, without as with, any such legislation or compact. Law and social organization, with its appliances, may confirm and protect him in his right, but do not create it.

Different Theories. — According to the view now taken, it is the labor expended in originally acquiring, or subsequently improving any object of possession, that constitutes the right of property in the same. In the case of land, the labor of cultivation renders it more valuable, and so confers the right of continued possession on him who has created that value. This is the view maintained by Locke, and many others.

Another view of the matter is, that, inasmuch as God, the Creator of all things, provided the gifts of nature for the use of all his creatures, therefore every one has a right originally to all he needs. In this manner, land, as well as other things, comes to be the property of the individual. This is a rule of somewhat indefinite application; and if carried out, would lead, perhaps, to the disorganization of society as at present constituted. As regards strictly the gifts of nature, it is doubtless true that they were intended for all. Light, air, rain, sunshine, and the like, are free to all, and in their nature cannot, under ordinary circumstances, be appropriated. But it is otherwise with that on which, by my toil or skill, I have conferred a value. Water is free to all; but not the water of the well that I have dug for my own convenience. Fire is a commodity which nature places within the reach of all; but not the fire which my labor has kindled for my own use. So land may originally have been free to the first comer; but when he has once taken possession, and expended labor and created value, it is not free to others, so long as he chooses to occupy it.

Paley's View.— Paley makes the foundation of property to be the law of the land, as carrying out the will and intention of the Creator. "It is the intention of God that the produce of the earth be applied to the use of man. This intention cannot be fulfilled without establishing property. It is consistent, therefore, with his will that property be established. The land cannot be divided into separate property without leaving it to the law of the country to regulate that division. It is consistent, therefore, with the same will that law should regulate the division; and, consequently, 'consistent with the will of God,' or 'right,' that I should possess that share which these regulations assign me."

This resolves all right into the will of God, — which is Paley's theory of right, — and it also supposes that the laws of the land are in all cases an expression of that will, — which is by no means certain. Now, it is perfectly clear that law regulates the conveyance of property, defines what is and what is not property, maintains and secures to the rightful owner that which properly belongs to him. It maintains and defends, but it does not *create* the right to own. It regulates rather than originates that right.

Constitution of the Mind. — The right, in itself considered, or in the abstract, is found, if I mistake not, in the nature and constitution of the human mind, — just as society itself originates from that same nature and constitution. This, indeed, reduces itself ultimately into the divine will; inasmuch as the nature and constitution of men are from God, and it was for him to form us with what nature, and endow us with what propensities, he pleased. Still, we need go no further than to the constitution of human nature to discover the origin of the principle in question. The desire to possess, to appropriate, lies among the native and implanted principles of the mind.

It shows itself in earliest life. The child appropriates to himself the toys that are given him, and feels injured if they are taken from him by another. The structure of language shows that this is a universal principle. Wherever we find in human speech the use of possessive pronouns, or other forms of language fulfilling that office, we find the expression of this principle. Men, universally, feel that there is a right violated, a wrong done, in taking by violence or fraud that which has been appropriated by another. Hence, they demand not mere restitution, but the punishment of the offender.

But while we seek in the structure of the mind itself the origin and foundation of the right of property in general — of the right to appropriate, in itself considered — the condition on which that right depends — *i. e.*, the right to appropriate this or that thing, in any given case — is the circumstance already pointed out: namely, that labor has been originally bestowed in the acquisition of these things, and value created as the result of that labor, to which value the laborer is justly entitled, as something he has himself produced.

Objection. — If it be said that we possess many things, which we call property, on which we have not bestowed labor, — many values which we have not ourselves created, as, for example, property inherited or bequeathed, or the gifts of friendship, — I reply, these values were originally acquired or created by labor; they became the property of the original owner in that way; and the right of possession has been conferred by him on the present possessor.

The only exception to this rule, which occurs to my mind, is the accident of discovery: as when, walking by the bank of a stream, I find a piece of gold ore, or a pearl, among its sands. In this case, there is certainly no labor bestowed on the acquisition further than that of picking up and appropriating what I have discovered. The act of appropriation constitutes my right in this case, and holds good as against others, on the ground that no one else has bestowed labor on the things in question, and therefore no one else has any claim to them. Were it otherwise,—were the treasure found not a natural product, but the result of human labor, as, *e. g.*, a bracelet of pearls, or a purse of gold coined for use,—my discovery of the article would not constitute a right of possession against the claim of the real owner. Even in the case supposed, the owner of the soil in which the gold ore or the jewels is found, may present a counter claim, on the ground that, in purchasing the soil, he purchased whatever value it may produce or contain. The soil itself is his property, and no one else has a right to take away from it any of its values.

In like manner, were a meteorite to fall from the sky upon my land, my right to that value would depend not merely, or so much, upon the accident of discovery, as upon my previous right to the premises,—a right purchased by labor in some form.

View of Whately.—Archbishop Whately, in his Logic, has made use of this very illustration to prove the opposite doctrine, viz., that the right of property does *not* depend, ultimately, on labor. The labor expended in the production of values is, according to him, not essential to the existence of value and to property in the same, but is merely *accidental*,—a circumstance that, indeed, usually, but not always or necessarily, accompanies the possession of wealth. The meteorite that falls in my yard has a value quite independent of human labor.

It seems to me, however, that in this instance, Whately, while attempting to correct a popular fallacy, as he regards it, has himself fallen into a still more serious error. If we look at the real wealth of the world, the chief values that constitute the property of men, we certainly do find them to be, in great proportion, the result of human labor. The exceptions are so few and so slight, as compared with the whole amount, that they scarcely deserve to be taken into the account; and instead of calling labor an *accidental circumstance* sometimes accompanying the possession of wealth, it were certainly much nearer the truth to call it the *rule*, and its exceptions the accident.

Relation of the State to private Property.—According to the view of some, the state is the supreme and *ultimate* proprietor and controller of all property. The natural right must, in all cases, be held subordinate to the public authority. It is for the state to determine what shall be considered as the property of every citizen, and no man can hold any property, or call it his own, except as under the law of the land. All individual right is thus resolved into state right. Such is the view maintained by some able writers, among others by Dr. Hickok.

According to this view, the individual right to property is derived from the state. The natural right is no right unless the state sanctions it. This view seems to destroy individual right and liberty,—to merge the individual citizen, with all his rights and powers, in the state,—thus making the state all in all, as in that theory of political organization which Plato has left us.

In reality, the state confers no right, as to property, which did not previously exist, and which would not have existed even had there been no such thing as a state. It confirms and establishes existing rights. It regulates the sale and transfer of property. It inquires into the validity of titles and the terms of contract, and takes care that those terms shall be fulfilled. The state is merely a social organization, contrived for the purpose of more effectually securing and maintaining the rights and liberties of the whole body of individual citizens, — in other words, the public good.

It has no power, except that of the individual arms that compose its aggregate strength; no rights or authority, except such as may be conferred on it by the body politic. It owns, and can own, no property, except such as belongs to the citizens that constitute the state, either in their private, individual capacity, or as a public body. Whatever right or control of property the state has, it derived originally from the people.

In order to carry out the purposes for which the state is created, it must have control and disposal of so much of the public property as is necessary to the subsistence, defence, and well-being of the state; must have power to lay out roads, levy taxes, etc.; and, whenever, in pursuance of such objects, the public claim comes into conflict with individual claim, the latter must yield to the former, on the principle that the majority govern. When, for example, the land held by any citizen is needed for some public purpose, as a road, for instance, the state has the right to take it from him for that purpose; but not without equivalent to the full value of the property taken. Otherwise, government becomes a despotism, and there is no longer security for individual right.

§ II. — Advantages of the Institution of Property.

Granting the right, which has been already discussed, the question may still arise, Of what use is the institution of property, or private possession? Why may not society hold its goods in common, every man taking from the common stock that which he needs for his own present wants, and that only? Why should one particular portion of the soil, for example, be set off to my share, with its various products, and another to my neighbor? What advantage results from such distribution?

Contributes to the Comfort and Happiness of Man. — That there are some disadvantages resulting from the distribution of property, cannot be denied. On the other hand, there are many and obvious advantages; prominent among which must be reckoned the contribution thus made to the comfort and happiness of the race. Man is so constituted, as we have already seen, that he naturally desires to possess, and call his own, the objects that minister to his wants. He enjoys that which is his own and not another's. The waters from his own spring, the fruit from his own tree, that he has himself planted and nurtured, the game which his own bow has brought down, or his own net captured, are sweeter and pleasanter than any other.

He not only enjoys more what he thus possesses, but he possesses more in consequence of this arrangement. Were there no such thing as property, there would be no division of labor; every man would be obliged to hunt, and fish, and cook, for himself; to make his own clothes, and his own hut, or tent; to provide for all his own wants. He would, in consequence, be very poorly provided. His implements of labor would be rude and clumsy; his conveniences of living, scanty. His time and attention being divided among so many pursuits, he would acquire little skill in any of them. By devoting himself to some one art or profession, he becomes expert in that; and by exchanging the products of his skill and labor for other commodities, which in like manner have been produced by other laborers, the objects of enjoyment at his command become greatly augmented. But this implies prop erty in what is thus produced, as otherwise there can be no right of exchange.

Augments the Produce of the Earth. — It is a further advantage of the arrangement in question, that it greatly increases the products of the soil. In order to fertility, and the greatest productiveness of the earth, there must be labor and due cultivation. It produces little spontaneously. But where there is no property in the soil and its products, where they are the common possession of all, where those who do not labor share equally with those who do, there is no incitement to labor — no inducement to put forth the exertion requisite to the proper cultivation of the soil. Tillage will inevitably be neglected, and the community will grow poor together, in proportion to that neglect. The products of the earth, as every one knows, are our chief source of national wealth — the foundation, in fact, on which other modes and sources of productiveness must ultimately rest.

The effect of leaving land and produce to be held in common, is seen in the neglect of agriculture by the North American native tribes — gathering a precarious and scanty support from an amount of territory sufficient, under proper management, to feed and clothe a hundred-fold greater population. It has always been observed, also, that where, among civilized communities, a piece of ground or other property has been held in common, it is of little use to any body. The fruit of a tree that grows by the roadside, and is regarded as public property, is seldom allowed to come to maturity. It would be much the same with all other products, in like circumstances.

Promotes Civilization. — Without individual possession and right of property, there can be no division of labor, as I have said; and without division of labor, there can be little progress in civilization. The advantages of civilized over savage life, depend in a great measure on those mechanic arts which supply the conveniences and luxuries of refined society, and which, in turn, can never be carried to any degree of perfection, where the workman is not permitted to derive the benefit of his own skill and industry.

The state of Europe during the middle ages, when despotic power prevailed, when the laborer belonged to the soil that he cultivated, when the rights of private property were little regarded, and the wish of the strongest was law, as compared with the state of the same countries at the present day, when peace and constitutional law have given security to private rights, is a striking illustration of this truth. We see the same thing illustrated also in the present state of Syria, and other countries of Asia and the East. Despotic power prevails, and the laborer is not sure that he shall be permitted to enjoy the product of his field. His grain, his flocks, his produce of whatever kind, are liable to be taken from him at any moment, by the rapacity and extortion of the lawless agents of government. There is, consequently, no inducement to labor, more than is necessary for absolute subsistence. Agriculture is neglected, and the mechanic arts. Society lingers in the twilight of barbarism. On the contrary, wherever, under free and well-ordered governments, we find the rights of private property respected and secured, there we find the arts and agriculture flourishing, property accumulating, society rapidly advancing.

Inequality of Distribution. — But, while the institution of property has its obvious advantages, it is not to be denied that certain disadvantages, and perhaps abuses, flow from it. Nothing seems, at first sight, more unjust than the extreme *inequality* with which property, the actual wealth of the world, is distributed among men. One man has a fortune, another is reduced to beggary. One rolls in luxury, and counts his millions, and measures his estates by the square mile; another toils for the merest pittance, and barely subsists on the soil which he cultivates for another. Nor is it always the most industrious, the most talented, or the most deserving, that reap the largest reward. The weak, the profligate, the idle, the vicious, may be, and often are, the favorites of fortune, revelling upon the proceeds of the sweat and toil of honest industry.

Paley's Illustration. — This anomaly has been very forcibly represented by Dr. Paley, in the well-known allegory of the flock of pigeons: "If you should see a flock of pigeons in a field of corn, and if (instead of each picking where and what it liked, taking just what it wanted, and no more) you should see ninety-nine of them gathering all they got into a heap; reserving nothing for themselves but the chaff and the refuse; keeping this heap for one — that, the weakest, perhaps worst pigeon of the flock; sitting round and looking on all the winter, whilst this one was devouring, throwing about, and wasting it; and if a pigeon more hardy and hungry than the rest, touched a grain of the hoard, all the others flying upon it, and tearing it to pieces; — if you should see this, you would see nothing more than what is every day practised and established among men. Among men you see the ninety-nine, toiling and scraping together a heap of superfluities for one (and this one, too, oftentimes the feeblest and worst of the whole set — a child, a woman, a madman, or a fool); getting nothing for themselves but the coarsest of the provision which their own industry produces; looking quietly on while they see the fruits of all their labor spent or spoiled; and if one of the number take or touch a particle of the hoard, the others joining against him, and hanging him for the theft."

Fallacy of this Statement.—It is important to be borne in mind that, in the present constitution of things, all property represents, and is the product of labor, performed at some time, and by somebody. The labor expended in the product may not have been put forth by the present possessor of the product, but at some time long previous, and by some one whom he has never seen. It may have come into his hands by inheritance from some remote ancestor. However that may be, it is none the less the product of labor. So far as other men are concerned, it is the same thing as if the present possessor had acquired it by his own industry and skill. So much industry, so much toil, so much skill, lie embodied and represented in this wealth which is accumulated in the coffers of the present proprietor. His lordly mansion, his noble acres, his fine grounds and estates, are the product for which a full price has been paid, in that which is the ultimate price of all requisitions, viz., human labor.

The illustration of Paley overlooks this fact. The pigeon which he describes seated in the midst of the flock, enjoys the products of the labors of those around him, to which he has no right. It is not his labor; it is not his product. He has no claims to it; it belongs to those who are engaged in heaping it together. But in the distribution of property among men, it is not so; the rich man has that only which he has acquired by his own toil and economy, or which has rightfully descended to him from those who in the first instance acquired it in this manner. He has a claim and a right to all that he calls his. The poor man, on the other hand, has equal claim and right to all that he produces, be it more or less; and, so far from hanging him if he touches it, or preventing him from the full enjoyment of it, society protects him in that right. So far as designed to represent the unequal distribution of property, then, the illustration of Dr. Paley, while amusing and ingenious, is by no means a fair and correct representation of the case. The argument which it conveys is sophistical.

§ III.—Modes in which Property may be Acquired.

The First Ownership. — The first ownership of all things lies with the Creator of all, and is his gift to his creatures. So far as I have need of these things, and no one else has, by any reason, a higher claim to them, I may regard that which I find ready at my hand, and adapted to my wants, as the gift of the Creator to me, his creature. That I need it, and can have it without interfering with the rights of others, in itself constitutes in some sort a title to the thing. Such is the case as regards the spontaneous productions of the earth, game running wild in the forest, unclaimed lands, etc. Such, in the primitive state of society, was the case with most of those values which were in that rude stage of civilization possessed.

Acquisition by Effort. — But, aside from this primitive acquisition by gift from the Creator, the chief mode in which property may be acquired is by labor. As society advances, and man's wants increase, he no longer depends on those spontaneous productions of the earth found ready at his hand, and which may be regarded as the direct gift of God to man. The cave which has hitherto sheltered him, is exchanged for a more comfortable abode; the simple fruits that have satisfied his hunger, are replaced by food of greater variety and abundance; the skins of animals, that constitute as yet his clothing, are laid aside for some more convenient apparel; and these advances are all the product of labor. To obtain these better accommodations he fells the forest, he builds, he tills the ground, he plants, he weaves, he spins; and what he thus acquires as the result and reward of labor, becomes his own, because the labor with which it was procured was his own; and no one has a right to take it from him without his consent, and without just compensation.

There is, however, a limitation to be here considered. He who acquires property by labor is entitled to the proceeds of that labor only, and not to the proceeds of those previous values on which that labor may be expended. If I cultivate land belonging to another, or make use of tools and implements which are the property of another, this land, these tools and implements, are already existing values, on which the labor of others has previously been bestowed; and when I unite my labor with theirs, as I do in making use of these things, I am entitled manifestly not to the whole, but only to a share of the proceeds. It is right that he who has bestowed labor on the land, in acquiring possession of it, and preparing it for cultivation, and on the tools and implements which he has invented and manufactured, and which I have used, should receive the benefit of his labor, as well as I of mine.

Acquisition by Exchange.—That which I have acquired, and which is rightfully my own, I may not choose to keep. It may be more in quantity than I need for my own use; or I may prefer some other value in place of it. I may part with it, therefore, for something in return; and this is *exchange.* This is still another mode of acquisition; and what is thus acquired, becomes my property as really and rightfully as if my own labor had been expended originally and directly in its production.

A great part of the actual possessions of any man in civilized society are thus acquired; comparatively few of the things which he calls his own are the direct product of his own industry. For the most part, we neither build our own houses, nor make our own garments, nor prepare our own food, but employ the labor of others for these purposes.

Acquisition by Gift and Inheritance.—Another mode of acquisition is by the conferring of value gratuitously, as when I receive a gift from a friend, or when property is left me by inheritance. The rightful owner of any possession may, if he chooses, part with the same without receiving an equivalent in return. It is at his disposal, and he may convey the right of ownership now vested in him to whomsoever he pleases. When this is done informally, it is called a gift. When property is conveyed by will, or by due forms of law, at the decease of the original owner, it is termed *inheritance.*

Question as to Right of Possession.—Does mere possession, in any case, confer the right to possess? Suppose I have, by dishonest means, obtained possession of valuable property; suppose, moreover, that the rightful owners are all dead, and that no one has now any better claim than myself to this property—that is, no one has any claim at all;—does my possession, the fact that it is now in my hands, entitle me to keep possession of it? Dr. Wayland answers yes; I have no moral right to the property, but I have the right to exclude others from it, who have no better claim than I have. This may be; and yet I may have no right to retain possession of it myself. The state, in such a case, becomes the proper recipient. I may not be under obligation to give up the property to any individual claimant, but I may be under obligation to give it up to society for the benefit of the whole. The mere fact that the property is now in my hands gives me no right to retain possession, inasmuch as it came into my hands unlawfully. There may be cases where simple possession entitles the holder to retain; as where no right of another is violated in the original acquisition; where the object acquired is, previous to its acquisition, the property of no one individual, as in the case of fruits growing by the roadside, or nuts in the forest, or game on the prairie, or land lying unclaimed in a new and uninhabited territory. In such a case, simple possession holds good against all subsequent occupancy by another. But such is not the case now supposed.

The principal modes in which property may be acquired, are those now stated — viz., by the direct gift of the Creator, by labor of acquisition and production, by exchange, by donation and inheritance.

§ IV. — Different Kinds of Property.

Personal and Real. — It has become usual to divide property into two kinds or classes — personal, and real; the latter including possessions in land, houses, etc. — whatever is in its nature a fixture, not easily moved; the former including all other species of property, such as admits of transfer from place to place. That which we term real estate, was not probably, at first, recognized as property at all, but became so only as society and civilization progressed. The cave that sheltered the wanderer, and the pasture that fed his flocks, were *his* only so long as he occupied them. After that, they were free to the next comer.

History of Property. — The first objects of property were probably the fruits of the earth, the spontaneous products of the soil, which became the property of the individual by the simple act of gathering and appropriation to his own use. The labor of acquiring these fruits might have been very slight; but it was sufficient to constitute a difference between him who had, and him who had not, in this manner acquired possession. Soon the products of the chase would be added to the list of rightful possessions; and these, as they would require more labor and skill in the acquisition, would for that reason belong, by a still clearer right, to the individual who had acquired them.

In like manner, tools and implements for the chase, or for the gathering and preparing of the fruits of the earth, tents, weapons of protection, and whatever of the like sort was early found necessary to the comfort and subsistence of man, would come to be regarded as property. In the progress of time, flocks and herds of domestic animals would constitute a portion of the wealth of man. Not until the country became somewhat thickly inhabited, and man began to turn his attention to the cultivation of the soil, would land itself come to be regarded as property; and then only as each occupant expended labor on the soil, and mingled his products with it, would he acquire a right of individual appropriation.

Accordingly, among the earlier and less civilized nations, we find no trace of property in land. The North American native tribes seem to have known nothing of it. The Scythians, while they appropriated cattle and horses, left their land in common. When Cæsar invaded Britain, he seems to have found no traces of property in land. This species of property came to be a permanent possession, probably, not until the organization of society, and of civil government, fixing by law the right of the individual to the soil he cultivated. Previously, it was property only by possession and actual occupancy.

Property as Regulated by Law. — Inasmuch as land is less obviously the property of an individual than are those possessions which he can carry with him from place to place, and as the right of ownership is, therefore, maintained with more difficulty, this species of property is made more directly and peculiarly the object of legislation. The ancient law of England regards land as the chief part of property, all other things being treated as only appendages to persons. Hence the distinctive terms, *real* property, and *personal* property.

The cultivator and the proprietor of the soil are not always the same person, nor of the same class. In such a case the rights of each are determined by law — the cultivator giving to the proprietor a certain share of the proceeds, which is termed *rent.* This may be given in *produce,* as in Asia, where the proprietor, usually the sovereign, receives one-fifth, commonly, of whatever is raised on the land; or, it may be in labor, as in Russia and Germany, where the peasant pays his rent by working a definite portion of his time for the exclusive benefit of the landlord. The cultivator is then termed a serf. In other countries of Europe one-half the produce of the land goes to the owner of the soil, one-half to the cultivator. In England, between the landlord and the cultivator, we find an intermediate class, termed farmers, who give to the owner of the soil his rent, and to the laborer his wages, retaining what is left after these deductions as their own profit.

Feudal System. — There prevailed for some centuries in Europe, a system of land tenure, according to which the proprietor held himself bound to protect the laborer as against other persons, and the laborer in turn was bound to render to his superior certain fixed and valuable services. The relation of the two was one of mutual dependence, the lord requiring the service of the vassal, and the latter the protection of the lord. On this condition the vassal held certain lands as, in a modified sense, his own—paying fixed dues to the lord, and yielding also personal service as a soldier in arms. The land thus held by the laborer was termed a *Feud*, or Fee; hence the expression, *Feudal System.* The land thus held was not the absolute property of the laborer, however, nor yet even of the lord; but its ultimate ownership vested in the sovereign. The laborer who held no fees or feuds, was termed a *Villein*, and was little better than a serf.

§ V.—Crimes against Property.

There are three principal modes in which the right of property may be violated. One may take what belongs to another, clandestinely, without the owner's knowledge. This is *theft.* Or, he may take it by violence, as when a highwayman presents a pistol and demands money, or when a band of armed men storm a castle, or ravage a territory, and plunder its treasures. This is *robbery.* Or, yet again, the consent of the owner may be *fraudulently* obtained, by deceiving him as to the real nature, or the market value, of the commodity offered.

Theft.—To take the property of another without his knowledge, and full, free consent, with design to appropriate it to our own use, is a violation of the right of property, and is justly regarded as a crime. It matters little whether the amount thus clandestinely appropriated be large or small, whether it be of great or trifling value, whether its loss will be severely felt by the owner or not; in any case it is a violation of right, and, as regards the moral character of the act, it is essentially one and the same. Even if it should so happen that the owner has no objection to the transfer, still, so long as we presume upon this willingness, without first obtaining his consent, we are guilty of theft.

Robbery. — In case of violence offered for the purpose of obtaining consent not otherwise given, the crime is aggravated. The double offence is committed, of violence to the person, and violation of the property. I have no right to threaten the life or personal safety of another; no right to take his property; still less a right to accomplish the latter object by means of the former. The offence is aggravated, and deserves, and is everywhere held to deserve, the severest punishment. To compel consent by means of violence, is a greater crime than to take the property by force, and without the semblance of consent.

Cheating. — But it is not enough that consent be attained, and that it be freely given; this may be, and still the right of property be violated. That consent must be honestly and not fraudulently obtained, else the transaction is criminal. The greater part of the crimes against property are of this nature. The number of burglars, thieves, highway robbers, is small, in comparison with the number of those who, in business transactions, hesitate not to cheat and defraud their fellow-men. The latter are as really guilty of crime, though not perhaps, in some respects, of so great a crime, as the former; nor is the one a more respectable and honorable mode of procedure than the other. The command, "Thou shalt not steal," is as really broken in the one case as the other. Nor has he who cheats his fellow in a small way, and under cover of a business transaction, the same apology for his crime that the more daring offender may often urge. The man who breaks into my house, or who demands my purse on the highway, may be driven to his desperate course by want and absolute starvation. The man who, pretending fair and honorable commerce, cheats me out of a few pennies, can plead no such apology for his dishonesty and meanness.

Modes of Cheating. — There are various modes in which this species of dishonesty may be practised. It may be done by presenting for sale goods that are damaged, or in some way inferior to what they seem and are taken to be, deficient in quality or in quantity, a poorer article than we represent, and than we intend that the buyer shall suppose. This is as really a fraud as if we were slyly to abstract just so much in value from the pocket of the purchaser.

Another mode is to mislead the buyer as to the market price of the article sold. When a man devotes himself to the business of exchanges, he is understood to possess some skill in the matter of purchasing, and to receive a fair compensation for that skill, as well as for his time and trouble; he is understood also to furnish goods at the ordinary market prices. If, now, his skill in any particular instance fails him; if he finds that he has purchased at a given price what is not really worth so much; or if, the article being good, the price falls while it is upon his hands, he has no right to remunerate himself at the expense of his customers — no right to take advantage of their ignorance, and sell to them at a price beyond the real value, on the ground that it cost him at that rate. This is to deceive the customer, and, in reality, to defraud him. If the trader is at liberty to reap the benefit of a rise of prices while the goods are in his possession, he is, on the same principle, bound to give the buyer the benefit of an accidental decline of prices. If, on the other hand, he adopts the rule of selling as he bought, he is bound to apply it equally to both cases, and give the customer the benefit of a purchase below the present market price.

It is always understood that the trader furnishes his goods at the ruling price in the market. He takes care to have this understood. His credit and success depend on it. Hence he is bound to fulfill an expectation in itself so reasonable and universal, and which he has himself contributed to form. This obligation is violated, not merely by assuring the customer that he can procure the article in question nowhere at a cheaper rate, — which, in the case supposed, would be a direct falsehood, — but equally by silence; since where nothing is said, the buyer presumes, and has a right to presume, that he is giving only the ordinary market price.

False Information. — Closely allied to this very common species of dishonesty is another — the circulating false information respecting the value, quantity, or price of any kind of goods, with a view to effect the sale; as, for example, when the stock broker, by false reports circulated on 'Change, seeks to raise or depress the price of stocks; or when the speculator, monopolizing a given article, conveys the impression of a scarcity, when in reality there is an abundance of that commodity. This latter method of procedure becomes the more culpable when it affects, not the luxuries and conveniences, but the very necessaries of life, as in the case of monopolies of flour and grain.

Monopoly. — The question may here arise, whether, aside from any false impression thus conveyed of a scarcity which does not really exist, the monopolizing an article of trade for the purpose of raising the price, is in itself a species of dishonesty. Suppose a merchant, for example, to purchase all the ivory, or all the indigo, or saltpetre in the market; suppose him to extend his transactions in this line to all the commercial cities in the country, purchasing all that can be procured, wherever found; suppose him then to raise the price of the article, depending on the demand to ensure a sale at the advanced rate. Where, it may be asked, is the dishonesty of such a proceeding? Everything is fair and open in the transaction. The merchant has simply to say, I hold in my possession such and such goods, and you can have them if you like at such a price. It is true they have been often sold at a much lower price, but they are not now to be obtained except at the rate mentioned. Buy, or not, as you please. What is there of dishonesty in this?

I cannot see that there is, properly speaking, any dishonesty or fraud in such a proceeding. It is not deception; it is not cheating. The goods are offered at what is, for the time, the market value, — that is, they cannot, for the present, be obtained for less, in other markets. In a word, the merchant in question has it in his power to fix the market value of the goods, and does so. This he certainly has the right to do, in the case supposed. If the articles in question were necessaries of life, he would have no moral right to establish a monopoly, and then fix on them a price that should place them beyond the reach of all except the rich. But such is not the case supposed.

But, while we may not class such a transaction with the various forms of dishonest dealings, it must be admitted that public sentiment, and the common sense of mankind, very generally disapprove of this method of procedure, as not altogether just and honorable. It is taking what seems to be an undue advantage of the community. The profession of the merchant is one that is supposed to be for the public good. He comes between the producer and the consumer, for the advantage of both. It is better for both that there should be a class of men who shall devote themselves to the business of exchanges. But when the merchant, taking advantage of his position, puts upon his goods such a price that the community is rather injured than benefited by his transactions, no reason can be shown why such a business or profession should exist. The public good requires that it should cease to be.

Dishonesty of the Buyer. — It is hardly necessary to remark that the same rule applies to the buyer as to the seller. He is under obligation to pay a fair profit to the trader, in remuneration for the skill, labor, and capital employed by the latter in the business of purchasing; and any attempt to defraud him of this remuneration, by any of the tricks of trade, or by underrating the true value of the goods, is a species of dishonesty.

Excuses. — The various modes of dishonest dealing which have been mentioned, are frequently justified, by those who employ them, on the ground that such practices are nearly universal; that if they did not practise them, others would; that the competition is so great, that they could do no business; that in no other way can they live, and support their families. I reply: these excuses — even granting the validity of the statements — make the practices in question none the less immoral and dishonest. If every other person employed in the traffic cheats his customers, by giving them light weight and short measure, diluted and adulterated liquors, damaged in place of perfect articles, or by selling at a higher than the true market value, it is none the less a fraud for me to do the same. If the competition is such that I cannot carry on the business without resorting to such artifices, it is quite time that I was out of it, and in some more honest employment. As to the argument from the necessity of living and supporting one's family, "it is obvious," says Dr. Wayland, "that, were this plea allowed, it would put an end to all questions of morals; for there never was an iniquity so infamous as not to find multitudes who were ready to justify it on this plea."

Limitations of the Right of Property. — In this connection may be noticed certain questions respecting the limitation of the right of property. Cases may arise in which there shall seem to be a necessity for taking the property of others without their consent. Of the right of the state to take so much of the land of any citizen, with the buildings and improvements thereon, as may be necessary for the public good, in laying out roads and constructing other public works, I have already spoken. Such right must be conceded, and that irrespective of the owner's consent, though not without a fair equivalent. On the same principle, the individual is bound to meet his given proportion of the public expenses, in the shape of taxes; and if he refuses to do so, the state may take so much of his property as is necessary for this purpose, without his consent.

But, aside from these and the like instances, in which the state comes into conflict with the citizen, cases may arise in which the private individual, or a company of individuals, may find it necessary, in order to the preservation of life, to appropriate the property of another. A ship is in a storm at sea, and, in order to the preservation of all on board, it may be necessary to throw overboard a portion of her cargo. That, however, is private property, and to obtain the consent of the owner is, under the circumstances, impossible In such a case, no one can hesitate. Life is more valuable than property; and even if it were not, the property fares no worse than it would if the ship went down with all on board. It will be lost, in either case. Nothing is gained to the owner by the attempt to save it.

In like manner, and on the same principle, if the provisions fail in a ship, and the passengers are in danger of starving, there can be no question that they have the right to appropriate so much as may be necessary of the ship's cargo to their own support. These, and the like, are cases of necessity, against which there can be no law. Jurists accordingly, both ancient and modern, have admitted that, under such circumstances, the right of property must give way to higher rights and interests. Whether, under other and ordinary circumstances, a starving man has the right to take food not belonging to him, may admit of question, inasmuch as society usually makes provision foı his relief in another mode.

CHAPTER IV.

DUTIES PERTAINING TO REPUTATION.

Reputation a Right. — Among the springs of human action, there is none more powerful, or more universal, than the love of esteem. It has its seat in the constitution of our nature. Reputation is one of the goods which every man desires to get and to keep; among the first and greatest, indeed, of those goods — than which no possession is more valuable, no right more sacred. A good name is better than gold. No wealth can purchase it; once lost, no treasure can replace it. Hence it is held always among the dearest and most precious of earthly possessions. Its loss may entail the most serious consequences.

Society is bound to protect every man in the possession and enjoyment of whatever justly belongs to him; hence it is bound to protect him in this, as one of his most valuable and sacred rights. This is a principle recognized by the laws of civilized society, both ancient and modern. "Est enim famae, ut et vitae, habenda ratio" — Reputation, as well as life, is to be regarded in law — was a maxim of Roman jurisprudence. The laws of England and of our own country, in like manner, take cognizance of injuries affecting the reputation, no less than of injuries affecting the property and the life. There is reason and justice in this. One who by industry, skill, and patient toil, has built up a fortune, is justly entitled to the possession and enjoyment of the same. If now, by the same industry and skill, he has acquired a reputation, as artist, merchant, or professional man, is he not by every principle of justice and right entitled equally also to that? And is not the latter often much the more valuable acquisition of the two? To diminish the esteem in which he is held, and rob him wholly or in part of his justly earned reputation, is to inflict on him a much more serious injury than to rob him of money.

The violation of the right now under consideration is known under the general name of *slander;* and in treating of this crime, it will be to our purpose to define what this term properly includes; to inquire further what the law of reputation requires and forbids, and in what cases it is allowable to speak to the injury of others; and, finally, to show reasons why we should not, without cause, speak evil of any one. These topics will be severally discussed in the following sections.

§ I. — Slander Defined.

I understand this term to include all forms of detraction. It is the utterance of anything calculated to injure the good name and character of another, without due cause, whether maliciously, or inconsiderately. The utterance may be *malicious* — designed to injure. An enemy, or a rival, may take that way to gratify his revenge, or to pull down a competitor whom he cannot successfully encounter in a more open and honorable way. This is the height of meanness, and a crime of no ordinary turpitude.

Or the act may be an inconsiderate and thoughtless one. There may be no special, set design to injure another's reputation. The mere love of gossip, the desire to say or to hear some new thing, and especially the gratification which it affords to one's self-esteem and self-complacency to dwell upon the foibles and weaknesses of others, may be the real motive and spring of action; and the injury which is to result to the good name and character of the person spoken of, may not occur to the speaker at the moment. This is, however, none the less slander. There may be a difference in the degree of guilt in the two cases, but both are crimes. The consequences are much the same in either case. We cannot excuse ourselves by saying, the mischief was not intended. A proper regard for duty, and for the rights of others, would have led us to pause before we uttered the injurious words, and to look at the consequences of what we were about to utter. Our forgetfulness and thoughtlessness of consequences by no means frees us from responsibility from those consequences, be they what they may.

Nor is it essential that the thing said should be false, in order to constitute it a slander. It may be a true thing; yet, if maliciously spoken, with design to injure, or even thoughtlessly uttered, without due and sufficient cause why it should be said, it is none the less slander. No one has a moral right to injure his fellow, without cause, even by publishing what is strictly true of him. Doubtless there is more guilt in uttering *falsehood* maliciously, than in uttering *truth* maliciously; more guilt in intentional than in inconsiderate slander; all these, however, are forms of slander, — all are crimes.

Perhaps the most common form of slander is that where one seeks to detract from the good opinion which a friend, or benefactor, or the community, entertain of a person whom he dislikes; to awaken suspicion or distrust with regard to him, and so change his relation to the parties concerned, and to society. In a thousand ways this mischief may be done, this object accomplished. With due secrecy, and injunctions of secrecy upon those to whom the disclosure is made; with every precaution to avoid detection; what is more, with great apparent *reluctance* to make the statements which are made, and with professions of friendship for the injured party, may the work be done. These are the usual subterfuges and pretences of the slanderer. All such disguises are more or less hypocritical, and, as Paley has well remarked, they are all so many aggravations of the offence, inasmuch as they indicate deliberation and design.

§ II. — What the Law of Reputation Forbids.

From the definition already given of slander, as including all forms of detraction, the rule itself, of which this is a violation, becomes evident. The law of reputation forbids us, in general, to say anything, without imperative reasons, that shall detract from the good name and reputation of another; it requires us, on the other hand, to sustain that good name and reputation by all due and proper means.

Making public the Faults of Others. — More specifically, it forbids us needlessly and without cause to give publicity to the faults, or even the aggravated offences of others. We may know that which the public does not know, and which, if it were known, would tend very greatly to the injury of the individual concerned. Now, there may be circumstances which would require us, from a regard to the public good, or for other reasons which will be hereafter considered, to disclose the facts which have come to our knowledge. But, aside from these, we have no right, thoughtlessly, needlessly, without weighty and sufficient reasons, to make use of our information to the discredit and injury of the offending party. Whatever publicity he may give to his own actions, and whatever, in the natural course of justice and of divine providence, they may acquire, is another matter; but the mere knowledge, on my part, that he has acted dishonestly, is not a sufficient reason why I should speak of it to his injury, and gives me no right to do so. "One man," says Dr. Hickok, "has no right to be injuring the good name of another, even by reporting that which may be true of him, unless some grave interest of the public may demand it." The person to whose injury we are tempted to speak, may be himself deeply conscious of his own faults, and earnestly making efforts to overcome them. Or the particular offence that we have in mind may have been committed in former years, and under circumstances of peculiar temptation; it may be something of which he has long and bitterly repented, and from which his whole subsequent life has turned away utterly. To give publicity to the matter, under such circumstances, would be to work infinite mischief and causeless ruin.

Judging of the Motives of Others. — On the same principle, and by the same law of morality, we are forbidden to judge of the motives of others, either by assigning to their conduct wrong motives, where right ones may reasonably be supposed, or by suggesting that the action proceeds from some other motive than that which is apparent and professed. We have no right to suppose or presume any such thing. The motives of men are for the most part known only to Him who sees the heart. We do great injustice to the character of others, when, on such imperfect and insufficient data as we have, and without due cause, we set aside the professed intent and design of an action, and attribute it to some unworthy source. We like not to be ourselves judged in that manner, and have no right thus to judge the motives of others.

Holding Others up to Ridicule. — Any deliberate attempt to bring others into contempt, by ridicule and raillery, and thus to detract from the esteem in which they would otherwise be held, is likewise a violation of the rule. The shafts of ridicule are, of all weapons with which one's reputation may possibly be assailed, the most fatal and venomous. They are the most difficult to meet, and for this reason both the more mischievous and the more cowardly. On this point the remarks of Dr. Wayland are forcible and just: "It is but a very imperfect excuse, for conduct of this sort, to plead that we do not mean any harm. What *do* we mean? Surely reasonable beings should be prepared to answer this question. Were the witty calumniator to stand concealed, and hear himself made the subject of remarks precisely similar to those in which he indulges respecting others, he would have a very definite conception of what others mean. Let him then carry the lesson home to his own bosom."

Misinterpreting Others. — The law of reputation forbids

us likewise to put a wrong construction on what others say and do, — to interpret their language or conduct as meaning one thing, while in reality it is susceptible of a very different interpretation, and then to make use of this false and forced construction to the injury of the party concerned. This is a course of procedure at once mischievous and despicable. When intentionally done, it is dowright dishonesty; when inadvertently, it is still a wrong and a crime. This is a form of slander to which the critic and literary reviewer, the disputant, the controversial writer, are too frequently tempted to resort, in answering an opponent, or pointing out what they may regard as error. The words and statements of an author are wrested, whether consciously or inadvertently, from their true meaning, and he is held up to public odium, on charges not less false than injurious. Even the records of theological controversy are not, it is to be feared, wholly free from this fault.

In what Cases Silence not required. — Here the question may arise, whether, in all cases, we are bound to observe silence respecting the faults or crimes of others. Does the law of morality, as regards reputation, require us in all cases to conceal from the public eye what we may happen to know that is derogatory to the character of another? If not, then what are the exceptions?

I reply, whenever the good of the community imperatively requires the exposure of the faults or follies, the mistakes or crimes of another, then is the law of reputation superseded, set aside by a higher claim, and we are at liberty to make known what has come to our observation; but not otherwise. Thus, for example, a man may be enjoying a higher reputation as a scholar, a man of science or for virtue and general worth, than he may seem to me to deserve. That gives me no right to diminish his reputation, and bring him down to the level which, in my opinion, he ought to occupy. His reputation is his own acquirement and possession, and he has the right to enjoy it. If, however, this involves manifest injustice to another, then there is adequate cause for interference, and for setting the matter right. So, in like manner, if I have reason to suppose that any person is plotting the injury of another, or of the community, I have no right to keep silence, out of regard to his reputation. Or if a crime has been committed, and I know the authors, I am not at liberty to be silent where the ends of public justice and the public good require the disclosure of the guilty. These ends are of still higher moment than personal reputation, and the law of procedure in all such cases is plain.

§ III. — Reasons for Observing the Law of Reputation

The law which has been stated as binding upon us, in the matter of speaking to the injury of others, is by no means a law without a reason. On the contrary, it is enforced by considerations of the most weighty and imperative character.

Baseness of Slander. — One reason why we should not, without adequate cause, speak evil of any one, is, the *baseness* of so doing. Slander is justly regarded as one of the basest and meanest of crimes. Some crimes find their apology in the strength of the natural appetite which prompts to their commission. But no man can plead, I suppose, a natural appetite for slander; and even if he should, it would not be likely to raise him in our esteem, or to be taken as an excuse for his crime. Slander injures another, without benefit to one's self; destroys and lays waste without cause, wantonly, and for the mere sake of mischief. It is evil inflicted gratuitously, and for the evil's own sake. It is a course prompted by envy, or the desire of revenge. It has its source in the darkest and most malignant passions and principles of our fallen nature. There is nothing noble or magnanimous about it. It is a false, dishonorable, cowardly thing. No man can be guilty of it and retain self-respect, or the respect of others. He sinks himself in the estimation of all honorable men, and brands himself with the ignominy which he vainly seeks to fasten upon his victim.

Effect on the Community.—It is to be considered, also, what would be the effect on the community, were men to indulge freely in the habit of speaking evil one of another, and exposing one another's faults and follies, without adequate cause. Manifestly such a state of society would be almost intolerable. No one is free from faults; and if every one were at liberty to expose to the public gaze the imperfections and weaknesses of all with whom he is conversant, scandal must become the order of the day, and the great staple of conversation. Universal suspicion and distrust would be awakened; the tenderest and most sacred relations of life would be involved; and all social intercourse and organization must speedily come to an end. Nothing so weakens the restraints of crime and the regard for public virtue, as free converse of the failings and follies of others, especially of those who stand high in public estimation as persons of worth and character.

Duty of the Citizen and of the Press.—It is incumbent, then, on every good citizen, as he values the public welfare, the order and harmony and virtue of the community, to abstain from the needless utterance of that which would tend to derogate from the respect in which another is held; and not only to abstain from this himself, but to discountenance it in others, and brand it with his disapprobation and scorn. Especially is this incumbent on the public press. It is bad enough to give publicity to the failings of others in the limited circle of one's private acquaintance; it is a greater mischief and a greater crime to publish them to the world. How sad the spectacle, when the press of a nation debases itself to the low work of slandering a political opponent or party, or of giving needless publicity to the failings of men high in authority and public esteem!

CHAPTER V.

DUTIES PERTAINING TO VERACITY.

Evidence that Veracity is a Duty. — Among the duties which we owe to society, is that of speaking the truth in our varied intercourse with our fellow-men. That this is a duty, is evident from the demands of our moral nature, from the whole structure and framework of society, which in a measure depends on and presupposes this duty, as well as from the explicit commands of God's word. We are so constituted as to place confidence in the testimony of our fellow-men; and our moral nature, our sense of right and justice, is violated when we find ourselves deceived. We are also naturally inclined to speak the truth, and it is only under strong temptations to the contrary that we are induced to pursue an opposite course. Whenever we yield to these inducements, our moral nature is violated; we are conscious of wrong and self-degradation; we are cast down from our integrity. This moral nature, this disposition to credit others, this impulse to truthfulness, this loss of self-esteem and consciousness of wrong when we deviate from the truth in our statements, is in itself an indication of the will of the Creator, too plain to be mistaken. This nature of ours is his workmanship.

The effects, moreover, which would result if truth were to be abandoned in the intercourse of man with man, the disastrous consequences to society of that general distrust and want of confidence which would necessarily ensue, may be taken as evidence of the will of the Deity, and of the obligation of veracity.

To this have been added the explicit declarations of Scripture, forbidding, in the plainest and most positive terms, deceit and falsehood, and assuring us that lying lips are an abomination to the Lord. Into that heavenly felicity which awaits the righteous, there can in nowise enter, we are told, anything that maketh a lie.

We can hardly be mistaken, then, in regarding veracity as a duty.

In treating of it, our inquiries may have reference to truthfulness in ordinary discourse, or as regards the promises made between man and man, or in the more solemn form of the judicial oath.

§ I. — Truthfulness in Common Discourse.

Where lies the Obligation to this. — That we are under obligation to speak the truth in the ordinary conversation and social intercourse of life, is hardly to be questioned. A question may arise, however, as to what *constitutes*, or where lies that obligation. Dr. Paley places it on the ground of *virtual promise.* Truth is expected, and conversation implies a tacit promise to meet that expectation; otherwise we should not be at the trouble of conversing. "A lie is a breach of promise."

The pernicious consequences which, directly and indirectly, result to society and to the individual from the want of truthfulness in discourse, may also be regarded as constituting an obligation to veracity. A lie destroys the confidence of man in man, and so strikes at the very foundations of society. It is pernicious, and wholly so in its tendency. The business of life would be at once interrupted, and all social intercourse destroyed, if falsehood, and not truth, were to become the rule and basis of human discourse.

The individual suffers, no less than society, from any violation of the law of truth. The spiritual nature is degraded, and moral principle weakened, if not destroyed, by every such violation. At the same time, the highest indignity is offered to the moral nature of others. The attempt at deception and imposition which every false statement involves, is in itself an insult of the grossest nature, to whomsoever it is offered. Every honorable man so regards it.

We need, then, inquire no further for the ground of obligation to speak the truth in all our converse with our fellow-men.

Lies Defined. — The crime against the laws of veracity in common discourse, is known under the general name of a *lie*. But what exactly constitutes a lie? Are *all untrue statements* lies? Evidently not. A lie is the utterance of an untruth with *intention to deceive.* The deception is the essential element. Now, in very many cases, where statements are made that are not according to strict truth, there is no intention to deceive, and no actual deception. Of this nature are parables, fictions, dramas, allegories, and all that class of writings, as also the burlesque, and other species of wit. The intention of the author is simply to amuse, or, at most, to convey instruction, through the medium of the fiction, and the interest thus awakened; and it is understood, from the first, that the course of the story is not an exact narrative of events that have actually happened, in the precise order and manner as there described. The statements are not according to strict truth, yet there is no intention to deceive. They are in one sense false, yet they are not lies.

On the other hand, there are some lies that are not properly falsehoods. Some truths, even, are lies. When uttered with intention to deceive, they are virtually lies. A statement may be true literally, and in the exact sense, and yet not true in the sense in which the hearer or reader is likely to understand it; and if I take advantage of this purposely to deceive him, although my statement may be strictly true, yet, as I use it, and intend it to be taken, it is really a lie. Of this nature are very many of the prevarications, subterfuges, and reserved meanings, which have been justified by casuists, especially of the Romish faith.

Not of necessity Oral. — It is not essential to a lie, that it be an oral, or even a written statement. It may be expressed in signs, which are intelligible as a medium of communication, and which, as in the case of the deaf mute, may constitute in fact a language in themselves. A lie may be acted, as well as spoken. When, in answer to a question, I reply by means of a look, a movement of the arm, a turning of the head, a pointing of the finger — that is my statement, my answer; and it is either true or false. In the latter case it means deception, if it means anything, and is, therefore, a lie. Nay, more; even silence may be itself a lie. The simple omission or suppression of the truth, may be as real deception, and may as really be so intended, as the statement of the opposite. If, in the statement of evidence before a jury, I omit some part essential to the real merit and aspect of the case, my omission — my silence — is a virtual falsehood, and that with intent to deceive. So of the instance mentioned by Dr. Paley, of the historical writer, who, in his account of the reign of Charles the First, should suppress any evidence of that ruler's despotism; he is understood to be relating the whole truth, and the omission of an important part of that truth may justly be regarded as a lie.

Whether Justifiable in any Case. — Are lies ever justifiable? Are we in all cases bound to speak the truth, be the consequences what they may? Suppose, for example, I meet a madman, or a robber, who threatens personal violence: shall I divert him from his object by telling a falsehood, and thus save my property, or my life, or, perhaps, the lives of others? According to Paley, a falsehood in such a case is not a lie, — that is, is not criminal, — because no great harm is done. The immediate consequence is, by the supposition, beneficial; and the worst that can happen is that these men, once deceived, will not be likely to trust me again. But then, as they are not likely to come again in my way, this disadvantage, he maintains, does not outweigh the positive advantage gained by the falsehood.

It may so happen, however, that some one else shall meet this madman, or this robber, even if I do not; and in consequence of my falsehood, and the distrust thus awakened, this person may lose his life. I purchase my own safety, in such a case, at the expense of the safety of others. Because my statement has proved false, the statements of another, even when speaking the truth, may not be believed.

A False Principle. — Besides this, the principle here assumed is a false one. It makes the obligation to speak the truth depend on the *inconvenience* resulting from false statements. This is by no means the case. If this were so, there were an end to all morality. If the truth may be set aside, and falsehood uttered in its place, whenever it shall seem to be, on the whole, for the advantage of the speaker so to do, — when there is some end to be gained by it which to him is of some importance, — the law of veracity is not merely weakened, but essentially destroyed. If there is no higher obligation to truth, or any other virtue, than the advantages immediately resulting from it; and if it is left to the individual, in every case, to decide whether it is, on the whole, more expedient for him in the present instance to practise virtue or its opposite, — then the whole system of morality rests, it must be confessed, on a very precarious basis. Under the influence of passion, of fear, of strong temptation, it can hardly be doubtful how, in most cases, men will decide. The present gain will outweigh the ultimate advantage, and vice will be preferred to virtue. Men will do evil that good may come; they will justify their crimes by the plea that great advantage is to result. This is the principle of the casuist and the bigot, in all ages, that the end justifies the means.

But, it may be said, the person to whom we speak has *no right* to demand information: are we, in that case, under obligation to inform him? I reply: we may be under no obligation, perhaps, to give him information which he is not entitled to ask; but this does not authorize us to tell him a falsehood, in place of the truth. We are not obliged to answer his inquiries at all; but, if we do, we have no right to tell him a lie.

It should be remembered, moreover, that even though there may be no obligation on our part to the *questioner*, we may, nevertheless, owe it to *ourselves*, to speak the truth, and that only. He who puts the question is not the only person to be regarded in the case. Something is due to our own sense of honor and self-respect, and to that unblemished integrity of character, at the loss of which even life itself were dearly purchased.

Objection. — It may be said that, where life is in danger, the right of self-defence, which has already been conceded, involves the right of deception and falsehood, if necessary to the preservation of life. If I may justly kill my assailant, in order to save my own life, why may I not lie, in order to save it? Falsehood is surely not a greater crime than the taking of human life. To this I reply, that the right of self-protection from lawless violence does not necessarily imply the right to defend ourselves in all possible ways, and under all circumstances. There may be methods of defence which are not justifiable, and this may be one of them. It is only in extreme cases, as when I must either kill or be killed, that the law of self-defence allows me to take the life of my assailant. In such a case, by the very supposition, falsehood will not answer the purpose. But, even if it would, it does not follow that the right to defend myself or others from lawless violence, by opposing force to force and weapon to weapon, involves the right to protect myself or them in another and a very different manner, viz., by falsehood. There is a meanness and dishonor about the latter course, in stooping to which, even to save life itself, I incur a self-degradation and self-contempt, which, to the high-minded and honorable spirit, will justly seem one of the greatest calamities. It does not follow, that because I have the right to protect my person and my life by a manly and vigorous defence, I therefore have the right to do so by resorting to a mean and dishonorable artifice. It may be better to forfeit life itself, than honor and self-respect. It may be better to take the life of the aggressor, already forfeited, than to do either.

Treatment of the Insane.—The question may arise, whether the law of veracity is strictly to be observed in our treatment of that unfortunate class in whom reason no longer holds her seat. The practice, if I mistake not, very generally prevails, of resorting to deception and direct falsehood in such cases, in order to effect an object not otherwise readily attained. Such a course can be justified only on the ground that the insane person is, by reason of his condition, an irrational and *irresponsible* being, and, as such, an exception to all ordinary rules; and that a regard to his own highest good requires him to be so treated. In such a case, the law of benevolence may possibly set aside the law of veracity. How far such a course is actually wise and expedient,—how far it is likely to be successful in accomplishing the objects in view,—whether honesty and veracity are not, even in such cases, in the long run, the best policy,—is, to say the least, an open question.

Importance of Truth in Trifles.—It is of the highest importance to form a habit of speaking the truth, even in matters of little moment. Such a habit, securely and firmly fixed, is one of the surest bulwarks against the encroachments of vice. It is essential to a truly noble and virtuous character. Untruthfulness in little things, leads to deception in more important matters, and on a larger scale. "White lies," it has been well said, "always introduce others of a darker complexion. I have seldom known any one who deserted truth in trifles, that could be trusted in matters of importance." "There is no vice," says Dr. Wayland, "which, more easily than this, stupefies a man's conscience. He who tells lies frequently, will soon become an habitual liar; and an habitual liar will soon lose the power of distinguishing between the conceptions of his imagination, and the recollections of his memory. I have known a few persons who seemed to have arrived at this most deplorable moral condition. Let every one, therefore, beware of even the most distant approaches to this detestable vice."

§ II. Veracity as Regards Promises.

Whence the Obligation. — The obligation to keep a promise, according to some writers, arises from the necessity of such a course to the well-being and even existence of society. Men act from expectations founded upon the assurances of others; and if no confidence could be reposed in such assurances, the varied intercourse of life could not go on, and society would be at an end.

This is doubtless true, and it furnishes a strong and in itself imperative reason for the fulfillment of promises. In the absence of any other and higher principle, this would of itself constitute an obligation to such a course.

But it is by no means true, that there is no higher principle applicable to the case. The law of expediency, however weighty, is not the only law, nor is it the ground of obligation in the present case. It is not a sufficient account of the matter. Aside from all considerations of this nature, from all results of evil to the community and to the individual, have I a moral right to awaken expectations which I do not intend to meet, and thus to disappoint and deceive my fellow-men? Is it not a species of fraud, of dishonesty, which is in itself a crime, aside from its ruinous consequences to society? Does not the law of veracity, which makes it binding on me to speak the truth in my ordinary conversation, oblige me also to keep my promises?

In what sense to be interpreted.—How is a promise to be interpreted? Shall it be as the promiser himself understands it? But he may intend to deceive. He may so frame his explanations as intentionally to convey a false idea to the party receiving the promise,—saying one thing and meaning another. Is he, in that case, bound only by his own meaning and intention? A man promises to pay me a certain sum of money for certain services, really intending to make payment in some worthless or depreciated currency. Is he bound, in that case, only to fulfill his original intention? This, of course, cannot be conceded.

Shall we say, then, that the promise is to be interpreted as the party to whom the promise is made understands it? But here again there is a difficulty; for the receiver may, on his part, misunderstand the promise, and the real meaning of the promiser. In the case supposed, I may understand the promise of my employer to be that I shall be paid in gold, while he really means and promises nothing of the sort. It would be manifestly unfair to hold the promiser bound to fulfill his promise, not according to its real meaning, but according to any construction that the whim or fancy of the other party chose to put upon it.

Obviously the only just rule is to take the words in their natural and proper signification, as meaning just what they would naturally be understood to mean by any one not specially concerned in the matter; in other words, as he who made the promise supposed that it would, and intended that it should, be understood. The promiser is bound to abide by this interpretation, and to meet the expectations which he has thus formed, and which he intended to form. If he fails to do this, he is guilty of dishonesty.

In illustration of this principle, Paley refers to the historical incident of the treachery practised upon the garrison of Sebastia, who were promised that, if they would surrender, *no blood should be shed;* but who were, on surrendering, buried alive; — the promise being kept as to its letter, but broken in reality.

In what cases not binding. — As a general rule, there can be no doubt of the obligation to fulfill a promise once made. And yet there are exceptions to that rule. Not every promise is binding. What, then, are these exceptions?

Suppose, for example, I have promised to do what is in itself unlawful, — to commit a crime, to lie, to steal, to commit murder, in any way to violate the laws of society or the laws of God, — am I under obligation to keep such a promise? Unquestionably not. There can be no obligation on any man to do wrong. It is a contradiction of terms to say that a man *ought* to do what he ought *not* to do. In case the unlawfulness of the act contemplated was *known* at the time the promise was made, then the promise itself was a guilty one, and the sooner it is broken the better. The guilt of such promises, it has been well said, lies not in the breaking, but in the making. In case the unlawfulness was *not* known, but the thing promised was, at the time, supposed to be lawful, this supposed lawfulness was manifestly an implied *condition* of the promise; and a failure of the condition, implies a failure of the obligation. The promise is to be taken in its plain and obvious intent; and if there was no intention to do a wrong act, no promise to do a known wrong, of course there is no obligation in the premises. This was the case with Herod, whose promise was to give his daughter whatever she might ask; but who, in making that promise, had no thought of her asking what she did. In taking the life of John the Baptist, under such circumstances, that ruler committed the crime of murder in order to avoid breaking a promise which, in reality, he never made; and which, if made, he had not only no obligation but no *right* to keep.

In like manner, a promise obtained by any misrepresentation or fraud on the part of the person receiving the promise, is not binding, when such fraud or misrepresentation is discovered, inasmuch as the condition on which the promise was made proves false. If a beggar, for instance, obtains my signature for a sum of money to relieve his apparent distress, and I afterwards discover that he is an impostor, and his distress counterfeit, my promise, which was made on the strength of that representation, is no longer morally binding.

Impossibilities.—Nor can a promise bind any man to perform what proves to be an impossibility. "We cannot be under obligation," says Dr. Wayland, "to do what is plainly out of our power." If, however, at the time the promise was made, we ourselves *knew* that it was an impossibility to perform the same, we are really guilty of fraud; since a promise is an implied belief that the thing promised is possible. Here, again, it is not the breaking, but the making of the promise that is criminal. No one has a right to promise what he does not believe can be done, much less what he knows cannot be. Thus, for example, the proprietor of a stage, steamboat, or other vehicle, has no right to promise to convey me to a certain place within a specified time, if he knows, or has any reason to believe, that, owing to the state of the roads, or state of the weather, it will be impossible to reach the given point until after the time specified. The builder or contractor has no right to promise that the house which he is erecting shall be ready for occupancy at a given time, when in all probability it cannot be completed, as he very well knows, until some weeks, or even months, after that date. All such promises are dishonest.

I am well aware that nothing is more common than promises of just this nature; insomuch that it has come to be almost proverbial that no dependence is to be placed, in regard to such matters, upon the word of those who perhaps would scorn to be guilty of falsehood in other things. It is none the less a falsehood and a fraud, however, because of frequent occurrence. Nor is it any justification of such a course, to say that the thing promised was in its nature impossible of fulfillment. This we should have thought of before we promised. We had no right to promise an uncertainty, much less an impossibility.

Extorted Promises.—A promise may be extorted by violence—by an appeal to fear. Placed in imminent peril, I promise the highwayman or the assassin that, if he will spare my life, I will not betray him, or give information that shall lead to his arrest. Am I bound to keep that promise? This is a point upon which moralists have greatly differed, and which it is not easy to decide. On the one hand, it may be said, that were such promises in a few instances broken, confidence would no longer be reposed in them, and whoever should fall into the hands of the highwayman would be murdered as well as robbed. On the other hand, justice and the safety of the public demand the arrest of the criminal. My silence may cost many lives. I have no right to purchase my own safety at the expense of the lives and safety of others. And then, aside from this, — the advantage or disadvantage to the community, — am I under obligation to keep a promise forced from me under such circumstances? As the obligation of one party always implies a corresponding *right* of the other, I am surely not bound to give what he who extorts the promise has no right to demand. Nor has he the right to demand the fulfillment of a promise which he had in the first place no right to procure. But, had he any right, under the circumstances, to make me promise what I did? Had he a right to my life, a right to put me in peril and in fear, a right to the violence and threats by which he extorted the promise in the first instance? If not, then what becomes of his right to demand the fulfillment of a promise thus extorted; and if he has no right to demand it, then, as far as he is concerned at least, I am under no obligation to keep it.

Were the circumstances otherwise — had I, by my own carelessness, or curiosity, or folly, placed myself in the power of such a person, and then purchased my life by promise of secrecy, the case had been different, and the argument, as above given, would no longer hold.

Contracts. — A contract is a mutual promise between two parties, — one engaging to do one thing, provided the other will do another thing. It comes, therefore, under the same general rule with promises. I am bound to fulfill a contract, for the same reasons that I am bound to keep any other promise that I have made.

The same rule which applies to the interpretation of promises, applies also to contracts. They are to be taken according to their plain and obvious signification, as meaning that which they would naturally be understood to mean by any intelligent and unprejudiced person. The rule given by Paley is to the same effect: "Whatever is expected by one side, and known to be so expected by the other, is to be deemed a part or condition of the contract."

The failure of the party, with whom we contract, to fulfill his part of the obligation, releases us from ours, since it is the failure of the condition on which the contract was made, and on which it entirely depends.

A society, or company of men, it hardly need be said, is under the same obligation to fulfill its contracts, as an individual; the state, as the citizen. Nations and states, in their dealings with each other, are under the same laws and obligations of veracity and honesty in regard to all their treaties and compacts, as those which bind the conscience of the private citizen.

§ III. — Veracity in Respect to Oaths.

I. *Significance of the Oath.* — It is often of the highest importance to secure the most exact truthfulness of statement—to make sure that what is asserted is not false. To secure this most effectually is the object of an oath. This is calling on the Supreme Being, the omniscient and omnipotent ruler of the universe, to witness that what we say is true, and to deal with us in strict justice if it be not true. We thus place ourselves under the highest conceivable obligations and motives to truthfulness; since, to make this solemn appeal to the majesty of Heaven, and then directly, and in the face of it, to utter that which is false, in the very ear of Him whom we have called to witness our truthfulness, would be an act of impiety the most daring and reckless of which we can well conceive. He who has any just, or even remote idea of the value of the divine favor, and the danger of incurring the displeasure of Him who holds our very breath in the hollow of his hand, will not for the sake of any present advantage, venture to offer so deliberate an insult to the Supreme Being. By imprecating upon ourselves the divine displeasure and curse if we speak falsely, we place ourselves under the highest possible motives to truthfulness. And this is the theory and significance of the oath.

Form of Expression. — The usual form of expression in the English oath is, "*So help me God*,"— in which the emphatic word is the particle *so;* that is, may God be my helper and friend, in all things wherein I need his help, now and hereafter, in life and in death, in time and eternity, only so far as, and on condition that, I now speak the truth. To add still further solemnity to the act, the juror places his hand on the word of God, or lifts it to heaven in sign of solemn invocation and appeal. This latter was the ancient Jewish custom, whence ours is probably derived. With the Greeks and Romans it was customary to slay a victim, on solemn occasions, when it was desired to give special importance to the transaction. Hence, from the striking down of the beast, the expression *ferire pactum*, whence our own phrase, to *strike a bargain.*

II. *Different Applications of the Oath.* — There are two different kinds, or, more properly, different applications of the oath. I may take oath that I will testify truly, or that I will perform some engagement. The oath of *testimony* places me under the most solemn obligation to state that which I know respecting a given matter, without addition, or suppression, without exaggerating, or mitigating, or falsely coloring aught. The oath of *engagement* binds me to the faithful performance of any duty which may be assigned me, or the fulfillment of any office of trust committed to me, or of any engagement which I voluntarily assume. More frequently, oaths of this class are either oaths of office or of trust. As regards the latter, it seems an obvious propriety that, where interests of great moment are intrusted to the keeping of successive guardians, in, it may be, successive generations of men, every precaution should be taken to secure the fidelity of those thus trusted. This is the case with corporate bodies, to whom is committed the business of executing an instrument, or appropriating a charity according to the designs of the testator or founder. Our institutions of learning, and other benevolent and charitable institutions, which depend, for the most part, on funds given for the purpose, are managed by boards of trust, the members of which, when they enter upon their duties, take oath to administer the trust according to the intention of the instrument, and the will of the donor.

Oath of Office.—The common oath of *office* is, perhaps, of more questionable propriety. When the duties of the office assumed are of such a nature as to require the added security and solemnity of an oath; when the office is one of great importance, or of unusual difficulty; and when much depends on the fidelity and skill with which its duties are performed,—there can be no doubt as to the propriety and utility of the oath. Such is the case when men are called to the high and important offices of the state—to the administration of public affairs. Whatever can add to the sense of moral obligation, and quicken the conscience, should be brought to bear in such a case.

The oath should be imposed, however, only on occasions of importance. Its too frequent imposition tends rather to weaken than to strengthen the sense of obligation, and the restraints of virtue. In proportion as it becomes a familiar and common thing, its sacredness is impaired, its efficacy destroyed. It comes to be regarded as a mere form, and takes no hold upon the conscience. Such a use of it must tend greatly to obliterate all moral distinctions, all nice perceptions of duty and sense of obligation, from the mind.

This effect is very greatly increased by the senseless and unmeaning manner in which the oath is, in such cases very generally administered by the official whose duty it is to induct into office the new incumbent. The words are hurried over with extreme rapidity, and in the most careless manner, as if they were the merest form, or as if whatever meaning they had were something to be ashamed of, rather than to be carefully pondered. It were much better that all such oaths should never be administered. They are productive of more evil than good.

Even aside from this irreverent and senseless manner which too frequently accompanies the administration of the oath of office, why, it may be asked, is it necessary to make use of the solemn sanctions of religion to secure fidelity in the discharge of every petty office and employment to which men may be called in the details of public duty? "Why should one man," it has been well said, "who is called upon to discharge the duties of a constable, or of an overseer of common schools, or even of a counsellor or a judge, be placed under the pains and penalties of perjury, or under peril of his eternal salvation, any more than his neighbor, who discharges the duties of a merchant, of an instructor of youth, a physician, or a clergyman?" On this point, the remarks of Dr. Paley, with reference to the frequency of oaths, are worthy of consideration, as equally applicable to our own country. "This obscure and elliptical form, together with the levity and frequency with which it is administered, has brought about a general inadvertency to the obligation of oaths, which, both in a religious and political view, is much to be lamented; and it merits public consideration, whether the requiring of oaths on so many frivolous occasions, especially in the customs, and in the qualification for petty offices, has any other effect than to make them cheap in the minds of the people. A pound of tea cannot travel regularly from the ship to the consumer, without costing half a dozen oaths at the least; and the same security for the due discharge of their office — namely, that of an oath — is required from a church-warden and an archbishop, from a petty constable and the Chief Justice of England."

III. *Lawfulness of Oaths.* — There are certain religious sects, as the Moravians, and the Quakers, which regard the oath as unlawful on any occasion, and, on the ground of these scruples, refuse to swear. In support of this view they cite the words of our Saviour, in Matthew v. 34, 37: "I say unto you, swear not at all," "Let your communication be yea, yea, and nay, nay; for whatsoever is more than these cometh of evil." That our Saviour intended by these words to prohibit the solemn judicial oath, there is not the least evidence. On the contrary, his words evidently refer to the use of oaths in common conversation; that is, to profane swearing, and to all irreverent and unauthorized appeals to Heaven in confirmation of our veracity, without judicial form and sanction. The Jews seem to have distinguished between swearing by the name of God, and swearing by other and less sacred objects, as the heaven, the earth, Jerusalem, the head, etc., — regarding the latter forms as less sacred and binding than the former one. Christ forbids all such use of language, as irreverent to the Supreme Being, and his direction therefore is, swear *not at all;* that is, not in *any* of these ways: they are *all* improper and profane. That, in so saying, he intended to forbid the judicial oath, there is no evidence, but the highest improbability.

Sanctioned in Scripture. — No attentive reader of the Scriptures can fail to observe the fact, that the solemn oath is repeatedly recognized and sanctioned in the sacred writings. Our Saviour himself was once put on oath by the high-priest, and made reply, when "adjured by the living God," to declare whether he was the Christ, the Son of God. God repeatedly swears by himself, in the Old Testament Scriptures. In order to show the immutability of his counsel, he confirmed his own covenant with the Jews by an oath. "For when God made promise to Abraham, because he could swear by no greater, he sware by himself." "For men verily swear by the greater; and an oath for confirmation is to them the end of all strife. Wherein God willing more abundantly to show unto the heirs of promise the immutability of his counsel, confirmed it by an oath" (Heb. vi. 13, 16, 17). "I have sworn by myself, the word is gone out of my mouth in righteousness, and shall not return" (Is. xlv. 23). "The Lord God hath sworn by himself, saith the Lord the God of hosts" (Amos vi. 8). "For I have sworn by myself, saith the Lord, that Bozrah shall become a desolation" (Jer. xlix. 13).

Among the precepts of the law given on Sinai we find the following: "Thou shalt fear the Lord thy God, and serve him, and shalt swear by his name" (Deut. vi. 13). The same is repeated in Deut. x. 20. The judicial oath is probably referred to in these passages. Still more explicitly in the following: "Then shall an oath of the Lord be between them both, that he hath not put his hand unto his neighbor's goods" (Ex. xxii. 11). Paul, in his epistles, repeatedly calls God to witness, in the most solemn manner, for the truth of what he says. "For God is my witness" (Rom. i. 9). "Moreover, I call God for a witness upon my soul" (2 Cor. i. 23). From the above examples it is evident that oaths, solemn and judicial, are by no means condemned in the Scriptures, but, on the contrary, sanctioned both by precept and example.

Necessity of the Oath. — That the frequent and irreverent use of the oath, on trifling occasions, tends to evil, has already been admitted; that its use can be, or need be, entirely dispensed with in judicial transactions, and on public occasions of solemn moment, I am not ready to admit. The state needs to employ it; nor can the ends of justice be well secured without it. Reputation, property, life itself, and all the interests that are dear to man on the earth, depend on the sanctity of the oath. So long as human nature is what it is, it is absolutely necessary to throw around the forms of justice, and the offices of high public trust, the solemnity and sanction of a direct appeal to the omniscient and omnipotent Ruler of men and things.

Where Religious Belief is wanting. — The state may have occasion for the testimony or public services of those who have either no religious belief, or a widely different one from the commonly received faith; as, for example, of one who believes in Mohammed, or in the deities of the pagan world; of one who, as the Jew, believes in God, but not in Christ; or of one who rejects the doctrine of a future state, or of future retribution. In such cases, of what avail is the oath, in its usual form and significance? I reply: if the faith of the testator in God, and in the retributions of the future, be not wholly wanting, his oath may be upon and according to his faith, whatever that may be, — whether Jewish, Pagan, or Mohammedan; and, as his religion is more or less practical, and pure, and exerts more or less restraint and influence on his life, so his oath will be more or less binding on his conscience, and his testimony will be more or less worthy of credence, in that proportion. If, however, either the existence of the Supreme Being, or a state of future rewards and punishments, be not an object of earnest belief to the testator, it is difficult to see of what validity the oath can any longer be. It has lost its significance, so far as he is concerned, and his testimony, if taken, must be taken with allowance, and for what it is worth.

PART III.

DUTIES TO THE FAMILY.

We have as yet considered only those duties which man owes to himself, to society, and to his fellow-men in general. There are other duties, not less important, of a more specific character. There are in the world two great institutions, — both of divine origin, both founded in man's moral and social nature, both placing him in new and peculiar relations, and requiring of him new and peculiar duties, — I mean the *Family* and the *State*. Of the former I am now to treat.

The duties which belong to this class divide themselves naturally into those of the *marriage* relation, and those of the *parental* relation; or, the duties of husband and wife, and those of parent and child.

CHAPTER I.

DUTIES OF THE MARRIAGE RELATION.

The family is a distinct and peculiar institution, standing by itself; a distinct organic community, complete within itself; — having its own laws, its own rights and privileges, its own interests, its own duties. The family is, in an important sense, the *foundation* of the state, which is a community or society of families, gathered into one organization, rather than a casual combination of individuals otherwise isolated. At the basis of this arrangement stands the marriage relation, itself an institution of divine origin, while, at the same time, its foundation is in the constitution of our nature. It is the origin of all the domestic relations, and of all civil society. The continuance and progress of the race from age to age depends upon it.

Nature of this Relation. — Marriage is the union for life of one of either sex with one of the other. It is a mutual compact, and a voluntary one, having for its basis, not mere personal respect and regard, not merely the convenience and interest of the parties, but mutual affection. Where this is wanting, with whatever forms the rite may be celebrated, and whatever advantages or disadvantages it may ensure, it is after all but a form, a solemn mockery.

The ground of this relation exists in the very constitution of our nature. Those natural desires and propensities which relate to the intercourse of the sexes, look forward to this relation as their end, and are at once regulated, refined, and chastened by it. Without such an influence, and such an end, these desires would constantly tend to the degradation of man, and the disorganization of society. Under the influence of the marriage relation, these disturbing forces are curbed and tranquillized, security and confidence are imparted, society is established on a firm basis. The parties united in this sacred relation — joined, not in person merely, but in heart — become one in all the interests and duties, the joys and the sorrows of life.

But, while founded in the constitution of our nature, the relation of which I speak is not the less a divine institution. That nature is itself the work of the divine Creator, having reference to this end, and terminating in it. He who designed the constitution of the human mind, and the human body, and planned all the circumstances of his earthly condition, designed also that man should not live alone upon the earth. Hence the social nature and wants; and hence marriage, which is the result of that nature, may be regarded as an institution of divine origin.

But while nature lays the foundation for such an institution, and that in accordance with the design of the Creator, it is still a matter to be regulated and ratified by public authority. The parties are not alone concerned. The public welfare demands that a relation of this kind should not be formed clandestinely, or without official authority and due forms of ratification. The law takes cognizance of this relation, prescribes the due forms and conditions, and concerns itself with the due observance of the same. This it is the proper business of the state to do, through its appointed legal authorities, in order to the permanence and security of the rights and interests involved in the new relation of the parties.

The relation thus formed and authorized is for life. Only one crime — that of infidelity to the marriage bond — can rightfully be made the ground of separation.

Such, in brief, is the nature of the marriage relation: a compact between two persons of different sex, freely and voluntarily formed, by the mutual consent and choice of each, on the ground of affection, — a union of heart and person and interests, authorized by due forms of law, and to continue while life continues.

Different Views of Marriage. — The conception of the nature and rights of the marriage relation, and of the duties which it imposes, has varied in different ages and among different nations. With some, polygamy and concubinage have been tolerated, and divorce has been allowed on frivolous grounds. Still, the idea of complete and perfect marriage has, with almost all nations, been that now indicated, — the exclusive union of one man and one woman for life.

The practice of polygamy seems to have been more or less prevalent in the early periods of Jewish history. Still, in the beginning it was not so; but the marriage institution, as it came from the hand of God, was the union of a single pair, and they two were one flesh. It has been well remarked by Dr. Hickok, that, "If polygamy was practised by the patriarchs with God's permission, it still had no divine sanction; God's legislation has been always against it, even when, for other reasons, he has not enforced it."

By the Roman laws, polygamy was not allowed. The Institutes define marriage as "the union of a man and a woman, so as to constitute an inseparable, habitual course of life;" and in the Digest it is spoken of as "partnership for life — the mutual participation of divine and human rights." The law of Justinian expressly forbids having more than one wife. "It is not lawful to have two wives at the same time." Concubinage was, however, allowed. So, also, in the Grecian states. The heroes of Homer, it has been remarked, appear never to have had more than one spouse, — ἄλοχος, — while sometimes represented as living in concubinage. This shows that even in that early period and rude stage of society, the true idea of marriage was still entertained.

English law regards the husband and wife as but one person, — the legal existence of the woman, during marriage, being incorporated in that of her husband. She can bring no legal claim or suit in her own name alone; nor can the husband, by legal act or conveyance, grant anything to his wife, — she being one and the same with himself in the eye of the law. Even in criminal prosecutions, husband and wife cannot be evidence for or against each other, on the ground that, according to established maxims of law, "no one can be a witness in his own cause," and "no one is bound to accuse himself." This differs from Roman law, in which husband and wife are two distinct persons, and each may hold property, contract debts, etc.

According to Roman law, Roman citizens could only marry Roman citizens, — union with those of other nations not being regarded as valid marriage. Restrictions of a similar nature exist, or have existed to some extent, among other people, limiting the marriage union to the families of the same nation or tribe. It is for the laws of every state to prescribe the limits within which marriage may be contracted; and in most, if not all, civilized nations, there are certain restrictions of this sort, as respects marriage within certain degrees of kindred.

As marriage is not merely a civil but also a religious institution, the state is not alone concerned in its due observance; hence, in the ceremonies attending its public authorization, civil and religious rites are usually conjoined. A mere legal contract does not express its true idea and full import. The sanctions of religion are combined with the sanctions of law, in its true and proper solemnization. The sentiment of duty is addressed, as well as the sentiment of citizenship. The custom of performing the marriage ceremony in churches, however, does not seem to have prevailed prior to the thirteenth century.

Divorce. — Divorce, or the separation of the marriage union, was allowable among the Jews, under certain regulations, whenever the husband for any reason chose to put away his wife. Such was not the original and true design of the marriage relation, which was intended to be permanent, holding the parties in union for life. It was a perversion of that design, *tolerated*, but never *sanctioned* by the Divine Law-giver.

There were reasons for this toleration. The cruelty and hardness of men, the barbarism of the age, rendered divorce a less evil to both, when affection no longer held the parties in mutual regard, than would be an inseparable union, from which all love had fled, and in which woman, as the weaker and more likely to be abused, would suffer the greatest inconveniences and injuries.

English law does not recognize the right of divorce. A special act of Parliament is necessary to provide for each case of the sort as it comes up.

In our own country, the facilities and occasions for divorce vary in the different states; but in all, it is to be feared, the tendency is to a separation of the marriage tie for reasons of too slight a nature. In proportion as divorce becomes easy, the security of the domestic relations is impaired, and woman is degraded from her true position. The law of God is explicit in this matter; and so far as state policy departs from this rule, it defeats its own end, which is, the highest welfare of the body politic.

Duties of the Marriage Relation. — Fidelity is the first law of the marriage state, — the faithful observance of the solemn contract. This is broken by whatever is contrary to the law of chastity. Not merely criminal intercourse with other persons, but whatever weakens or destroys that exclusive affection on which the contract is founded, is really a violation of that contract. The evils resulting from infidelity to the marriage vow are among the greatest and most serious with which society is afflicted. The peace and harmony of the domestic relations are destroyed, families are broken up, the most sacred ties are severed, discord and misery reign where all should be happiness and love. Hence, in all ages, and by all laws of God and man, it has been treated as an aggravated and serious offence. By the Jewish law it was punishable with death.

By the law of nature and of the Scriptures, the husband is the head of the family; with him is vested the chief authority: hence the duty of *respect*, and, so far as there is any occasion for it by reason of the conflict of opinion or diversity of choice, the duty also of *obedience*, on the part of the wife. This authority, of course, gives the husband no right to abuse his power by acts of unkindness and severity, or any harshness of demeanor; nor, on the other hand, does it derogate in the least from the honor and dignity of woman. To submit and obey, is not more the sphere than the highest grace and ornament of the gentler sex; as such, it is explicitly enjoined in the sacred writings. In ruder states of society, and in earlier ages of the world, as even now wherever barbarism exists, woman has been but the slave of man. His brute strength has prevailed over her weakness, and abused her gentleness and uncomplaining, patient endurance of ills and wrongs. The Roman law allowed the husband to treat the wife with severity, and even with personal violence. But where Christianity comes, it elevates woman from this degraded position, and makes her the equal companion of the stronger sex; and, while it still enjoins upon her the duty of obedience and subjection to the husband, it clothes that very subjection with a dignity and beauty more attractive than any outward adorning.

But, while it is the part of the gentler sex to yield, it is the part of the stronger to support, protect, and treat with uniform kindness and courtesy, the weaker. Strength and authority give the husband no right to tyrannize over the wife, or manifest his power by acts of unkindness, or any want of that respect and affection which are ever her due. He is to provide for her physical wants, her comfortable maintenance and support. He is to protect her, so far as possible, from injury and insult. He is to be her guardian and defender. She is to lean upon his strength, and feel secure, as the vine clings for support to the sturdy oak, whose rude, strong arms are able to defend it against the winds and storms.

Nor is the relation of the wife one of entire dependence, but rather of reciprocal aid. She has her part to bear, and to perform, of the duties and struggles, the cares and toils of life. She is not to hang as a mere useless weight upon the stronger arm, but rather to stay and strengthen that arm, and make it firmer and bolder for its work. The labors of providing for the physical wants and maintenance of the household, are to be shared in common; the duties of the husband lying, for the most part, in labors without, and those of the wife in labors performed within the house. In these she is to bear her part cheerfully, and with good courage; and whether in wealth or in poverty, in sickness or in health, in comfort or in distress, — whatever the varied lot of life may be, — she is in all to be a sharer and a helper. If the arm on whose protection and strength she relies is disabled and stricken down, she is, so far as possible, to assume the cares and duties which have hitherto devolved upon the stronger, — as the faithful vine still clings to the broken branch, — and hold up in its weakness that on which she has leaned for support.

Still another duty devolves on those who sustain to each other the marriage relation, — that of *mutual affection.* Where this is wanting, or where, having once existed, it is suffered to die out, the marriage tie becomes irksome, and that which should lend a charm to life, only adds to its burden. There must be respect, kindness, courtesy, honor, fidelity, from each to each, — these, but not these alone; there must be something more than these, or the principle on which the marriage contract is based is wanting, and the contract itself becomes virtually null. Where there is no true affection, marriage is but a form, from which the soul has fled. This, then, must in truth be regarded as one of the first and most imperative duties of the marriage state, — to cherish each that pure and true affection for the other which the sacred bond implies, and which is essential to the happiness, if not to the continuance of the relation. That bond and sacred vow are in reality broken, let it ever be remembered, not merely by unlawful intercourse with others, but by any neglect, unkindness, desertion, withdrawal of mutual confidence, and mutual regard. The want of affection is itself a violation of duty, and where it continues, amounts to a virtual sundering of the marriage tie.

CHAPTER II.

DUTIES OF THE PARENTAL RELATION.

§ I. — Duties of Parents.

It is the duty of the parent to provide for the physical wants of his children, and also to educate them, in such a manner as shall best prepare them for the duties of life, and the stations which they are to occupy in society, and best conduce to their happiness, temporal and eternal. The end in view, in all family nurture and training, is, directly, the welfare and happiness of the child, both present and future; indirectly, the demands of society and the state; ultimately, and as inclusive of all others, the claims of God.

The family, as we have already seen, is an institution peculiar and complete within itself—having its own laws, its own rights and interests, its own end. Nevertheless, it does not exist for itself alone. It has its relations to other objects and other institutions, its duties to perform, its office to accomplish. Prominent among these duties, and one chief end for which it exists, is the training and preparation of the children for those duties which they owe to *themselves*, to *society*, and to their *Maker*. Whatever tends to promote this, furthers the great design and end of the family as an institution; whatever interferes with and prevents this, frustrates that design.

This general object includes several specific ends or duties, for which the parent is responsible.

1. Maintenance.—The duty of the parent is to support the child during his years of minority, and provide for all his physical wants. Infancy and childhood are helpless and inexperienced, unable to provide for themselves, dependent of necessity on the watchful care and protection of the parent. Without that care and provision, they must inevitably perish, unless, indeed, some other takes the place of the parent. Parents are the natural guardians and providers for the wants of their children. The deep and strong affection which nature has implanted in the bosom, looks to this end, and was designed as the basis and security for the discharge of this important trust; nor can this trust be devolved upon another, except in case of death or inability, without positive violation of duty.

The manner in which this duty shall be performed must depend upon the circumstances of the family, and the general position in life which the child may properly be expected to occupy. The children of the rich and the poor cannot be alike provided for; the one will have more and better food and clothing than the other. The parent does his duty when he provides for the support of his children according to the best of his ability and judgment, and according to his own circumstances. Nor need he reproach himself, when this is done, because his limited means have not allowed him to bring up his children in that affluence which others can command; since the simple habits of frugality and industry, which the lessons of honest poverty are most likely to teach, are in themselves of greater value to the household, than any amount of wealth, or any degree of refinement.

2. Government. — The family is a little society, a miniature state; and every society, every state, must have its laws, its government. The government of the family is entrusted to the parents, both by the nature of the case and by divine authority; and the faithful administration of this government is a duty which they owe both to the household, to the state, and to God. For the manner in which they discharge this duty, they are directly responsible to Him who instituted the family relation, and who placed in their charge this solemn trust. The end of the family institution is to train its members for the service of the state, and the service of God, in whatever stations they may hereafter be called to fill; and both the state, or society in its organized capacity, and God, have a claim upon the parents for the faithful performance of this important trust.

"The family," it has been well said, "is but a nursery

for higher and broader spheres of action. In it are to be planted the seeds, and there are to be nurtured the germs, which are to have their full development, and bear their fruit, in future years, and in other worlds."

It is not merely, then, the happiness and welfare of the household, as such, while gathered under one roof, — although this is in itself a most important end to be secured, — but it is also the welfare and highest usefulness and happiness of its members, when they shall be no longer under the sheltering roof that covered them in the happy days of childhood, but shall have their own part to act, and their own, it may be, arduous and trying duties to perform in the busy, toiling world, — it is this higher and ultimate end that is to be reached, if at all, by means of family government. Where this is duly administered, the household is trained to habits of order and obedience; the child grows up under a system in which he learns the cardinal virtue of submission to authority, and is thus fitted to become a useful member of society. Where, on the contrary, parental government is not enforced, the lessons of obedience are not learned, and the child goes forth into society, unused to the wholesome restraints of law, untaught to submit to the will and authority of those whose right it is to govern, unfitted for the responsible duties of the citizen; in many respects, a useless, if not positively dangerous member of the community.

To whom entrusted. — The duty of maintaining authority, and administering the government of the household, is, by the law of nature, and the relation of the parties, entrusted to the parents. It is their province and right to govern — the province and duty of the child to obey. This is a divine arrangement, the foundation of which lies in the constitution of our nature. It is not a merely arbitrary and conventional arrangement, but the design and law of the Creator. No duty is more clearly enjoined in the Scriptures, and none entails a severer penalty on those who neglect and violate it.

The parent is not, however, to use this authority as abusing it. He is not to govern, merely for the sake and from the love of governing, in an arbitrary and unreasonable manner. He is ever to keep in mind the end of discipline, as already pointed out; that is, the highest welfare and happiness of all the members of the household. As a safeguard against abuse, Providence has wisely thrown around this delegated authority the restraints of parental affection. The power to govern is lodged in safe hands; the heart of the parent pleads for mercy, while his sense of justice demands the punishment of the offender.

As the parties united in marriage are one, the authority of the parents is a joint and concurrent authority; and inasmuch as the end of all family discipline is one of common interest to both the parents, there can, ordinarily, be little danger of any conflict of views or interests in its administration. Should such difference arise, as there must be some ultimate appeal, the supreme authority rests, by common consent, by the nature of the case, and by the laws of the land, with the father, as the rightful head of the family, and source of ultimate authority.

3. Education. — The duty of the parent is not entirely discharged when provision has been made for the physical wants of the household, and for its due government. The child is not only to be fed, and clothed, and governed, but suitably *educated;* and this education must have reference to the whole development and training, both ***physical*** and *moral*, as well as ***intellectual***,

Physical Culture. — It must have reference to the *physical training.* A good physical constitution is one of the greatest earthly advantages; and this, so far as it depends on any care and skill of treatment after birth, is to be secured by every means in the power of the parent. Parental ignorance and negligence have, doubtless, much to do with the feeble health, the broken constitution, the life of suffering, and the premature decay and death, of many a household. The physical culture, the health and strength of the child, is the first and most important object to be attained; and due attention to this object is the first and most imperative of parental duties. Care must be taken to regulate the food, the dress, the exercise, the hours of rest, the entire habits of life, as affecting the physical constitution; to avoid all such indulgence on the one hand, and all such hardship and exposure on the other, as shall endanger the health, or injure the constitution of the child. For all this the parent is responsible; and if, by carelessness, neglect, or want of skill, he fails in the performance of his duty, not himself only, not the child only, nor the family only, but other and wider interests receive an injury; society suffers, the state is a loser, and claims still higher than these are forgotten. As regards both the service of the state, and the service of God, the true end of family culture looks, first of all, at the physical health and vigor, — aims to secure that, — and fails of its grand and ulterior designs very much in proportion as it fails in that. If that is overlooked; if, by neglect, or mistaken indulgence, habits unfavorable to health and manly development are formed; if, as sometimes happens, the selfishness and avarice of the parent lead him to expose his child to an amount of toil and hardship unsuited to its tender years, — then, whatever suffering may ensue, whatever loss to the child in subsequent years of life, whatever to society, and to the cause of God, the responsibility and the guilt must rest with fearful weight upon that negligent, that indulgent, or that selfish parent.

Intellectual Culture. — *The intellect,* also, is to receive its education. The germs of whatever power and greatness it may afterward attain, lie in the mind at the outset; they are to be developed and nurtured by careful and skilful training. The intellect comes to maturity, and possession of its own proper strength, only by culture and discipline. Left in ignorance, its faculties imperfectly unfolded and developed, its condition will inevitably be that of weakness and imbecility, as compared with what it might be, and was designed to be.

A thorough education, if not invaluable, is, at least, of higher value to the child than any amount of treasure, or any position in society which mere wealth or the accident of birth can command. It is itself the highest fortune, the richest treasure. He who has it cannot well be poor; he who is destitute of it, whatever else he may have, cannot be truly rich. The parent has no right to send his child out into the world uneducated, and, in consequence, unfitted for the highest duties of life.

The process of education, wisely and well conducted, will always have regard to two things, — the habits and mental peculiarities of the child, and also the condition and station in life for which it is to be fitted. If either of these is overlooked, the great end of education — that is, the highest happiness and usefulness of the child in future life — will not be attained.

The care of this mental training, at first devolving chiefly on the parents, may, as the child progresses, be in part, but *never wholly,* transferred to other teachers; never so transferred as that the parent shall be no longer responsible for the manner in which the process is conducted, and for its ultimate success or failure. No pressure of other duties can atone for any neglect of this; nor can any fidelity and skill of the teacher compensate for the want of that time and attention which the parent should still bestow on the intellectual culture and progress of the child, and which are indispensable to the most successful results.

Moral Culture. — Nor is the *moral* education of the child to be overlooked. The manners, the disposition, the heart, the religious belief, are matters requiring careful attention and culture. If the mind is to be educated, not less the heart. Eternal destinies, and not merely the present welfare and happiness of the child, depend on the manner in which this part of his education is conducted. Those destinies of the future are in an important sense entrusted to the decision of the parent. He is to educate and train the child, not merely for honor and usefulness on earth, but for immortality and eternal life; not merely to be a valuable member of society, but a citizen of the heavenly kingdom, and a partaker of the heavenly felicity. This duty neglected, all is neglected; this lost, all is lost.

The moral education includes not merely the culture of religious feeling toward God, as the direct object of adoration and love, but of all morally right feeling and action — of all that is pure, and lovely, and of good report. It includes the checking and restraining of all the evil desires and propensities of the child's nature; the development and careful fostering of all generous, pure, noble sentiments and principles of action; the vigilant guarding against all evil and seductive influences to which the inexperience of childhood and youth may be exposed, and by which it may so easily be led astray. It includes precept; it includes example, without which precept will avail nothing. It includes the thousand influences of a well-ordered religious home, constantly, and to himself perhaps unconsciously, surrounding the child, and as by silken threads leading him in the way that he should go. Happy the child that is thus led; happy the home to which that child belongs, and in which such influences dwell.

§ II. — Duties of Children.

The duties of the parent and of the child are, for the most part, reciprocal — the obligation resting upon the one necessarily implying a corresponding obligation on the part of the other. The obligation of the parent to govern, implies the duty of the child to obey; the obligation of the parent to educate, involves the duty of the child to yield to and be guided by this care and culture.

There are also duties arising from the relation in which the parties stand. The superior wisdom and intelligence of the parent, no less than his authority, demand respect and reverence from the child. The care and love which have watched over the helplessness of childhood, and provided for its wants, and sacrificed much for its good, demand in return filial gratitude and affection. These, then, as determined by the nature of the case, are the principal duties of the child toward the parent, viz., *obedience, docility, reverence, filial affection.*

1. Obedience. — It is the duty of the child to yield unreserved and unquestioned obedience to the authority and commands of the parent; and this obedience must be irrespective of the why and wherefore of the command, of the wisdom and necessity of the course prescribed; it must be rendered as obedience to authority, and to the

will of the parent, *because* it is his will. In no other way can the end of family government be attained, the peace and order of the household be promoted, the welfare of the child secured.

The duty of obedience is manifest not only from the nature of the case, and from the end of family government, but from the word of God. No duty is more explicitly and emphatically enjoined in the Scriptures than this: "Children, obey your parents in the Lord; for this is right" (Eph. vi. 1). And again, "Children, obey your parents in all things; for this is well-pleasing unto the Lord" (Col. iii. 20). To disobey the commands of the parent, is, then, to be guilty of a double crime: it is to violate at once the law of the household, and the law of God.

Limit of Authority. — But here an important question arises, respecting the limits of parental authority. Are there any limits? Is the child under obligation to yield obedience to any and *all* commands of the parent, *whatever they may be?* Suppose the parent order him to do that which is manifestly wrong, as, to break the Sabbath, or to steal, or to lie, or in any manner to break the laws of the state, or the laws of God; is he then to obey?

I reply, by no means. The parent has no *right* to give such commands, and, therefore, they are not binding on the conscience of the child. Whenever the child is ordered to do that which he knows and fully believes to be wrong, he is under no obligation to obey; nay, he has no right to obey. When the law of the parent comes into conflict manifestly and directly with the law of the state, or with the law of God, these, which are higher laws, must be obeyed. The authority of the state is above that of the parent; and the authority of the Supreme and Almighty Ruler is above both. The child must do right, and suffer the consequences; the responsibility rests with the parent.

When there is any doubt as to the real character of the act required, — any uncertainty whether it is, in fact, a wrong act, and in conflict with the divine commands, — it seems to me that the authority of the parent should in all such cases be held as decisive, until at least clearer light can be obtained as to the path of duty. Under ordinary circumstances, the parent, from his superior intelligence, and greater experience, is certainly more likely to know what is right and proper than the child; hence, in matters of doubtful character, it is safer to follow the decisions of the parent, even at the risk of doing wrong, than to incur the at least equal risk of doing wrong by disobedience.

2. Docility. — As the duty of the parent is to teach, to educate, so the duty of the child is to learn. It is for him to yield, with docile spirit, to the culture and training which the parent sees fit to adopt. In physical nature, and mental discipline; in the education of the manners and the heart; in all that pertains to the culture, in its highest and most comprehensive sense, of body, mind, and soul, — the child is to hold himself ready, within those limits already specified, to be instructed, moulded, trained, by parental wisdom and care. In fault of this, all efforts of instruction will be unavailing, and the great end of family nurture and discipline will be unattained. A stubborn and unyielding spirit, that sets itself in opposition to the wisdom and the counsels of the parent, and refuses to be guided thereby, is in itself a sin most deserving of rebuke, and which incurs, wherever found, the special displeasure of God. Very marked is the condemnation bestowed upon this sin in the Scriptures. Under the Jewish law, it was even punishable with death. "If a man have a stubborn and rebellious son, which will not obey the voice of his father, or the voice of his mother, and that, when they have chastened

him, will not hearken to them: then shall his father and his mother lay hold on him, and bring him out unto the elders of his city, and unto the gate of his place; and they shall say unto the elders of his city, this our son is stubborn and rebellious, he will not obey our voice; he is a glutton and a drunkard. And all the men of his city shall stone him with stones that he die; so shalt thou put evil away from among you, and all Israel shall hear and fear" (Deut. xxi. 18—21).

Very full and explicit are the precepts which inculcate the duty of cherishing the opposite spirit. "My son, keep the instruction of thy father, and forsake not the law of thy mother. They shall be an ornament of grace unto thy head, and chains about thy neck" (Prov. i. 8, 9). "Keep thy father's commandments, and forsake not the law of thy mother" (Prov. vi. 20). "A fool despiseth his father's instructions" (Prov. xv. 5). "A wise son heareth his father's instructions, but a scorner heareth not rebuke" (Prov. xiii. 1).

3. Reverence. — It is the duty of the child to treat his parents with that deference and respect that belong to those who are his superiors in age and wisdom, as well as in authority. Nothing is more unbecoming in a child than any want of respect toward his superiors, and especially toward his parents. They sustain to him a relation which peculiarly demands of him this deferential regard. They are the authors of his life. To them he is indebted for the care and attention which have watched over him from infancy, provided for his wants, directed his education. To them he is rightfully subject by the laws of God and man; and to those sustaining to him this relation, and exercising this authority, he is bound, by the laws of nature

and reason, to yield a respect and reverence which are due to no one else on the earth.

Nor is this claim abrogated by any rank or attainments on the part of the child, or by any deficiency of intellectual, social, or even moral worth and rank, on the part of the parent. These circumstances alter not the relation of the two parties. The child, as he grows to maturity, may come to be wiser, wealthier, more distinguished, more virtuous even, than those who gave him birth, and brought him up from infancy to youth and manhood. He is not, on these accounts, excused from paying to them, so long as he lives, and they live, that respect and reverence which are still their due, and which every generous and manly spirit will esteem it a delight and an honor to show.

The end of the family institution, so far as the child is concerned, is to fit him for the service of the state, and the service of his God; to be an honorable and useful member of society, and a candidate for immortal blessedness. In no way is this end more surely defeated, than by the want of due respect toward the parents; in no way more directly promoted, than by the careful observance of this duty. He who has not learned, or who has scorned to pay due respect and reverence to his parents, will not be likely to bow with submission and reverence before the majesty of the law. He who is wanting in deference to his earthly superiors and protectors, will not be likely to yield the homage of the heart to his heavenly Father, or to humble himself, in adoration and lowliness of mind, before the Majesty of heaven and earth. He is poorly fitted for the duties of life, for the service of the state, and the service of his God, who knows not how to honor his parents.

Nothing is more graceful and fitting, nothing more honorable and ennobling to the character, than the exercise of this virtue; nothing, on the other hand, more unseemly, and dishonorable, than the opposite vice. The blessing of God attends the one; his frown and curse, the other. "*Honor* thy father and thy mother — which is the first commandment with promise — that it may be well with thee, and thou mayest live long on the earth" (Eph. vi. 2, referring to Ex. xx. 12). "Cursed be he that setteth light by his father or his mother; and all the people shall say, Amen" (Deut. xxvii. 16). And yet again: "The eye that mocketh at his father, and despiseth to obey his mother, the ravens of the valley shall pluck it out, and the young eagles shall eat it" (Prov. xxx. 17).

4. Filial Affection and Gratitude. — The duties which have already been named are incomplete without this. Those offices are to be performed not merely as duties, and because they are required by the laws and customs of society, by self-respect, and by the divine command, but from a higher principle than the single sense of duty, — from love, the pure affection and deep gratitude of the heart. The relation in which our parents stand to us, entitles them to our sincere affection and gratitude. To no human beings are we so much indebted as to them. They have given us being; they have provided for our physical wants; have fed and clothed us; have watched our steps by day, and our slumbers by night; have denied themselves, that they might make better provision for us; have educated us in whatever of useful learning and of good manners we have acquired; have done what they could — it is to be hoped — to train us for usefulness and happiness here and hereafter. As we grow up, we may possibly perceive faults of character in them, — faults, perhaps, in their mode of educating and governing us; but no such defects, whether real or imagined, can ever discharge the obligation on our part of true and earnest gratitude and love.

The character that is wanting in this, is wanting in all that is manly and noble. The heart that lacks this emotion, is essentially a mean and selfish heart.

Nor is this duty one that ceases to be required of us as we come ourselves to manhood. Time, in its never-ceasing progress, reverses the order in which life began: the child becomes a parent, and the parent by-and-by becomes again a child. The arms that held us in infancy, require now the strength of our more robust and vigorous forms; the hands that toiled and the feet that moved so readily for all our wants, must now depend on us for support. By every little act of kindness and attention, by all the sweet and soothing ministry of love, it is for us to discharge that debt. Happy for us, if, over the grave of a parent, we never have occasion to drop a tear of regret that we were in any measure negligent of this sacred duty.

PART IV.

DUTIES TO THE STATE.

CHAPTER I.

NATURE AND FOUNDATION OF CIVIL GOVERNMENT.

It has already been remarked that there exist in the world two great and distinct institutions, — the *Family* and the *State*, — having each its own organization, its own laws, its own object, its own proper duties. Of these, the former has already occupied our attention, and we approach now the consideration of the latter.

The State what. — In order to clearness, we must ascertain precisely what is meant by the state. I understand by the state, a community organized under one form or system of government, and dwelling together, under that government, in one and the same territory. Those thus associated for purposes of government, compose the state.

The word is frequently employed in a somewhat different sense from that now given, — sometimes, to denote the idea of civil government in the abstract, without reference to the aggregate of individuals that compose the state; sometimes, also, to denote the power that exercises authority and administers law in the community thus organized

— as when Louis Fourteenth of France declared, "I am the state."

The true idea, however, of the state, I take to be that already given. When we speak of the family, or of the state, as institutions, we do indeed use those terms abstractly; but when we come to define more fully our meaning, we say, the family is a little community, consisting of those related by ties of marriage and consanguinity, dwelling under one roof, and holding property in common; and, in like manner, we say, the state is a larger community, organized under one form of government, and dwelling together in the same country or territory.

Not every Community a State. — It is not every and any community, or company of men, that constitutes a state, even though they may inhabit the same territory. They must be an organized community, and that for the purpose of government — a united whole, bound together by one and the same system of civil administration. A herd of wild beasts roaming together over the western prairies is a community; a horde of savages, scarcely less wild and lawless, may dwell together without the forms of civilized society; but neither of these communities is a state. Those who came over in the pilgrim bark, the May-Flower, were a community, united in one and the same great enterprise, yet only a collection of separate families and individuals, and nothing more, until, in the cabin of that little vessel, there was drawn up the instrument that constituted them an organized community, and prescribed the form of their future government; that instrument drawn and signed, they became from that moment a *state*.

It will be to our purpose, in the further discussion of the subject proposed for consideration in the present chapter, to inquire as to the *origin* and *object* of civil government — how such an institution ever came to be, and for what ends designed; also, as to the *foundation* on which it rests — whence comes its authority. These topics will be discussed in the following sections.

§ I. — Origin and Object of Civil Government.

Origin of Civil Government. — If we inquire for the origin of this institution,— the manner in which such a thing as the state, or civil government, came to be, — we must go back, doubtless, to a very early period of civilization — to the first rude beginnings of human history. The germ of civil authority lies, if I mistake not, in the family; the members of which, united by closest ties of sympathy and common interest, are subject to the parental authority and control. This is the first form of obedience, and the first kind of government. "A family," it is well said by Paley, "contains the rudiments of an empire. The authority of one over many, and the disposition to govern and to be governed, are in this way incidental to the very nature, and coëval, no doubt, with the existence of the human species."

It is easy to see how, from this simple beginning, the principle of civil government, taking its rise, may have extended, till, as now, it embraces nations and centuries in its sweep. The respect and homage due to the wisdom and authority of the parent, do not cease when the children approach the maturity of riper years. Around the tent of the father gather, in process of time, the tents of the children; the government of the family becomes gradually the government of many families, all united by ties of consanguinity and common origin, all owing and owning allegiance to a common ancestor. The general direction and control of the little community, thus enlarged by successive generations, would, by common consent, be vested in the hands of that aged and honored ancestor, the *patriarch* of the flock, the chief of the tribe. And thus we have the second step in the formation of civil government.

The rapid increase of such a community would enlarge the boundaries of the original dominion, until, in course of time, the chief or patriarch of the tribe becomes the ruler of the nation. Large communities and empires would grow out of small ones, not only by the laws of natural growth, and increase of population, but by accessions of smaller and weaker tribes forming alliance with the stronger, for purposes of mutual advantage.

The patriarch of the tribe, or chief of the clan, would be likely to gather about him many followers, in the capacity of servants and retainers, dependent on his bounty, and obedient to his command. Possessions, also, of land, cattle, jewels, and other treasures, would accumulate in his keeping. To the aristocracy and influence of birth there would in this way be added the authority which wealth bestows. In process of time, as the wealth of the tribe increased, and its numbers augmented, the temptation would be felt to employ these resources in the subjugation of neighboring and weaker tribes. The chief who should thus employ his personal wealth and followers to enlarge the boundaries, and extend the power of his tribe, would add not only to the authority of his clan, but to his own power as ruler; and so to the aristocracy of birth and of wealth would be added that of military prowess. This latter, in process of time, and of human affairs, might come to be of more consequence than either of the former as an element of sovereignty.

It is easy to see how, in the natural course of things,

these causes, combined, or even singly, would lead to the formation of great and powerful empires, from such small beginnings as we have indicated. And it is easy also to see how, starting with the idea of paternal government as its source and germ,—that is, of a power lodged in the hands of *one*, to be administered at his discretion,—the form of civil government should have been, in theory and in fact, essentially the power and authority of *one* over the whole; that is, *monarchical.*

Whatever theory we adopt as the *foundation* of civil government,—whether we regard it as of direct divine authority, or as founded in social compact, or in the nature of man,—there can be little doubt that, as a matter of history, its origin and progress have been essentially what I have now indicated.

Object of Civil Government.—Viewing civil government as an existing institution, we may naturally ask what is the end or object which it proposes to accomplish; what is the use, the advantage, the necessity for anything of the sort; why should not every man be his own ruler and sovereign?

The sovereignty of the individual, I reply, would be inconsistent with the rights and freedom of the whole. Every member of the community has an interest in the conduct of every other member. Every man is a composite element of the whole, and is bound to consult the interests and wishes of the whole. If he were to have his own way, and consult only his own pleasure in everything, his choice would often interfere with that of others, and thus would result a conflict of choices; and not only would injustice thus be done, often, to the weaker of two parties, but the general peace and order of the whole would be disturbed. "The freedom of the individual," it has been well said, "is the bondage of the community."

Objection. — But will not the same thing occur if government exists? it may be asked. Will that insure to every man his choice? Will not government itself interfere with the choice of the individual, and restrain his freedom? So far as that freedom interferes with the general freedom and the general order, I reply, it will doubtless be restrained under any system of wise and efficient government; and so far as this, it *needs* to be restrained. In the nature of things, not every man can have his choice. The nearest approximation to this is, that the choice of the *greatest number* shall prevail; in other words, that the will of the majority shall govern.

In proportion as any government carries out the will of the majority, and legislates for the good of the whole, it accomplishes the great end of all civil government; and in so far as it loses sight of this, or fails of this, it fails of reaching that end.

Suppose, now, that, under existing government, an individual finds himself ill-suited, — his choices interfered with, his wishes disregarded, his rights taken from him, — what redress, it may be asked, remains for such a one? I reply: there will at least remain one resource, after all others have been tried in vain. If he finds it impossible to obtain justice, and to enjoy his rights in the community where he is, let him peaceably withdraw from it, and join some other which he likes better; or, if none such can be found, it is in his power to cut himself off entirely from his fellow-men, and live in a desert or a cave. It may be a hardship to do this; but it were better that a few should suffer hardship and loss, than that the many should be exposed to the dangers of lawlessness and anarchy.

Ends to be secured. — There are two leading objects ever to be kept in view and secured by civil government — public *order* and public *freedom*; — the former for the sake of the latter, and the latter in the greatest degree that is compatible with the former. These ends will be most effectually secured in connection with the highest civilization and most rapid progress of the state. Whatever promotes the one, promotes also the other. While, therefore, the state may not propose to itself, directly, as an end, the moral and religious culture and character of its citizens, it may, and must, aim to secure this as a *means*, and a necessary means, to the end which it legitimately pursues, viz., the public order and freedom. Virtue and religion are indispensable to the highest civilization and elevation of the people, and so to the public welfare, and cannot therefore be overlooked by any wise and intelligent government.

These not the only Objects of Civil Government. — I have spoken of *order* and *freedom* as leading objects to be secured by civil government; I would not affirm that they are the only objects for which government exists. It is possible, certainly, to conceive of a state of society in which every man should be upright and honest; in which the most perfect order should be realized; in which there should be, therefore, no crimes to punish, no lawlessness to rebuke, no irregularity or disorder to provide against. In such a community, as there would be the most perfect order, so also there would be the highest possible degree of public freedom; consequently, there would be no need of government for these ends. If these were the only objects for which civil government exists, then there would be no need of government at all.

Yet, even in such a community, there would still be

something for government to do. Its occasion and its proper functions would not wholly cease. There are certain matters of public utility and convenience — as, for example, the coining of money, the making of roads, the disposal of property left without heirs, the regulation of commerce and of intercourse with other countries — which could not well be arranged without the existence of some form of government. In such matters, it would be necessary that some persons should be authorized to act in behalf of the whole; and such authority would constitute, in fact, a government.

§ II. — Foundation of Civil Government.

Having considered, in the preceding section, the *origin* and *object* of civil government, we are prepared now to inquire as to its *foundation.* On what does this institution rest as its basis and support? Whence does it derive its authority? How comes government, in the person of magistrate, legislator, judge, and in the form of law, written or unwritten, to have power over me, to restrain and govern my conduct, — a power extending to my person, my property, and even my life? What right has it to do this, and whence does it obtain this right? Suppose I should deny this right, and refuse this control — what then?

Theory of Divine Right. — There have been various theories respecting this matter. According to some, civil government is founded in the *will of God:* it rests on the basis of a *divine right.* This theory supposes that civil government is an ordinance of God; that as marriage and the family relation were of direct divine appointment, so likewise the state; and that as we had no agency in instituting, so we have no choice in submitting to either of these arrangements, and no right to alter or dispense with either, but must take both as established facts, — part of the scheme of Providence and of the divine order of things, to which it is the duty of all men to conform. We are under government, and we must obey it, for the same reason that it is our duty to obey God in anything else that he may prescribe for us; and this obedience must be without hesitation or question.

This view derives support from the fact that civil government *originates*, as we have seen, from the family institution, — having its root there, and progressing, by slow and natural degrees, to its full and mature development. Now, unquestionably, the family is an institution of divine appointment, — a fact which exists by special arrangement and design of Providence. The paternal government is one under which we find ourselves on coming into the world, and which, whether we will or not, we are obliged to obey. And as, out of this existing fact, this authority independent of our will, civil government takes its rise, and by natural stages grows to be what it is, the inference seems plausible, that this also, like that from which it proceeds, is of special divine authority.

Paley's View. — A modified form of this theory was advanced by Dr. Paley, who bases the obligation to obey civil government on *the will of God as collected from expediency.* This view differs from the preceding, chiefly in that it assigns a reason for the will of God being what it is, viz., the expediency or advantage of such an institution to human welfare and happiness; whereas the former, somewhat more arbitrarily, refers the whole matter to the divine will, and leaves it there, without explanation or reason.

The argument of Paley is summed up, by himself, in the following propositions: "It is the will of God that the happiness of human life be promoted." "Civil society conduces to that end." "Civil societies cannot be upholden, unless in each the interest of the whole society be binding upon every part and member of it." Hence the conclusion, "that so long as the interest of the whole society requires it,—that is, so long as the established government cannot be resisted or changed without public inconvenience,—it is the will of God (which *will* universally determines our duty) that the established government be obeyed, and no longer." The argument is, not that government is expedient, and *therefore* we must obey; but that it is expedient, and therefore it is the will of God; and *because* it is his will, *therefore* we must obey.

Theory of Social Nature.—Dissatisfied with this manner of explaining the subject, others have taken a different view of the matter, and have sought the foundation of government in the moral and social nature of man. It is no longer, according to this view, the arbitrary and sovereign will of God, nor yet that will as governed by a regard to expediency, but rather the nature and constitution of man, that is the basis on which civil government reposes. That nature fits him for, and leads him to adopt such an arrangement. It is his own institution, his own choice, his instinctive, natural preference. He frames laws, and appoints rulers, and submits himself to the control of those laws and those magistrates, on the same principle that the bee and other insects observe a certain order in the arrangement of their social affairs, and maintain a certain government, following the direction of their leader, because such is their *nature*. In like manner, the nature and constitution of man fit him to be a member of society and of the state, even as they fit him to be a member of the family. He adopts this method, and continues it, not because he finds these institutions ready made, and imposed on him by the will of the Creator, arbitrary or otherwise, without choice of his own, but because he finds them exactly suited to his nature and wants. This theory was held by many of the ancient philosophers. It was the view maintained by Plato and Aristotle, among the Greeks. Aristotle calls man πολιτικον Ζωον — a political animal.

Theory of Social Compact. — There is still another theory of government, differing in some important respects from either of those already mentioned, — a view advocated by many distinguished writers, and, indeed, the prevalent one of modern times; I refer to the theory of *social compact*, as it is called. This view — advanced by Hobbes, adopted by several subsequent philosophers of note in England, and on the continent, by Shaftesbury, and essentially by Locke and his disciples — has come to be, if I mistake not, the prevalent view, both in England and our own country, and has been widely adopted by jurists and members of the legal profession, as the principle on which civil government is supposed to rest. According to this theory, civil government is of the nature of a *contract* between man and man, in which each binds himself to fulfill certain conditions, and abide by certain rules, mutually agreed upon; which rules and conditions are binding so long as the contract stands. To these conditions it is the duty of every member of society to conform, for the same reason that it is his duty to abide by any other obligation or contract, or to keep any other engagement.

Those who enter into this arrangement — and every one who lives in society, and enjoys its advantages, virtually and tacitly gives his consent and adherence to the arrangement — mutually agree to relinquish each certain individual and natural rights into the keeping of the whole, and for the benefit of the whole; in return for which, they are to receive certain privileges, and be guarded and protected in the full enjoyment of all their rights, personal and civil. It is for the advantage of each to abide by these rules, and that others should do the same; hence the institution exists, and is continued from age to age.

Objections to this Theory. — The view now proposed is by no means free from objections. If civil government rests upon a compact, — a mutual agreement, or engagement, formed among men, — then when, and where, and by whom, was this agreement made? Where are the records, and what the history of the transaction? "No social compact similar to what is here described," says Paley, "was ever made or entered into in reality; no such original convention of the people was ever actually holden, or in any country could be holden, antecedent to the history of civil government in that country. It is to suppose it possible to call savages out of caves and deserts to deliberate and vote upon topics which the experience and studies and refinements of civil life alone suggest. Therefore no government in the universe began from this original."

To this it may be replied, that the question is not now as to the *origin* of civil government — how it *began* — but as to its *basis* — on what it *rests* — what is the *ground* of the relation which we find existing between the citizen and the state, the governed and the governors. It is no answer to the theory under consideration, to say that no government ever *began* in that way. The question is not how and when it began, but, having a beginning and existence, as a matter of fact, does it, or does it not, rest upon the consent of the governed; is it, or is it not, of the *nature* of a contract?

Nor is it enough to say that no record of any such transaction exists — that no such contract in reality was ever made. Even if this were true, — which is by no means certain, — it might be none the less true that the existing governments are really of the *nature* of a contract or agreement among the people, that they virtually rest upon no other basis than the consent of the parties governed, even though we cannot point to any formal engagement, to that effect, drawn up in so many words, and at such a time and place. Whether we can point to such original transaction or not, the real nature of the bond that holds society together as an organized body, may be precisely that of a mutual contract; and it may be very important for us to know, and to admit this truth. No other form of expression may so well and truly indicate the precise relations which exist between the different members of the body politic, and the reciprocal rights and duties of each, as that now in question.

Further Reply. — It is by no means to be conceded, however, that there is not in existence, as a matter of fact, any such contract or mutual agreement as we are now speaking of. It is not a mere figment of the imagination, but a historic reality. There are, at least in every civilized nation, certain fundamental principles of law, and of civil polity, which, whether written or unwritten, are acknowledged, and acted upon, as the basis of all civil administration of affairs. These, modified from time to time, and gathered at last into complete form, compose the *constitution* of the country, or the state. This constitution is an existing historic fact, and the fundamental principles which compose it existed in the public mind, and were acknowledged as such, long before they were collected into one body, reduced to form, and adopted as a constitution. These principles and maxims, written or unwritten, are the *terms* of the social compact; and when, in the process of time, out of these principles, the constitution, as such, takes its distinct, manifest shape and form, *that* is the written, formal contract, by which all parties in the state agree to abide. As such it is regarded and treated by business-men, jurists, statesmen, lawyers — all, in fact, who have to do with affairs of state, whether in theory or practice.

The constitutions of the several states of this republic are such compacts; they recognize themselves as such, and contain in themselves the articles of compact. Thus the constitution of Massachusetts: "The body politic is formed by a voluntary association of individuals. It is *a Social Compact*, by which the whole people covenants with each citizen, and each citizen with the whole people, that all shall be governed by certain laws for the common good." The constitution of Connecticut recognizes the same principle: "All men, when they form a social compact, are equal in rights." So, also, the opening words of the constitution of New Jersey: "All the constitutional authority ever possessed by the kings of Great Britain over their dominions, was by *compact* derived from the people, and held of them for the common interest of the whole society." Nor is this use of language unauthorized; for the vote of the English Parliament which deposed James the Second, charges him with having broken the *original compact* between king and people.

It is not true, then, that no such thing as a social contract exists in reality. Every state constitution, whether more or less complete and formal, is, in fact, such an instrument; all its articles are articles of mutual agreement; and all those fundamental principles and maxims, of which it is the collection and embodiment, are, and were before they were thus collected, and while as yet they lay unexpressed in the common mind, a virtual compact, having for its object the defining and securing to every one his rights.

Another Objection. — It is also objected, by Dr. Paley and others, to the theory now under consideration, that it supposes, what in general is not true, that men have actually given their consent to the government under which they live; whereas, in fact, they have had, for the most part, no opportunity either to give or refuse their consent. The question has never been asked them, "Are you satisfied with this present arrangement of affairs, or do you desire a change?" But such consent, it is argued, is always implied in a voluntary engagement or contract; and where it is wanting, the transaction, whatever else it may be, is no contract. To call it so, is a misnomer — an expression both false and useless. Supposing that my ancestors framed and entered into such an agreement, called the constitution: how does their action bind me? What voice have I, what voice have I ever had, in the matter? Or what has any one of the fifty thousand or five hundred thousand inhabitants of the same city or state with myself, to do in the matter? And what right has any man, ancestor or not, to bind me in this way, without my consent?

It must be confessed there is no little force in this objection. It must be confessed that men find themselves, by birth, members of whatever form of civil society exists around them, and that they have usually very little to do with shaping and forming the government under which they are to live. In this respect the state is clearly analogous to the family. It is not for a man to choose whether he will belong to this nation, or to that; to this family, or to another, or to none. These things are decided for him. He is by birth a member of the family, and subject to parental rule. He is also by birth a member of civil society, and must take it as he finds it; at least, for a considerable part of his life.

Nor is it any answer to say, that such an arrangement is for the *best good* of the subject. Doubtless it is so. The question just now is, not whether it is a wise and beneficial arrangement, but whether it is *binding;* and if so, *why*, and on what ground? Suppose I do not choose to be trammelled by this arrangement, which somebody else, a few centuries ago, thought to be wise and expedient — what then? Suppose, even, I do not choose to submit to arrangements which are in reality for my own good? What right has one age and generation to bind another age, against its will, even to its own benefit?

The true answer to this reasoning I conceive to be, that, by the very nature of human society, the engagements of one generation must be held as binding upon those that come after, until at least they are directly rejected and annulled by the latter. Until such act of rejection, consent may fairly be presumed. Silence gives consent; the simple living under and complying with the conditions of such an arrangement, gives consent. As Paley himself says with respect to the laws which regulate the administration of justice: "The law of nature, founded in the very constitution of human society, which is formed to endure through a series of perishing generations, requires that the just engagements a man enters into should continue in force beyond his own life; it follows that the private rights of persons frequently depend upon what has been transacted in times remote from the present, by their ancestors or predecessors, or by those under whom they claim, or to whose obligations they have succeeded."

Now, this is true; but, as Dr. Whewell very justly remarks, it is no more true of *private* rights, than of any other; no more true of engagements which bind man and man, than of those which bind man and the state, since public rights, as well as private, and for the same reason, depend often on what was done by those who preceded us.

The True Explanation. — I am far from maintaining, however, that the theory of a social contract is free from objections. Nor, on the other hand, can this be affirmed of either of the theories previously adduced. Each of them expresses an important element of truth. Neither of them, as it seems to me, conveys the whole truth. Nor are these different theories necessarily exclusive of each other. On the contrary, it is only by combining whatever of truth is contained in each, with whatever is contained in the others, that we reach the complete explanation, the true philosophy, of civil government.

It is doubtless true, for example, that existing constitutions and forms of government are of the nature of a social contract, in which the parties bind themselves to observe certain conditions, for the sake of securing certain advantages; the parties being, severally, King and People; or King, Lords, and Commons, on the one hand, and people on the other, as in the case of the English government; or, as in our own country, every man with the whole people, and the whole people with every man. Nor is this the less a compact because formed and entered into by those who preceded the present generation.

This, then, is the first fact which meets us in our investigation, — starting from the present actual condition of civil society, — the first step in the explanation of the phenomenon of human government. But if we were to stop here, we should leave much unexplained. How *came* man to form such compacts — everywhere, in all ages, and nations? Is it accidental? Is there not rather a *foundation in his very nature* for just this condition of things? Is he not, even, as Aristotle said, a *political animal?* Here, then, we must bring in a second theory, and place it beside, or rather beneath the first, — civil government is founded in compact, but that compact is founded in the social nature of man.

Nor would I stop here. How comes he by this nature? Is it not the gift of God — an endowment conferred upon the creature by the all-wise Creator? Did not God, in making man as he is, and conferring upon him this social nature, *intend* that he should be subject to civil authority? Here, then, we bring in still a third theory, — that of the divine will, — and place it at the foundation of the whole Civil government is founded in compact; but that compact, again, depends on the nature of man; and this, in turn, rests ultimately on the will of God.

Of Divine Authority in what Sense. — According to the view now presented, civil government is of divine authority in this sense, and in this sense only, — that by the constitution of things, and of human nature, God has settled it that civil government, of some sort, there shall be; but of what sort it shall be, he has left it for men themselves to decide; and this they do decide, each community or people for itself, by some sort of social compact or agreement. It is not in the nature of things for any community of human beings to consent to live together without any form of government; and, in point of fact, the rudest and wildest community on earth will be found to have provided itself with some kind, and some degree of civil government.

§ III. — Historic Sketch. — Different Opinions as to the Nature of Civil Government.

In the preceding sections the nature and foundation of civil government have been discussed as regards their general principles. It may serve to fix these principles more definitely in our minds, and perhaps contribute to the clearer apprehension of them, if we trace, in its general outlines, the history of the topic now under consideration, as regards the opinions which have been held by writers of distinction respecting the nature of civil government.

Opinions of the Ancients. — The idea of the state as a natural and a necessary institution, having its foundation in the very nature and constitution of man, was familiar to the ancients. Thus *Aristotle:* "It is manifest that the state is one of the things which exist by nature; and that man is by nature a political animal. A man belonging to no state is less than man, or more."

This view, however, by no means prevented them from regarding civil government, at the same time, as of divine origin, founded in the will of Deity. "All laws," says *Plato*, "came from God. No mortal man was the founder of laws." Aristotle coincides with this view. "Law," says *Cicero*, "is nothing else but right reason, derived from the divinity, and government an emanation of the divine mind." The classical scholar need not be reminded that the writings of the ancient masters are pervaded with this sentiment.

Nor, again, does this divine origin of government preclude, in their opinion, *the consent of the governed*, as in reality the proximate source of power. Locke is not, as often stated, the author of this theory of government; on the contrary, it is a principle recognized in substance by the most distinguished political philosophers of the ancient world; and that in perfect consistency with their view of the divine origin of government. The idea of a social compact is no novelty in the world.

Plato makes "a tacit agreement between each member, and the whole community," to be the foundation of the state, and affirms that they who violate the laws, violate the agreement. "The civil law," says *Aristotle*, "is that which takes place amongst a number of free persons, who are members of the same community, in which they live on a footing of equality."

"The state," says *Cicero*, "is not every assemblage of men anyhow gathered, but a community united together by common laws, common interest, and a common consent." In like manner, *Livy* affirms that the force of the supreme command is based on the consent of those who obey.

Of the Moderns. — Among the moderns, the doctrine of the *divine origin of government* has been very generally held by English divines and statesmen. Subjection to the civil power, in the language of Bishop *Horsley*, is "a conscientious submission to the will of God." "Civil government," says Bishop *Butler*, "is that part of God's government over the world which he exercises by the instrumentality of men. Considering that all power is of God, all authority is properly of divine appointment." The view of *Dr. Paley* has already been stated. He bases the authority of government on the will of God as collected from expediency. The following is the language of *Edmund Burke:* "All dominion over man is the effect of the divine disposition. It is bound by the eternal laws of him that gave it, with which no human authority can dispense. * * * We are all born in subjection — all born equally, high and low, governors and governed, in subjection to one great, immutable, preëxistent law, prior to all our devices, and all our contrivances, paramount to all our ideas, and all our sensations, antecedent to our very existence, — by which we are knit and connected in the eternal frame of the universe, and out of which we cannot stir. This great law does not arise out of our conventions, or compacts; on the contrary, it gives to our compacts and conventions all the force and sanction they can have."

Coincident with the views now expressed is that of the great theologian *Calvin:* "The reason why we should be subject to magistrates, is, because they are appointed by the ordinance of God. Since it has pleased God so to administer the government of this world, he who resists their power, strives against the divine ordinance, and so fights against God. Because, to disregard his providence who is the author of civil government, is to go to war with him." These words are a comment upon a passage in the thirteenth chapter of the epistle to the Romans, in which the divine authority of civil government is very clearly set forth, and which may be regarded as not merely the Pauline, but the general Scripture doctrine of human government.

Not Inconsistent with Social Compact. — But, while maintaining the views now stated respecting human government, as founded in the will of God, and ultimately deriving its authority from that high source, the writers whom I have quoted by no means maintain that the *various forms* which human governments practically assume are also and equally of divine authority. On the contrary, they recognize the *form* as a matter of human invention and choice; and so, and that not inconsistently, they recognize, in many cases, the principle of the social compact. So, also, as we have seen, did Plato, Aristotle, and Cicero, while, in like manner, tracing back all law to a divine original, nevertheless admit the consent of the governed as the proximate source of authority in the state. Thus Bishop *Horsley*, whom I have already quoted, while maintaining "that all government is in such sort of divine institution, that, be the form of any particular government what it may, the submission of the individual is a principal branch of that religious duty which each man owes to God," is careful to admit "that all *particular forms* of government which now exist are the work of human policy, under the control of God's overruling providence." They have not thought it, therefore, at all inconsistent with their theory of the divine authority of civil government, to inquire into the origin and sources of political power, as a thing of human contrivance and social compact. For, as has been well stated by *Puffendorf*, in his *Law of Nature and Nations*, "he who affirms sovereignty to result immediately from compact, doth not in the least detract from the sacred character of civil government, or maintain that princes bear rule by human right only, not by divine."

The doctrine of *Social Compact* has been held, in fact, by almost all the chief writers on Morál and Political Philosophy in modern times. Puffendorf, Grotius, Montesquieu, Blackstone, Milton, Bacon, Sidney, Locke, Barbeyrac, Burlamaqui, John Q. Adams, Jefferson, are among the more prominent names which occur in this connection. Of these, it will be sufficient to quote as authority Grotius and Blackstone. The former says: "Men, not influenced by the express command of God, but of their own accord, having experienced the weak defence of separated families against the assaults of violence, united themselves in civil society, the effect of which was civil power, styled on this account, by St. Peter, the ordinance of man." Blackstone holds the following language respecting "the original contract of society." "This contract, though perhaps in no instance has it ever been formally expressed at the first institution of a state, yet in nature and reason must be always understood and implied, in the very act of associating together; namely, that the whole should protect all its parts, and that every part should pay obedience to the will of the whole; or, in other words, that the community should guard the rights of each individual member, and that, in return for this protection, each individual should submit to the laws of the community." The same authority, than which none is higher, pronounces the coronation oath taken by the monarchs of England on ascending the throne, to be, without dispute, an express and fundamental contract. This has always been the doctrine of the English Whigs. They acted on it when they brought Charles I. to the bar, and deposed James II. As already stated, the constitutions of these United States are based on the same great principle — the *Social Compact.*

CHAPTER II.

VARIOUS FORMS OF CIVIL GOVERNMENT.

The origin and object of civil government, and also the foundation on which it rests, have occupied our attention in the preceding chapter. A glance at the *various forms* which government assumes in its actual working, and at the *distribution* of its several *powers*, will enable us the better to comprehend the practical duties, growing out of these several relations, as they may come up for consideration in the subsequent chapters.

§ I.—Analysis of the Several Functions and Forms of Government.

It has been already observed, that every state is sovereign and independent—the power of directing its own affairs lying wholly in its own hands. The state, in its aggregate capacity, however, cannot administer government, nor enact laws, nor execute justice. The whole mass of the people cannot leave their places of business, assemble in one body, and so devote their personal attention to the affairs of government, the devising of suitable laws and regulations, or the trial and punishment of offenders. Evidently, this is out of the question. Hence the necessity for delegated authority. The state, which is the real sovereign,—that is, the people,—must commit its power, for the time, into the hands of those duly appointed and authorized to act for it, and whose acts, when thus commissioned, shall be in reality the action of the state. Now, as these officers, charged with the administration of government, vary as to number, and mode of appointment, and the nature and degree of the power committed to them, in this manner there arise so many different *forms* of government, in different countries, and different periods of history,—as monarchy, absolute or limited; aristocracy; republicanism, or unlimited democracy.

General Division of Functions.—Whatever may be the particular form which the government of a country assumes, there is usually a general division of the several powers and functions of the government into distinct departments, which are much the same under all varieties of state organization, and in all civilized countries. It is found desirable, for obvious reasons, to distribute the powers of government into three grand departments, — the Legislative, the Judicial, and the Executive, — and to keep these entirely distinct from each other.

The wisdom of such an arrangement will appear on a moment's reflection. Were the business of enacting and of executing the laws committed to the same hands, such is the imperfection of human nature, that serious difficulties would be likely to arise. There would be too much room for personal bias and prejudice. The executive would enact such laws as suited his own notions and plans of government. The legislator would execute the laws according to his own ideas of the importance of this or that enactment, which he might have favored or opposed, while it was under discussion, prior to its becoming a law. The judge could not, with impartiality, try offences against laws which he had himself made, and was himself to execute. It is never safe to entrust these several powers to the same hands. Hence, with most governments, not altogether despotic, the power of legislating, or making the laws, is entrusted to one body; that of judging them, or trying offences under them, to another; and that of executing the decisions thus made, to still another; and these are called the *Legislative*, the *Judicial*, and the *Executive* departments of government.

Upon these, again, certain checks are devised, for the prevention of abuse of power. The legislative body is usually composed of two parts, houses, or orders, differently constituted, whose concurrent action is necessary to the passage of any measure. Further, to guard against possible abuse of power, even under this arrangement, there is also the right of veto, — lodged usually with the executive, — by which it is in his power to check all rash and unwise legislation. In the *Judiciary* there is an effectual guarantee against intentional injustice, in the power of appeal from court to court, so that a case reaches its final decision only after having passed through successive trials, at different tribunals.

Different Forms of Government. — Besides the general divisions now indicated, and which are more or less common to all governments, not purely despotic in their nature, there are certain leading distinctions to be observed in respect to the various forms which the government may happen to assume. In different states, and at different periods of time, these forms vary widely and radically. The form of a government is determined by the character of its legislature or law-making power. As is that, so is the government. There are three principal forms which government assumes; or, more strictly, so many *elements* of power, which, either singly or in various combinations, enter into the structure, and determine the form, of all governments. These are the monarchic, or despotic, the aristocratic, and the democratic. According as one or another of these elements prevails, we have for a government, monarchy absolute, or monarchy limited, aristocracy, the representative republic, or the complete democracy. In the first, or *absolute monarchy*, the power is lodged in the hands of one. His will is law. The monarch is at once executive, and law-maker, and, if he pleases, judge also; that is, those who may be nominally entrusted with the functions of legislative and judiciary power, are so at his pleasure, by his appointment, and, therefore, under his complete control. To his power there are no constitutional checks or restraints. In the *limited monarchy* this supreme power of the king, or emperor, is modified, and held in check by the other departments of government, and by constitutional restraints, which affix certain limits, beyond which he may not go. The legislative, the judiciary, and the executive functions are kept distinct, and the prerogatives and powers of each are carefully guarded. Still, the monarchical element, or the idea of power in the hands of one, though in a modified form, prevails, and gives shape to the government.

In the *aristocracy*, we have a select body, sharing among themselves the powers and prerogatives of the government, or exercising the same in their collective capacity; filling their own vacancies, or coming into their places by inheritance, or by acquisition of certain titles, rank, or possessions. The law-power is lodged no longer now in the hands of one, but of the few, — descended from a line of noble ancestors, distinguished for their valor, their high birth, or their achievements in history, or themselves the architects, it may be, of their own fortunes, — taking rank, not by inheritance, but by the splendor of their own talents, their own fortunes, or their own services. These few stand forth from among the common multitude, and rule by virtue of conceded superiority.

In the *pure democracy* we have the simple reverse of pure monarchy, — power now in the hands of the many; not *ultimately*, merely — for ultimately it is always with the many, under whatever form it may present itself to the view — but *directly* and immediately; not in reality merely, but in *form*. The people at large make laws for themselves in assemblies of the whole, or by divisions and tribes. The will of the people is law, with no intervening instrumentality or agency to give it expression and validity. Or this democratic element, like the monarchic, may present itself in a modified form, — the people, instead of acting every man in person, in the assembly of the whole, delegating their power to certain persons authorized to act for them, or represent them; the real power still lying in the hands of the many, nevertheless, who choose only such persons as they please to represent them, and who have in some form the power of approving or revoking the decisions of the same.

We have, then, as distinct elements of government — monarchy, absolute or limited; aristocracy; and democracy, pure or representative. As a matter of fact, very few governments present either of these forms, however, in a simple or pure state, but more or less intermingled and combined with each other. Thus, we may have a monarchy, so far as regards the name and nature of the chief magistracy, along with an aristocracy or body of nobility, enjoying certain powers and privileges; and back of these, again, a representative body, acting for the people, and, to some extent, holding in check both nobles and monarch. Such is the actual constitution of the English government. The Commons have the power of voting or refusing all taxes and supplies, and also, they have the control of the army, — thus holding in their hand both the purse and the sword of government.

Our own constitution, also, while it dispenses with monarch and nobles, is by no means a simple and pure democracy, like the Athenian of old. The many are represented in legislative assembly. Over against this popular branch is placed the conservative element — a Senate — answering in idea, though not in form, to the Upper House of English Parliament; while in the chief executive, we have that concentration of authority in the person of one, which, under a widely different form, is still, so far as it enters at all into the political fabric, the essential element of despotic rather than democratic rule.

These different forms of government, now described, have each their separate and special advantages, and, also, disadvantages. In proportion as the monarchic element prevails, government becomes efficient, strong, united in council, prompt and decisive in action. The tendency is to greater and greater assumption of power by the one, to the injury of freedom, and the rights of the many. In proportion as democracy prevails, the popular will and rights are maintained; but often at the expense of wisdom in council, and of unity and efficiency in action.

The constitution of the English government, and, in a still higher degree, that of these United States, seem to me to present a combination of these several elements, wisely adapted to secure the most desirable results, with, perhaps, the fewest disadvantages.

§ II. — Historical Sketch of Forms of Government.

The various possible forms of government, and the several elements which enter more or less fully into the structure and composition of all forms, have been pointed out in the preceding section. Casting our eye now on the page of history, we shall find the various governments of the ancient and the modern time marked and characterized by the prevalence, some of one, some of another of these several elements, — in some the *monarchical*, in others the *aristocratic*, in others still, the *democratic* element prevailing, and giving character to the form of government. It may serve to fix in our minds the principles already indicated, if we take a rapid glance at the civil institutions of some of the nations prominent in history.

The Hebrew State. — The civil polity of this remarkable people was primarily a *Theocracy.* God was the supreme ruler and civil head of the state; in him was vested the law-making power — the sovereignty. Such a constitution of the state was no novelty, indeed, in the ancient world; but, on the contrary, was quite in accordance with the spirit of those earlier times. All the ancient law-givers — from Menes in Egypt, and Cadmus in Thebes, to Lycurgus in Sparta, and Numa in Rome — called in the aid of religion to strengthen the foundations of the civil power. With them, however, the religious sentiment was merely a *means* to an end: in the Hebrew polity, it was itself a chief end of the civil constitution. The recognition and adoration of one God, the supreme and rightful Ruler of the universe, was a fundamental law of the Hebrew state, a first principle of the civil polity. Idolatry was a crime against the state, punishable as such; and, on the other hand, the violation of the laws of the state was regarded as sin against God.

Democratic Element. — The Hebrew polity was not, however, a *pure* Theocracy. The sovereignty vested in Jehovah was not to the exclusion of the civil magistrate; it was an element of the government, rather than the government itself. Another and equally characteristic element of that government was *democracy,* — a magistracy elected by the people, and a constitution adopted by the people. Jehovah himself would not become the sovereign and civil head of the state, until he had been formally and solemnly chosen as such by the suffrages of the assembly. Summoned, at the call of the trumpet, to the heights of Sinai, Moses receives commission to propose to the people Jehovah as the national sovereign. The proposition is considered and accepted, in due form, by the people yielding their free and solemn assent. And all the people answered together: "All that the Lord hath spoken we will do." A solemn covenant is then entered into, — Jehovah, on his part, promising to be the ruler and protector of the nation; the people, on their part, promising faithful allegiance. Here, then, in due manner and form, is one instance, at least, of that which certain writers can find no trace of in history, viz., a *social compact.* It is a clear and manifest example of the manner in which, substantially, all free governments take their rise. As such it is recognized by the highest authorities, — Jahn, Lowman, Michaelis, Graves, Bossuet.

Further Democratic Element. — In like manner, the fundamental laws of the state were adopted by the people in assembly of the whole. The Hebrew constitution was submitted to and adopted by the Hebrew people, as really and formally as the constitution of the United States was submitted to and adopted by the several states of the Union. At the death of Moses, it seems to have been again subjected to popular suffrage; and once in every seven years thereafter, by statute law, it was, in like manner, to be ratified in assembly of the whole.

Such a government is, in the true sense, a government by the people, a democracy, — the constitution, the laws, the chief ruler, being subject to the popular will.

Not only the laws, and the chief ruler, were chosen by the people, but also the judges, and the chiefs, or princes of the several tribes. Each tribe seems to have been under the immediate direction of its prince, and to have been subdivided into several classes, or groups of families, each having its own chief or elder. These princes of tribes, together with the chiefs, or heads of families, were, in reality, representatives of the people, and constituted what may be called the popular branch of the government. Each tribe constituted, in fact, a separate state, in many respects independent, under its own prince and chiefs of families. It could even declare war, and make peace, for itself.

Equality of Classes and of Landed Property. — These several features constitute a strongly democratic cast of government, more nearly approaching a purely republican state than any other, perhaps, on record, except our own. To these characteristics should be added, also, the *social equality* of the people, — every person, whatever his birth, rank, wealth, or profession, being on a footing of entire equality, both socially and politically, with every other person in the state; — and also *the equal distribution of landed property* among the people; thus securing the political independence of the masses, promoting industry and a fondness for agricultural pursuits, giving dignity to labor, and cherishing the spirit of manly self-reliance, the love of home and of the soil.

Such were the leading features of the Hebrew polity.

The Egyptian State. — When we compare these institutions, so liberal, and, in many respects, so closely resembling our own, with those of other nations of antiquity, we are struck with the contrast. In Egypt, for example, — from which, if from any country, Moses must be supposed to have derived his notions of civil government, — the state was a despotism. The soil belonged to the monarch, and the people who cultivated it belonged more to the king, than to themselves. The institution of caste — that curse of oriental nations — prevailed in full rigor, separating the people into three great classes, — the priestly, the military, and the common people, or laboring class; which latter were a mere herd, without possessions or honors. The military were supported from the public lands, — one-third of the entire national domain being divided among them for this purpose. The priesthood was the ruling class — making, modifying, and interpreting the laws, and filling all the civil offices. The king was chosen either from the sacerdotal or the military caste; but the people had no voice in the election. Thus the king governed the nation, the gods governed the king (for Egypt, too, was strongly theocratic); but the priests governed the gods, by putting into their mouths such oracles as they chose.

THE ORIENTAL STATES. — Not unlike the Egyptian, in its general features, were the several chief oriental governments of the ancient world. The Assyrian and the Persian states, for example, were absolute monarchies, — complete military despotisms, — in which the will of the monarch, who was at the same time warrior and king, was the supreme law. He might be a just and humane man, like Cyrus, or the reverse; he might govern wisely and well, like Darius; or unjustly and arbitrarily, as many, if not most of the Assyrian and Persian monarchs; but in either case he was a despot — irresponsible, unrestrained by law or constitution.

THE SPARTAN GOVERNMENT. — Nor yet in Sparta, under Lycurgus, do we find much that corresponds to our idea of civil liberty and popular rights. The power of the state was lodged in the hands of the *senate*, a body of nobles, holding office for life. The people had, indeed, the right to vote on any proposition submitted by the senate; but it must be without discussion, or statement of reasons, — simply yes or no. It was for the senate to originate all laws; in them, also, was vested the whole executive power, and all the more important judicial decisions were likewise in their hands. Here we have an irresponsible oligarchy, — the centralization of power in the hands of a body of nobles, — one of the worst forms of despotism. In no nation, perhaps, was there ever less real freedom, as to the matters of state, and also of common life, than among the Spartans. All the affairs of social and domestic life, even the food and dress and manners of the citizens, were regulated by strict and stern decree.

The Athenian State. — In Athens, again, we find a tyranny hardly less despotic, but of another kind, — the despotism not of the one, nor of the few, but of the many, — the despotism of a turbulent, fickle, and lawless democracy. The Athenian State was, from the first, strongly democratic. Even under the monarchical form of government, this tendency was apparent. The kings possessed no absolute power, nor could they make or unmake laws at their pleasure. But not even the form of monarchy was suffered long to remain. By a clever artifice — the election of Jupiter as sole sovereign of the people — royalty is virtually abolished, and the chief power is lodged in the hands of archons, chosen by the people, or else by lot, at first for life, then for ten years, and, finally, year by year. These archons presided over the civil and military affairs of the state — over religion — its laws, its courts of justice. Still, the power was in the hands of the people. Every citizen, however poor, had his vote in the popular assembly; and with that assembly lay the power of peace and war, of trying appeals from the civil courts, of regulating commerce and finance; in a word, of general legislation. The people were complete masters of the state.

This had been well, if the people had only been masters

of themselves also; but, unfortunately, they were poorly fitted for self-government. Ever under the influence of designing men and demagogues; ever ready to be carried away, with or without due cause, by some new excitement; ever jealous of true greatness, and of distinguished service rendered to the state; ever impatient of restraint, and of all constitutional barriers;—liberty soon degenerated with them into licentiousness: the annual elections became scenes of disorder; and Athens, broken into contending factions, seemed on the verge of ruin. Draco and Solon were successively called to the helm, in this emergency; but neither the severity of the one, nor the genius and wisdom of the other, proved adequate to the task of imposing the needed restraints on this lawless element of popular will.

Various checks were indeed introduced by Solon into the constitution, such as the division of the citizens into classes on a property basis, and the restriction of offices to the more wealthy; the institution of a senate of four hundred, or council of state, to prepare business for the popular assembly; the reëstablishment of the Areopagus, as guardian of the laws, and of the public treasure, of education and of morals; and, finally, the appointment of courts of judicature, with juries taken from the people, and of itinerant judges for less important cases. These checks on the popular lawlessness were well devised, but in practice ineffectual. Neither senate of four hundred, nor Areopagus, famous for its wisdom, could withstand the tide of popular commotion. The popular will triumphed over all restraints of constitutional law; and, within ten years from its adoption, the constitution of Solon gave place to a military despotism.

THE ROMAN STATE.—The classical scholar will not need to be reminded that the history of ancient Rome is but the narrative of one continued struggle between Aristocracy and Democracy — the Patrician and the Plebeian blood. In the original constitution of the state, the former alone, of these two classes, was recognized as having place and privilege; the latter was an undistinguished herd, a mere rabble, a populace, occupying certain sections of the city, and forming a large portion of the rank and file of the army, but of no account politically; admitted neither to the senate, the magistracy, nor the deliberative assembly.

The senate, composed entirely of patricians, or nobles, with the king or the consuls at its head, was the administrative body, the executive power. The senate, together with the people,—*Senatus Populusque Romanus*,—constituted the deliberative and legislative body — an assembly of patrician families, distributed into curiæ or wards, according to the section of the city in which they dwelt,—thirty in all,—the decision of a majority of which, or of sixteen, was pronounced the will of the people. This assembly, or body, was called the *Comitia Curiata*, and was first instituted by Romulus. In this arrangement the plebeians — the common people — had no share whatever.

Comitia Centuriata. — It was not till the reign of Servius Tullius that the claims of this portion of the citizens came to be recognized in the administration of government, by the institution of an assembly called the *Comitia Centuriata*, composed of patricians and plebeians together. This gave them important advantages; but still they were excluded from all the higher offices, and from intermarriage with the patrician families. Nor was their share in legislation more than nominal. The constitution of the Comitia Centuriata was as follows: Tullius divided the people into six classes, on a property basis, — the first class consisting of all those whose estates, in lands and effects, amounted to one hundred thousand pounds of brass; the second, of those who were worth seventy-five thousand; the third, of those worth fifty thousand; and so on to the sixth class, which included all those worth less than twelve thousand five hundred. This last included, of course, most of the plebeians. These classes, again, were divided into centuries, one hundred and ninety-three in all; of which ninety-eight, a majority of the whole, were in the *first* class, while the whole of the *sixth* class, comprising a much larger number of the people than any other, constituted but a single century. As the vote was by centuries, this arrangement, of course, threw the whole power into the hands of the upper classes. Wealth predominated over numbers. The vote of the first class was first taken, and if the centuries comprising that class were unanimous, the question was decided, and the remaining centuries were not called. The great body of the people, in fact, never voted at all in this sort of assembly, except in case of a tie in the previous ballots; and it hardly ever happened that the lowest class was called. In these assemblies, the more important magistrates were chosen, — the consuls, pretors, censors, military tribunes, — the laws proposed by the higher magistrates were passed, war was declared, and all crimes against the state were tried.

Change of Constitution. — The disparagement and inequality of which I have spoken, came at last to be so deeply felt by the plebeian class, that they resolved no longer to submit to it, and withdrew in a body from the state. In order to persuade them to return, important concessions were now made. From the ranks of the plebeians two magistrates were appointed, to be chosen by the people themselves, called *Tribunes* of the Plebeians, as guardians of the interests and rights of that body. Their persons were inviolable, and they had full power to arrest all legal proceedings against any citizen. As another measure of relief, the debts of impoverished plebeians were also cancelled. The *Comitia Tributa*, or Assembly of the Tribes, was also instituted, which gave the plebeians some share in legislative affairs.

These comitia embraced, nominally, all the citizens; but, as the votes of all were here of equal weight, the patricians, or nobles, seldom attended, and the assembly was, in fact, a plebeian affair. In these assemblies, the inferior city and provincial magistrates were chosen, certain laws were passed, and certain trials, not of a capital nature, were held. The tribunes of the people were also elected in these comitia.

The specific powers and functions of these several assemblies — the Senate, the Centuries, and the Tribes — were probably not very clearly defined. The system, as thus arranged, was complicated and ill-adjusted, and, in its practical working, by no means harmonious. Patricians and plebeians were still in constant rivalry and altercation. The latter, however, by virtue of long-continued and determined struggles, were gradually gaining more and more power in the state. Step by step, important rights were secured. Intermarriage of the two classes was no longer forbidden. The senate, and even the consulship, were brought within reach of plebeian talent and ambition. Finally, of the two consuls, one was to be chosen invariably from the plebeian ranks, and the other high magistracies were thrown open to all classes of the people. The decrees of the Comitia Tributa were also invested with the authority of general law, and not binding, as before, merely upon the plebeians themselves. In fact, the political distinction of the two classes came to be of much less consequence than before.

These gradual and important changes introduced what

has been justly called the golden period of the Roman constitution. The regal, the aristocratic, and the democratic elements are at last more equitably and harmoniously combined,— the consuls representing the regal, the senate the aristocratic, and the comitia of centuries and tribes the democratic power of the state. Up to this time, these several powers had been in continual agitation and strife with each other for the ascendency.

The whole history of the Republic, in truth, from the expulsion of the kings until the point which we have now reached, was one continued struggle between these separated and inharmonious elements. The chief power had been in the hands of the wealthy and the noble, who were ever plotting against the rights of the people; consuls, pretors, senators, were clothed with the highest authority, even of life and death; the laws were severe, and often unequally administered; while the tribunes, set to guard the rights of the people, were ever aiming at the possession of power and honor for themselves, and so were often false to their trust. Such were the radical defects of the Roman constitution in what we may call the transition period of its history.

Further Change.— How long this better adjusted system might have continued, or how well it might have operated in the absence of disturbing causes from without, it is not for us to say. But as Rome enlarged her borders, and her power extended over the several provinces and states that lay round about her, the polity constructed originally for the government of the city, was found ill adapted to the government of an extended country. The people of the whole of Italy were too numerous to act in concert as a body. The representative system of modern times was not as yet invented. The democratic element of the state became unwieldy and unmanageable. Scenes of lawlessness and violence ensued; mobs prevailed; armies were necessary to preserve the peace. And so security was purchased at the expense of liberty, and military rule placed in the hands of the successful leader the sceptre of imperial power.

This power was unlimited. The oath of allegiance, which bound the soldier, by the most solemn imprecations, and in the most absolute manner, to the service and obedience of his commander, now bound him in the same terms to the emperor, as commander-in-chief; and this oath was taken, not by the soldiers only, but by all magistrates and citizens. The civil and military authority were thus united; the legislative and the executive powers reverted to one possessor; even the religious authority was added, — the emperor being invested with a sacred, and, in some sense, divine character; and so monarchy displaces at last the constitution, and assumes to itself the powers and rights of the people. Such, in brief outline, is the history, and such the termination, of the Roman State.

Feudal System. — Thus far, in our rapid survey of the progress of government among different nations, our attention has been directed to the ancient world. Glancing now at the more recent times, we find in the middle ages a system widely prevalent, and of marked peculiarities, generally known as the *Feudal System.*

The northern tribes, which, on the decline of the Roman power, overran and took possession of the provinces previously subject to the imperial sway, seem to have been, for the most part, of republican tendencies. Their chiefs, though sometimes designated by the title of king, possessed but limited power. The supreme authority was with the people, the freemen of the nation. The additional authority conferred upon the chief appointed to the command of the army in war, continued only till the return of peace. These German chiefs had each a band of followers, voluntarily attached to him, supported at his table, and devoted to his service. They were his *vassi*, his young men; hence the term *homage*, from the Latin *homo*. They who stood in this relation to the chief, or superior, held themselves ready to follow the fortunes of their leader, and sacrifice life itself for his interest. The connection was one of the most binding and sacred nature; and when the German tribes subdued the surrounding provinces, and established their own forms of government in the conquered territories, the relation now described became one of the chief features of the policy thus established. Thus arose the *Feudal* System, so called from the term Feud, or Fief, which was the name given to those landed possessions which the chiefs bestowed on their retainers, in the partition of the conquered lands. These fiefs were merely life-loans, the right of ownership being vested in the chief. If the son, however, devoted his person and service to the chief whom his father had served, he received, by custom, his father's fief; and this custom, in the course of centuries, came to be regarded as a right. This tenure of land by military service, which is one of the prominent features of the feudal system, and which in fact has given it its name, seems, however, to have been of earlier origin. It was, in fact, a custom borrowed from the days of the Roman Empire. Under Constantine, and the earlier emperors, the distant provinces of the empire were granted to certain military dukes, or counts, and their soldiery, on condition of their defending the same. These military leaders were magistrates, as well as commanders of the troops; and the military thus organized constituted a distinct and privileged class — a military aristocracy.

Thus arose the feudal system of the middle ages, — at first Germanic, afterwards extended over most of Europe, — a system of which the principal features were the two now indicated — the relation of Seignior and Vassal, and the tenure of land as fief, or feud, for service rendered. It was, on the whole, an advance on the arbitrary power of the Roman Empire. The inferior had his acknowledged rights, and the chief his acknowledged obligations. The service of the one was to be repaid by the protection of the other. Still, it was a system fraught with abuse and oppression. The lowest members enjoyed very little liberty, while to the peaceable inhabitants — those who were not included in the army — this system afforded no security or protection in their rights.

English Constitution. — The earlier Anglo-Saxon race seem to have derived from their Germanic ancestry a love of freedom, which infused itself into their laws and institutions. The Great Council of the nation — composed of prelates, abbots, aldermen, or *elder-men*, of the shires, and the noble and wise of the realm — gave its consent to all the important acts of government, and to all the laws of the land. The Norman Conquest introduced into England the feudal system, with even augmented rigor; but the conqueror so far relaxed his severity, subsequently, as to grant his subjects a charter, relieving in a degree the feudal oppression. Successive charters, under successive kings, granted still greater liberty; but it was not until the Great Charter of King John, that the English constitution can be said to have received its distinctive impress and character. This instrument has always and justly been regarded as lying at the foundation of English constitutional law. In the language of Mr. Hallam: "This is still the key-stone of English liberty. All that has since been obtained, is little more than as confirmation or commentary; and if every subsequent law were to be swept away, there would still remain the bold features which distinguish a free from a despotic monarchy." This charter guarantees security of person and of property to all freemen. "No freeman shall be taken, or imprisoned, or disseized of his freehold, or liberties, or free customs; or be outlawed, or exiled, or any otherwise destroyed. Nor will we pass upon him, but by the lawful judgment of his peers, and of the law of the land." The charter also limits and restrains the previously excessive power of the feudal lords over their vassals.

Further Safeguards. — Another safeguard of English liberty was the restriction of the right of taxation. Under the Saxon and the Norman dynasty, the king legislated only with the advice and consent of his Parliament; all new laws, and all new taxes, as well as other laws, must receive the sanction of this council of the realm. The Great Charter restrained somewhat the royal power as to taxes already established,—as, for example, the tax in commutation for personal military service, called *escuage*,—but it was not until Edward the First that the English constitution received its complete and definite form, as respects the right of taxation, requiring the consent of Parliament to all taxes imposed by the crown, and thus securing to private property that protection which was gained for personal liberty under the Great Charter of King John.

Already, however, had another and even more important step been taken in the progress of constitutional liberty in England. The same century that gave England the Magna Charta, and the concessions of Edward the First, as to right of taxation, witnessed the introduction of a new feature into her government, — the participation of the common people, with the nobles, in the deliberations and decisions of the Great Council; in other words, the establishment of the House of Commons. The first appearance of deputies from cities and boroughs in Parliament, was after the defeat of Henry the Third, by the Barons, in the battle of Lewes; and not until Edward the First were they permanently connected with that body. In successive reigns the power of this body was enlarged, and more fully established; its concurrence with the House of Peers became necessary, in order to any alterations of the law; and it exercised the right of inquiry into public measures, and abuses, and even of impeaching the king's ministers. In the fifteenth century, under the reign of the House of Lancaster, these powers were still further developed: the exclusive right of taxation by Parliament was secured, and so the right of controlling the national expenditure; the right of making the supplies of the crown depend upon redress of grievances; the right of controlling the royal decisions in questions of peace and war; of punishing unworthy and corrupt ministers; and, what is quite as important, the right of liberty of person, and liberty of speech, to every member of Parliament.

These were measures of great moment, and proved an effectual security against the encroachments of arbitrary power. From that time onward, though subject still to many abuses and reverses, the English constitution became the great bulwark of liberty defined and protected by law. The great elements of monarchy, aristocracy, and democracy, were so adjusted, and set over against each other, as to afford due check and balance each to the other. Constitutional government, though sometimes overborne by the arbitrary power of a monarch more bold and assuming than the rest, never failed to regain its former possessions and rights. The power of Henry the Eighth, of Mary, and of Elizabeth, was still a power limited and controlled by established law. As Whewell justly remarks: "Elizabeth frequently spoke to her Parliaments in an imperious manner; but they, too, had members, who spoke boldly on the other side; and though she exercised a large power in some instances, she yielded in others. The voice of English freedom was never silenced in the Houses of Parliament, nor the voice of English law in the Courts of Justice."

The great Revolution of 1688, which declared the throne of James the Second *vacant*, and placed William the Third upon that throne, as the representative of constitutional liberty, was the final death-scene of the doctrine of absolute power, and of the divine right of kings in England.

Constitution of the United States.—Our historical sketch of the different forms of civil government would be quite incomplete if we were to pass without notice the constitution of our own country. A very brief survey of its more prominent features is all which the limits of the present section allow.

The British colonies of North America — the germ of the states which compose the Union — brought to the formation and settlement of their political and civil institutions, a wisdom and experience in such matters not always enjoyed by the founders of new states. They had the history of Europe and of the world to guide them. They brought with them from the mother country a love of liberty, and just ideas of human rights; while, at the same time, they were far from those restraints which ancient customs and usages, and the regard for what is once established, impose on the progress of opinion and improvement in the Old World. The first principles of freedom they had learned in the father-land; while the errors of that government, and their own personal injuries and sufferings under it, rendered them deeply sensible of the dangers and evils to be avoided. When, in the progress of events, their independence of all foreign power left them at liberty to choose their own form of government, the constitution which, after mature deliberation, was adopted, may be regarded as the united act and will of the whole people.

Principle of Representation. — The distinguishing feature of the government — the basis on which the whole system rests — on which all free institutions must ever rest — is the principle of just and equal representation, — a representation extending to all interests, and to all classes of the people. There is no privileged class, no excluded class. The people are the nation, and the nation governs itself. With trivial exceptions, the elective franchise belongs to the whole body of free citizens, without distinction. The principle of representation, as we have already seen, is indeed recognized in other countries, especially in England; but in the constitution of the United States we find it, for the first time in history, fully and fairly carried out, and made the foundation of free government. It is only in this country that, at this moment indeed, a genuine representation of the people exists.

Relation of the several States to the General Government. — Within certain limits, the powers of government are exercised by the respective states within themselves; beyond these limits, the power is vested in the general government. The relation of the several states, therefore, to the general government, is not that of so many independent communities united for certain purposes in one confederation. The constitution is more than a compact between independent powers: it is a union of the people, as a whole, into one nation and one government. Those powers and offices which more properly belong to the nation, as such, — as, for example, the treaty-making power, the declaring of peace and war, the coining of money, the regulation of revenues and the postal service, the regulation of commerce, and other like powers of a general nature, — are under the control of the general government; while, in other matters, each state administers its own affairs, independent of all others.

The constitutions of the several states, and that of the United States, must therefore be viewed in connection, as parts of one system, in order to a complete and just conception of our government as a whole.

Distribution of Powers. — The constitutions of the several states, and that of the United States, are in general modelled on the same plan, — comprising, as their essential features, a legislative authority vested in two houses, and an executive, with prescribed and definite powers; — all chosen, either by the people directly, or through their representatives.

In the national government, the legislative body — a Congress, as it is termed — is composed of a Senate, and House of Representatives; the former elected for the term of six years, by the legislatures of the several states, two for each state; the latter chosen by the people directly, every two years — the number varying according to the population of each state. The Executive, whose term of office is four years, is chosen by electors appointed for the purpose, as the respective state legislatures may direct.

All bills for revenue must originate in the house of representatives. All cases of impeachment of public officers must be tried by the senate. Every bill passed by the senate and house of representatives must be submitted to, and approved by the executive, before it becomes a law. In case he refuses his approval and signature, it is returned, with his objections, in writing, to the house from which it originated; and if, upon reconsideration, it is still approved by two-thirds of the house, it is then sent to the other house, and if passed by two-thirds of that also, it then becomes a law, irrespective of the presidential veto.

Congress has power to levy taxes, duties, etc.; to borrow money; to regulate commerce with foreign nations, and between the several states; to raise and support armies, and provide a navy; to organize the Supreme Court, and appoint tribunals inferior to the same; to punish treason, piracy, and offences against the laws of nations; to coin money, and establish post-offices and post-routes; to make all needful rules for the government of the territories of the United States; to admit new states to the Union, and to propose amendments to the constitution by vote of two-thirds of both houses,—such amendments to be ratified by the legislatures, or by conventions called for the purpose, in three-fourths of the states.

Besides the negative power already mentioned, the executive, by consent of the senate, may make treaties, and appoint ambassadors, and the principal officers of the government. A pardoning power is also lodged in his hands.

Neither congress nor the executive has any power to interfere with, or prevent, the largest freedom of speech, and of the press, nor the utmost liberty of religious belief and worship.

Points of Contrast.—If one were asked to point out the essential advantages of this constitution over those of other countries,—as, for example, of England, or of the ancient republics,—the limited outline already given would furnish an answer. In no other country, ancient or modern, will he find the great principle of popular representation, which underlies all free government, so fully carried out, and completely embodied into the whole structure of government; in almost no other, such unlimited freedom of speech, and the press; in no other, such entire absence of all church, or other religious establishments, prescribed by law — such entire freedom of all men to do as they please in matters of religious belief and worship; in no other, such entire exemption from military establishments, and a standing army; in no other, the rights of citizens, without distinction of persons and classes, so fully and effectually secured.

Résumé. — We have, in the preceding pages, as was proposed, passed in brief review the leading features of some of the more prominent forms of government, as developed among the chief historic nations of ancient and modern times. Everywhere we find the three great elements of all government — monarchy, aristocracy, democracy — more or less fully developed, more or less in conflict with each other, more or less checking and balancing each the other. We find the simplicity and unity of patriarchal rule — the germ, doubtless, whence all civil governments originally sprang — tending naturally to the concentration of power in the hands of one; in other words, to monarchy: and this we find the predominant element, as we might expect, in the earlier and oriental governments. As we pass on down the line of nations and of ages, we find this monarchical power more and more limited and circumscribed by the power of chiefs and nobles; the *aristocratic* element thrusting itself into prominence; at times displacing even the kingly power altogether, as in Sparta, and the Roman Republic. In the progress of time, the popular will learns its strength, and asserts its rights; the democratic element comes into view as an important factor; wages, for a time, unequal strife with the antagonist forces of kingly and aristocratic power; gains for itself, in the end, important rights and privileges, as in the long-continued struggle between the plebeian and patrician classes in Rome; and, finally triumphant, secures for itself charters, and constitutions, and laws, guarding forever its liberties against all aggression, as in England.

One thing is noticeable in this brief outline of the history of civil government, — the entire absence of that most important feature of all free governments — the *representative principle* — in all the ancient systems, with the exception, perhaps, of the Hebrew; and even in that, the principle, if recognized, was not very clearly defined. The systems of Solon and of Lycurgus are ignorant of it. In Rome, it was the very thing wanting to secure the rights of the people, and put an end to the incessant conflicts of plebeian and patrician factions. It is only in the history of the English constitution that we find this great principle first distinctly brought forward, as the basis of just legislation.

Nor can I forbear to mention yet another thing, — the close resemblance, in many respects, between the ancient Hebrew Commonwealth and our own. The Institutes of Moses give us the first truly free and republican state, of which history retains any record. Ages passed away before another appeared worthy to be compared with that, — ages of conflict and turmoil, and manifold but too often futile experiments. Not from Athens, Rome, or Sparta, have we derived the essential principles of our constitution. The cradle of American liberty was rocked, not in ancient Greece, or sunny Italy, but in the deserts of Arabia, and at the frowning base of Horeb.

CHAPTER III.

DUTIES OF THE SUBJECT TO THE STATE.

We have already defined the state to be any community dwelling together, and organized for the purpose of civil government. We have found it, as an institution, closely analogous to, and probably originating in, the system of parental government in the family; we have seen it to be founded, immediately and primarily, on the consent of the governed, regarded as contracting parties, freely entering into and abiding by certain arrangements for the general good; mediately and ultimately, on the social nature of man, and so, on the will of God, as the author of that nature. The way is thus prepared for the consideration, in the present chapter, of the duties which this relation imposes upon the subject, or citizen, to the state of which he is a member, and the government under which he lives.

These duties are various; prominent among which may be named the duty to *respect* and *honor*, to *obey*, to *support*, and to *defend* the government whose protection he enjoys.

1. Respect.—It is incumbent on every citizen to *respect* and *honor* the state and its constituted authorities,—to treat with becoming deference its laws, its established forms and usages, its magistrates and officers, whether executive, legislative, or judiciary. It is only through these, its laws, its usages, its constituted authorities, that the state, as such, comes into practical relation to the citizen, as such. To honor these, is to honor the state; to dis-

honor these, is to cast contempt upon the whole institution and fabric of civil government.

These laws, forms, and constituted authorities, demand respect, as being in themselves the expression of the popular will, and the popular sovereignty. That will and sovereign power, find their material embodiment and expression in these forms, just as the thought, or feeling, that agitate and lie hidden in the breast, find their utterance and expression in the spoken word. The laws of the state, its established usages and institutions, its appointed officers, are to me the visible representation and the uttered voice of the state itself. I am bound to respect them, as I respect the majesty and collected wish and power of the whole people. If it is fit and proper that I should respect and honor any individual man, as such, and for what he is in himself, much more that I should honor the collective wisdom and dignity and worth of the whole nation,—that is, the constitution, laws, and officers, which represent and embody these.

Especially is this duty incumbent on those who live under a free and republican government. There is, if I mistake not, in the very nature of such institutions, that which makes it the special and imperative duty of their subjects to cherish towards them sentiments of respect. A free, and especially a republican government, is peculiarly exposed to danger, from the prevalence of erroneous views and sentiments among the people; peculiarly dependent on their respect, and earnest, honest attachment. In a monarchical, and especially a despotic government, there is comparatively little danger from this source. There are elements of power in such a government which can command, if not the love, at least the respect of the subjects. The pomp of royalty; the splendor of the throne; the power of military forces; the prestige of kingly birth and name; the associations of the past, and the visible majesty and strength of the present, — these all speak to the senses of the common mass, to the dullest understanding, and make themselves respected and feared.

In a republican state, these elements are wanting. There is no royalty; no splendor of court and throne; no ancestral honors; no regal dignity of birth and lineage; no standing army, to enforce obedience and command respect. The foundation of every *free* government is laid in the hearts of the people. The pillars of the republican state are the virtue, intelligence, and loyalty of her sons. She is strong only as they stand around her in their united strength — reverent, filial, and firm in her defence. When they become disaffected and disloyal, the state is in peril; when they withdraw their respect and confidence, it falls; — the fair fabric, reared with so much care, and treasure, and toil, — the goodly temple of liberty, — lies in ruins. No accumulation of physical resources can save it; no multiplied strength of numbers, and of sinewy arms, or of military weapons, can save it from such a fate, when once the respect and attachment of the people for their civil institutions is gone. The love of law and order, and of our own forms of government, as such, — this is our strength, our safety, our right arm of defence. A despotism, or limited monarchy, — almost any other form of government, — may continue to subsist without this element; a republic, never.

2. Obedience. — One of the first and most imperative duties of the citizen to the state of which he is a member, is to obey its just laws and requirements. Whatever reasons there are for the existence of the state, and of such a thing as civil government, be those reasons more or less numerous and weighty, the same, and with equal force, are to be urged in favor of obedience to that government,

within its just bounds. Not to obey, is virtually to annul, and abolish, both law, and the authority that makes law. Every citizen is bound to submit to the civil authority, then, because, in the first place, the public good requires it. Society cannot prosper, nor even long exist, without government. No community can dwell together in harmony without the recognized principle of law to regulate its movements, and balance its otherwise conflicting interests. As well dispense with gravitation in the physical world, and expect mountains and seas and all things to keep fast their places, as with law in the moral world, and expect human affairs to move on harmoniously and in order.

This is sufficiently attested by the experience of all times; by the fact that no community is known to exist on the face of the earth, entirely without any principle of law, or any form of government; by the universally observed truth, that in any community, just in proportion as the arm of state is inert and inefficient, crime prevails, injustice abounds, the best interests of the whole people suffer.

Additional Reason.—In every free government, the citizen is under an additional obligation to obey the laws and uphold the institutions of his country, from the fact that those laws and institutions are the expressed wish and choice of the whole people. This circumstance gives them additional authority. Every individual is under obligation to respect the wishes and the rights of the whole body, of which he is a member, and to submit to those rules and requisitions which the collective wisdom and will of the whole body have appointed. Nations may be independent of each other, to some extent; but not so with individuals dwelling together in the same community. But, suppose I am dissatisfied with existing arrangements: what is my remedy? I have the right, in that case, to do all I can, peaceably, to effect a change in those arrangements, and in the public opinion that sustains them. This is my undoubted privilege. But I have no right, simply because the existing laws and government do not suit my notions of what the laws and government should be, to cast off all allegiance, and refuse submission to them; for this is to say, the people shall not rule. When the voice of the millions, rising in majesty, is heard to say, "Let such things, such rules, such rulers be," it is not for the individual voice to say, "No, they shall not be." This is a principle, however, which applies only to such governments as are in reality the choice and will, expressed, or implied, of the people governed. When the laws and rulers are not of the people's making, but imposed upon them by arbitrary power, the duty of submission must turn upon other considerations.

I find, then, that my duty to my fellow-citizens, and my own, no less than the public good, require of me obedience to civil authority. It might be added that, inasmuch as I have enjoyed for a considerable time the inestimable advantages of civil society and a good government, I am bound in gratitude to do what I can to sustain and uphold the same, as but a reasonable return for favors received; and furthermore, that by living under this system, and taking some part, it may be, as a citizen, in its affairs, I have in a manner, tacitly, but virtually, pledged myself to such a course.

A Question. — But, here it may be asked, is the obedience of the subject to be unconditional and unqualified? is he to obey any and all laws and requirements, whatever they may be? This I cannot affirm. I have spoken of the duty of obedience only to such laws as are just and right; such as do not exceed the proper province and prerogative of the state; such as do not come clearly into conflict with that revealed will of God, which is above all human legislation, and to which alone we are ultimately accountable. Whatever enactment of human authority conflicts with this prior and supreme law, carries with it, at the bar of conscience, no power of obligation — becomes to every intelligent and devout mind, so soon as it is perceived to be contrary to the divine will, null and void. There can be no question on this point, which will not lead to practical atheism, to the deposing the Supreme Ruler from the throne of the universe, and placing thereon the merely human lawgiver and magistrate instead. When the state to which I hold allegiance so far forgets itself as to step beyond its proper province, and command what it has no right to command, my obligation ceases; when it goes further even than this, and commands what God has forbidden, its commands must be disregarded. In the former case, I may obey or not, as I please; in the latter, I have no *right* to obey: obedience becomes a sin.

Further Question. — But, it may still be asked, in what cases is resistance justifiable? Suppose the acts of government, though not, perhaps, specially in conflict with the divine commands, are, nevertheless, arbitrary and oppressive; the service required, the taxes levied, the disposal made of the public resources, the administration of justice, are all such as to occasion discontent among the people; a series of systematic encroachments is made upon the public rights, and the intention is evident to crush out the spirit of liberty from the nation, and establish despotism in place of free institutions; — suppose such a state of civil affairs to occur in any country, — a condition of things which, unfortunately, is of too frequent occurrence in the history of the world, — are the people, in such a case, under obligation still to yield obedience? I reply, that, according to the doctrine maintained in the previous chapter, government exists for the good of the governed: not the people for the king, the governor, the magistrate; but king, governor, magistrate, for the people: not society for the law, but the law for society. The end of law and government is the public welfare, — that, and that only. And when, in any case, the existing system no longer subserves this end; when the public good is not promoted, but hindered by it; when either the public freedom or the public virtue, or both, are in danger from the arm that is appointed to protect them, — then it may become not only the right, but the duty of the people, to resist the power that proves itself false and recreant to its trust, and to effect a change of government.

The right to such resistance and change becomes still more apparent, if we adopt the view, maintained in the previous chapter, that government is, in its essential nature, a species of contract between the different members of the body politic. If this be so, then surely, when, by any dishonesty or negligence of any of the parties to this engagement, the essential terms and conditions of the contract are violated, and the end which it was designed to accomplish is no longer secured, they who make the contract have the right to unmake it, or change it as they like.

Objection. — It may be said, this leaves too wide a door for faction and revolution to come in, encourages discontent, and endangers the stability of all government. Dr. Paley has urged this objection as of force against the theory of social compact; he regards that theory of the nature of government as leading, in this way, to dangerous conclusions. That the principle now stated is one liable to abuse, must be confessed; but what principle, it may be replied, that we could substitute in its place, would be less so. Shall we, then, deny to the people the right, under any circumstances, of resistance and of revolution? Shall we say it is *always* the duty of the subject to submit to government, no matter how oppressive and tyrannical, how unjust, or even how impious? Does the mere fact that a corrupt and tyrannical government exists, give it the right always to exist?

This will hardly be maintained, even by the most conservative theorist. Indeed, Dr. Paley himself, when he comes to consider the practical question of the right of resistance, goes quite as far as the most earnest advocate of popular rights would care to go in this direction. Regarding government, as he does, to be purely a matter of expediency, and not of the nature of a social contract, the justice of every particular case of resistance, he affirms, "is reduced to a computation of the quantity of the danger and grievance on the one side, and of the probability and expense of redressing it on the other."

"But who shall judge of this?" he continues. "We answer, '*Every man for himself.*' In contentions between the sovereign and the subject, the parties acknowledge no common arbitrator; and it would be absurd to refer the decision to *those*, whose conduct has provoked the question, and whose own interest, authority, and fate, are immediately concerned in it."

Indeed, Dr. Paley claims it as a special advantage of the doctrine of expediency over that of all implied compacts and covenants, of whatsoever sort, that it furnishes an easy answer to the question, under what circumstances resistance and revolution are allowable. He states the following, among other inferences from that doctrine, bearing upon the present question: "*It may be as much a duty, at one time, to resist government, as it is, at another, to obey it;* to wit, whenever more advantage will, in our opinion, accrue to the community from resistance, than mischief."

"The lawfulness of resistance, or the lawfulness of a revolt, does not depend alone upon the grievance which is sustained or feared, but also upon the probable expense and event of the contest."

And again: "No usage, law, or authority whatever, is so binding, that it need or ought to be continued, when it may be changed with advantage to the community."

This is surely sufficiently explicit, and sufficiently revolutionary. It is difficult to see how the doctrine of a social compact could lead to results more thoroughgoing, and more radical, than these. With the general doctrine here advanced, that resistance is, at times, a duty, I fully agree; and also that it must be left with the people to decide when the proper time has come for such resistance. But that, in deciding this important point, we have only, or chiefly, to take into account the expense, and the probable issue of the contest, as weighed against the amount of grievance, admits of question. There may be other and more important considerations, as it seems to me, than even these; and I can conceive of cases, not of improbable occurrence, in which resistance would be the duty of the people, or the citizen, against the most powerful odds, and with but the slightest prospect of success.

The Rule and the Exception. — It must be borne in mind, however, in all discussions of this subject, that the general duty of the subject is *obedience*, not *resistance*; that the latter is the exception, the former the rule; and that, while cases may occur which shall render the exception justifiable, a steady adherence to the rule is, under ordinary circumstances, the only wise and safe course. There is certainly more danger, at least in any free and intelligent community, that the people, jealous of their rights, and forgetful of their obligations, will be lacking in the duty of obedience to constituted authority, than that they will be wanting in the spirit of manly resistance to unjust and arbitrary rule. The tendency, it must be confessed, in our own country, at the present time, is rather to a want than to an excess of reverence for and loyalty to established institutions and forms of government, and especially for that which is the foundation of all, the *constitution.*

Obedience enjoined in Scripture.—The word of God is very explicit on this point. We are directed to submit ourselves "to every ordinance of man for the Lord's sake; whether it be to the king, as supreme, or unto governors, as unto them that are sent by him for the punishment of evil-doers, and for the praise of them that do well. For so is the will of God," etc. (1 Peter ii. 13—15). And still more explicitly: "Let every soul be subject unto the higher powers. For there is no power but of God: the powers that be are ordained of God. Whosoever, therefore, resisteth the power, resisteth the ordinance of God; and they that resist shall receive to themselves damnation. For rulers are not a terror to good works, but to the evil. Wilt thou then not be afraid of the power? do that which is good, and thou shalt have praise of the same; for he is the minister of God to thee for good. But if thou do that which is evil, be afraid; for he beareth not the sword in vain; for he is the minister of God, a revenger to execute wrath upon him that doeth evil. Wherefore, ye must needs be subject not only for wrath, but also for conscience' sake. For, for this cause, pay you tribute also; for they are God's ministers, attending continually upon this very thing. Render, therefore, to all their dues, — tribute to whom tribute is due, custom to whom custom, fear to whom fear, honor to whom honor" (Rom. xiii. 1—7).

These passages might seem, at first sight, to teach the doctrine of unlimited and passive obedience. Such, I think, cannot be the intention of the sacred writers; but rather, as Paley justly remarks, to set forth the *duty* of obedience to civil government, without describing the *extent* of it.

They place before the Christian disciple the duty of submission and obedience, not to this or that particular form of government, but to the established authority of the land in which he dwells. They inculcate this duty in the same way, and on the same ground, as the duty of obedidience to parental authority in the family. It was no part of the object of the writers, in these passages, to point out exceptions, but only to enforce the rule. We are not to infer from this, however, that in all cases whatsoever obedience is a duty, and resistance a sin. In the words of an able, but cautious and conservative writer, —Whewell, — "These passages do not at all show that in any state it may not be the duty of *the powers that be* to alter the laws, to appoint new magistrates, new magistracies, and the like; and allowable in extreme cases, in cases of necessity, to alter the constitution of the country, or to depose the sovereign."

3. Support and Defence. — To obey, is not the whole duty of the citizen. The civil authority is to be maintained by needful supplies, and, if need be, defended against foreign aggression. To this end, taxes may justly be levied, whether directly, or in the shape of duties imposed on articles of commerce; and to all such regulations looking to the necessary fiscal revenues of the gov-

ernment, the citizen ought willingly to submit. The state cannot exist for any length of time, nor the affairs of government be administered, without resources. In some form, its expenses must be provided for by the citizens; and in whatever mode this may be done, it is the duty of every man to bear his fair proportion of the expense. Evasion of the laws which regulate this matter, is as really dishonorable, and immoral, as evasion of any laws respecting property. To cheat the government, is as really a fraud as to cheat a private person. It is even a greater dishonesty, and a more serious crime, inasmuch as the rights of the state are of more dignity and importance than those of the individual. When my dishonesty goes no further than to take the property of my neighbor, I defraud one man only; when it extends to the property of government, I defraud the whole community. Tribute to whom tribute is due, is the rule of the sacred Scriptures. We are to render unto Cæsar the things that are Cæsar's, no less than to God the things that are God's.

Not less is it the duty of the citizen to *defend* the state, if need be, from personal violence. In repelling aggression from without, or sustaining, by personal service, civil or military, the authority of government against sedition and rebellion, — against lawlessness and anarchy within its own borders, — the aid of the citizen may be necessary. The good and true citizen, who understands well what he owes to himself, and to society, will never hesitate in such an emergency. At the call of his country, in defence of law and justice, in defence of the state to which he owes allegiance, he will be ready to sacrifice, if need be, all personal considerations of ease, safety, or profit, and lay upon the altar of freedom and of the right, himself and whatever he has.

CHAPTER IV.

DUTIES OF THE STATE TO ITS SUBJECTS.

It is to be borne in mind that the state, as already defined, is simply a society or community, dwelling together in the same territory, and organized for purposes of government. When we inquire, then, for the duties of the state to its subjects, we are simply inquiring what duties the whole society, or the aggregate of individuals, as thus organized, owes to each of its members. To this, a plain and obviously correct reply, comprehensive of all, is this: *It is the duty of the state to protect every one of its subjects in all his proper rights;* in other words, to do what it virtually engages and promises to do, by the terms of its constitution, or social compact.

The question, What *are* the proper rights of the subject? may admit of various opinions. They may be more or less expressly guaranteed to him in the laws and constitution of his country; and in different states these may vary. There can be no question, however, as to the general position that it is the duty of the state to carry out and fulfill the specific objects for which it was created. *Whatever is necessary to secure the great ends for which it exists,— whatever is necessary for the highest good of all,* — this it has the right to do, and ought to do. This is a duty which it owes to the whole, and to each individual.

General Sphere of State Authority. — Within the limits now specified, the authority of the state is complete and supreme. So far as the constitution allows, and the public good requires, it may coerce, restrain, and punish; may impose taxes; regulate the tenure and transmission of property; promote industry, education, religion; declare war; personally, it may, in all suitable ways, secure to each citizen the enjoyment of the highest freedom consistent with the freedom and rights of others. These, in general, are its rights and duties.

Beyond the limits now indicated, the state is out of its proper sphere. It has to do with its subjects, not as men, but as citizens. Its end and aim, as a state, are single, — that is, to secure the liberty and the rights of all its members. It is wholly a political organization. With the intellectual elevation and culture, the moral character, the religious opinions, the personal prosperity and happiness of its subjects, — except so far as these are related to the one specific end, the civil liberty and rights of the whole, — it has no direct concern. It desires and promotes all these things, not as ends, but only as means to an end. As such, they come properly within its cognizance, and are of the highest moment in its councils and consideration.

Even within these limits the state has no right to demand impossibilities; nor yet, in securing its object, to legislate against the principles of moral right, or against the known will of God. When it oversteps, or comes into collision with these immutable and eternal principles, its authority ceases, its sceptre is broken — the sword is stricken from its hand, and the crown from its brow.

We shall obtain a clearer and more definite view of the proper duties of the state with respect to its own rights, if we consider specifically some of the more important objects which fall directly, or indirectly, within its sphere of action, — among which may be included right of taxation; prohibitory laws; personal freedom of thought, speech, and action; prevention and punishment of crime; promotion of industry, in its various branches; education, and religion.

1. Taxes. — It is the duty of the state to sustain itself,

and to take whatever measures are necessary in order to this. For this purpose, it has the right to impose taxes and imposts, so far as may be necessary for its own support. The *manner* in which its revenues shall be raised, whether by direct tax, or by a system of duties on exports, or on imports, or in any other mode, and also the *amount* of revenue that shall be thus granted, are matters which may be safely left to the wisdom and discretion of each state to determine for itself. In no case, however, has the state a right to levy taxes that are oppressive and severe, or to distribute the burden of them unequally and unjustly upon any class or portion of the community. The tax ought, moreover, to be strictly for *public*, and not for private ends; and the persons thus taxed have the right to be in some way represented in the state. In the case of non-residents, or foreigners, and also of widows, and unmarried women possessing property within the state, the tax may perhaps be justly required, without such representation, on the ground of a fair equivalent for the protection of the property.

2. Prohibitory Laws.—It is the duty of the state to prohibit and prevent whatever is injurious to the public welfare, whether directly, as affecting the civil rights and liberties, or indirectly, as affecting the health, morals, or lives of the community. Its office is to guard all these interests and rights against encroachment; and in order to this, it must, if needful, enact and enforce laws prohibitory and sanitary. No member of society has a right to pursue any calling or profession, or make any use of his property, that shall put in jeopardy the safety, the property, the lives, of others. Neither his property, nor even his life, is his own in any such sense as that; and when, disregarding the rights and interests of others, he persists in that which is

to the common injury, the state, through its proper officers, may and ought to restrain him. This extends to all branches of manufacture and of trade that may be of hurtful tendency; to gaming-houses, and all establishments of vice and dissipation; to immoral publications; to whatever is injurious to public peace and virtue — to the health, happiness, and freedom of society. It embraces, also, such laws and regulations as may be for the health and safety of town or city in time of pestilence or prevailing disease. All these are matters of the highest importance to the public good, and they are of such a nature as to require the attention and energy of the public authorities. Merely private effort cannot accomplish, in most cases, the end that is desired. Even if individuals of sufficient benevolence and wisdom could be found to undertake such measures, private interests would almost inevitably come into collision with any plans they might adopt. The strong arm and authority of the state are necessary in all such undertakings.

3. *Personal Freedom.* — The state ought to leave the individual free to do anything not inconsistent with the general good. It ought not only to abstain in its own transactions from whatever would interfere with this freedom of the citizen, but it ought to secure to him this freedom, and protect him in it, so far as regards his relation to other persons. It has no right to deprive him, or to allow him to be deprived by others, of personal liberty, unless for crime, or insanity, or the like cause, which would render his going at large dangerous to the community.

On the same principle, it ought not to deprive him of the privilege of laboring at whatever honest employment or profession he chooses; nor to throw obstacles in the way of his changing his trade or profession, if he is disposed to try some other. These are matters which should be left open to the choice of the citizen, and with which government has no right to interfere.

Nor has the state a right to prevent the citizen from changing his place of residence, or even to throw obstacles in the way of his leaving the country altogether, and migrating to some other land, if he sees fit. This power is exercised by many of the arbitrary governments of the Old World, but it is a despotic and unjust power. The state has no right to say to its subjects, "You must live here, and not elsewhere."

The law of personal liberty applies also to freedom of speech, and of the press. These are undoubted rights of the citizen within the limits already indicated. I have no right, indeed, to say or to publish that which will be to the injury of others, in respect to business, social standing, or moral character; and whatever of this sort one is disposed to utter, or to print, that shall tend to the public detriment, it is the duty of the civil authority to forbid and prevent the same. Aside from this necessary restriction, it is the duty of the state to ensure and maintain the utmost liberty of thought, speech, and action, to its subjects.

4. Encouragement of Industry. — It is the duty of the state to foster and encourage every branch of honest industry. Much may be done by the public authority to this end. Agriculture, commerce, manufactures, the mechanic and the liberal arts, — every pursuit, indeed, in which men engage, may be materially aided, or seriously embarrassed, by the action of government. Wise or unwise legislation has much to do with the prosperity of the country in all branches of industry. It is the duty of government, by all suitable and proper methods, to encourage and aid every industrial pursuit which is not clearly incompatible

with the public welfare. It should, at least, throw no obstacles in the way of an honest calling. It ought to administer its affairs with impartial and even-handed justice, toward all sections of the country, and all the various pursuits and conflicting interests of the same, favoring no one at the expense of the others; but, by wise and impartial legislation, extending, so far as possible, to all, the utmost facilities and encouragements. It should never interfere with private enterprise, nor seek to turn the trade and industry of the country in any other than the natural channels, for political or party purposes. In all such measures and attempts, it is clearly out of its proper sphere.

There are, moreover, certain great public improvements, which cannot well be carried on by individual enterprise, and which, therefore, require the aid of government. Harbors may be improved, light-houses constructed, rivers rendered navigable, and various works of great public benefit be set on foot, which would be either too arduous, or two little remunerative, for private capital and enterprise to undertake. It is maintained, however, by many, and apparently with justice, that in no case ought works of this character to be undertaken by the state, where private or corporate action is available; inasmuch as the public resources may be more profitably employed in other ways; and inasmuch, also, as these very enterprises, when not too arduous to be undertaken by private capitalists, will be much more economically managed by individual enterprise than by the state.

5. Prevention and Punishment of Crime. — This is one of the most important duties devolving upon the state. Whether we regard civil government as founded in expediency, or the divine will, or in social compact, or

as resting on all these combined, in either case there rests upon it, as a first and most imperative obligation, the duty of protecting its subjects against the lawlessness and violence that would otherwise endanger person, property, and life. This is one of the chief objects to be secured by the institution of civil government — one of the chief ends for which it exists. For this purpose laws are enacted, specifying and forbidding all violation of the rights of others. Whatever is thus forbidden, becomes, in the eye of the law, a crime. But law without sanctions or penalties annexed, is no law, but only counsel, and more or less plausible advice. It becomes law only when, in addition to the precept, there is affixed a penalty for transgression. And the value of the law depends mainly on two things, — its inherent rightness or justice as precept or prohibition, and also the firmness and certainty with which its sanctions are enforced. If either of these conditions fail, it becomes a virtual nullity.

To call in question, then, the right of government to punish crime, is virtually to call in question its right to exist. Take away this, and society relapses into barbarism — every man taking the defence of his rights into his own hand.

But, aside from the general view now presented, there are two or three points requiring more particular consideration, such as the proper *end* of punishment, its proper *mode* and *degree of severity*, and the *amount of evidence* necessary to convict of crime.

End of Punishment. — And first, as to the proper end of human punishment. What is the object in view, in the infliction of punishment for crime? Is it the satisfaction of justice, which demands the punishment of the offender as, in some sense, a compensation for the crime?

Or, is it disciplinary, aiming at the reformation of the offender? Or, is it simply with a view to prevent future offences, by impressing the public mind with a just and salutary fear of the consequences of evil-doing? Here are three different explanations, or theories, of the proper end of human punishment; the first makes it *retributive*, the second *reformatory*, the third *preventive*.

At the hands of a strictly righteous God, guilt is expected to receive, and justice demands that it should receive, punishment; and the penalty must be in proportion to the guilt. Such penalty, or suffering inflicted on account of guilt, is termed retributive.

It is not, however, on this principle that human governments proceed. The object of society, in the infliction of punishment, is not to satisfy the abstract demands of justice; nor yet is it to vindicate the injured sovereignty of the law; nor to make amends for the mischief done,—for that is often irreparable, and the punishment of the offender has no tendency to make good the injury already committed. Punishment then, as inflicted by human governments, is not in its nature *retributive*.

Much less is it reformative in its character and design The end for which punishment is inflicted is not the repentance and reformation of the criminal, however desirable that may be. It is not for this purpose that government exists. It has a higher end than the discipline of individuals. There are other influences and institutions that look to that, and exist for that. Government has to do, not with the reformation and moral culture of the individual, but with the public welfare, and the public freedom; and these may often require that the benefit of the individual who has committed the crime should be disregarded, for the sake of the public benefit. Imprisonment, confiscation of property, or death, may be of no benefit personally to him, but quite the reverse; that is not the question; there are higher ends and interests to be promoted, than his own good. Were it otherwise, the more hardened and depraved the criminal, the less reason for his punishment, since the less prospect of his reformation. On this principle, moreover, our prisons and penitentiaries, our courts of justice, and all the machinery of government, are but so many benevolent and charitable institutions, and are to be ranked in the same category with sabbath schools and missionary operations. This is certainly a very inadequate idea of the nature of civil government, and of the object of legal sanctions. Punishment is not reformative.

The simple reason why society inflicts punishment on those who disturb its peace, is, that it finds it necessary to do so for its own safety, in the prevention of crime. It *inflicts penalty* upon the evil-doer, because it has *threatened* to do so. It *threatens* penalty, because, without such declaration, *law* would be inoperative and null. It makes *law*, because, without it, there were no government, and no such thing as society. If there be government at all, there must be law; if law, there must be legal sanctions; and if sanctions, then they must be rigidly enforced. The same reasons, then, which make civil government a necessity, make punishment a necessity, — *i. e.*, the safety of the community, and the prevention of crime.

Not only is the criminal himself, or he who is already disposed to transgress, deterred from so doing by the certainty that, if detected, he will suffer the inevitable penalty and just desert of his offences, but by every example of this sort a salutary fear is awakened in other minds, by perceiving the ruinous consequences of a course of crime. By all such influences is society the gainer; nor is it possible to dispense with these influences, and still conserve the peace and welfare of society.

Mode and Degree of Punishment. — The end for which punishment is inflicted goes far to determine the proper mode and degree of its infliction. If the guilt of the offender be the motive for punishment, or the satisfaction of justice the end in view, then the punishment should be, of course, in proportion to the guilt. The simple inquiry that should regulate the whole proceeding should be: what, and how much, does the criminal *deserve* to suffer. And this might seem to be the just and true mode of procedure. A little observation, however, will be sufficient to convince any one that such is not the principle on which civil government administers its penal sanctions. The most guilty, and those most deserving of punishment, are not always most severely punished. Reference is had, not so much to the degree of guilt in the offender, as to the nature of the offence, the danger of its repetition, the difficulty of detecting and of preventing it, and the like circumstances. The man who betrays a solemn trust confided to him, or who habitually exercises unkindness and severity in his family government, or who refuses an act of benevolence, to save human life, or to relieve human suffering, may be really more guilty, or more deserving of punishment, so far as strict justice is concerned, than he who counterfeits a bank note, or steals to satisfy the cravings of hunger. But for the former, law has no penalty; for the latter, a severe one.

The *facility* with which any crime may be committed, and the consequent difficulty, and at the same time necessity, of preventing it, are the considerations chiefly in view in the regulation and distribution of punishment. The end of human government, of law, and of penal sanctions being one and the same, — *i. e.*, the protection of the community, and the prevention of crime, — whatever tends most directly to this end, is the measure most likely to be adopted, and that rightly. If the end can be accomplished, that is, the crime prevented and society protected, by some other means than by the punishment of the offender, then punishment may be dispensed with, notwithstanding the guilt and ill-desert of the offender in a moral point of view. If the offence be one liable to occur at any time, difficult of detection and of proof, and yet of great mischief to society, punishment becomes necessary as a means of prevention; and the punishment must be more or less severe, according as more or less may be required in order to effect this end. Thus, by the laws of some countries, the stealing of a sheep, or a horse, is punished with death — not because these crimes are considered as involving equal guilt with that of murder, but because, on account of the ease with which these and the like offences can be committed and concealed, nothing short of the severest penalties seemed sufficient to deter the evil-minded from their commission. This disproportion between the degree of punishment and the degree of ill-desert, is, perhaps, a necessary part of the imperfection of all human governments. The supreme and omniscient Ruler and Judge, whose eye penetrates the darkest recesses of guilt, from whose vigilance nothing can escape, and whose justice will bring to certain punishment whatever crime is committed, may, and will, doubtless, graduate that punishment according to the real guilt of the criminal. But no human government can do this.

Frequency of Punishment. — As to the frequency with which the severest punishments — as, for example, capital punishment, or imprisonment for life, at hard labor or in solitude — should be employed, there is room for question. It is a matter of expediency, and must be determined by careful observation. Beyond doubt, the severest penalties are fully within the power of civil government, and may be justly and rightly called into requisition, whenever they are necessary for the true purposes of government, — that is, for the safety and welfare of the state. The laws of many countries — of England, for example — seem to me to have erred, by the too frequent use of the severest penalties; on the other hand, our own may not improbably have erred in the other extreme. In the words of Dr. Hickok: "Life itself is not so sacred as that for which life is given; and if the opportunity to attain the ends of human life cannot be maintained but by the infliction of death upon such as disturb it, the state is bound, by its mission to humanity, to inflict that extreme penalty. If the state refuse to do this when the public sentiment demands it, the populace, in its frenzy, under the excitement of some fresh deed of cruelty and blood, will take the work into its own hands, and summarily despatch the obnoxious malefactor. It may be argued that summary punishments tend to make the people barbarous; but, in the one crime of murder, it is a more important and probable opinion that a disuse of capital punishment will directly tend to demoralize the public. The conviction that the murderer deserves to die, must be met by the civil sanction, or the very teachings and influence of the law will be to lower the standard of pure morality, and deprave the public sentiment, by making the life of man less sacred in the statute-book than it is in the natural conscience."

Evidence Necessary to Conviction. — It becomes a serious, and often a difficult question, what amount of evidence is requisite to conviction. On the one hand, there is the danger that, by the mistake or dishonesty of the witness, or the prejudice of the juror, the innocent may be punished in place of the guilty; on the other hand, the equal, or even greater danger, that, by some flaw in the evidence, or some artifice of the pleader, the criminal, of whose guilt there can be no reasonable doubt in the mind of judge or jury, shall be turned loose upon society, and thus the real power and proper office of justice be thwarted.

It is ever to be borne in mind, that the prevention of crime depends not so much on the *severity*, as on the *certainty* of punishment. The laws of England, for example, which prescribe the penalty of death for a great number of offences, but actually inflict it on but a small portion of the number, seem but poorly calculated for the prevention of crime, inasmuch as the criminal presumes, in the first place, — in common with most of those who meditate any violation of the laws, — that he shall not be detected; and then, that, if detected, the extreme penalty will in his case be remitted, as it has already been in so many others, and some milder punishment substituted in its place. Were that milder penalty threatened in the first instance, and then invariably executed, the certainty of the result would probably be more effective than the present uncertainty of a much more severe infliction.

Now, nothing tends so directly to destroy all certainty of punishment, as any difficulty attending the conviction of the guilty. Whatever stands in the way of the conviction of the criminal, stands in the way of his punishment. If such an amount of evidence is required, in order to conviction, as shall in most cases be impossible, or next to impossible, to procure, the effect is the same as if the law, with its penalties, were blotted from the statute-book, and society left unprotected against crime.

Viewed in this aspect, it admits of serious question, whether, in our anxiety to avoid the infliction of unjust punishment, we have not, in this country, carried to a dangerous extreme the doctrine that the accused is entitled to the benefit of any and every reasonable doubt of his guilt.

There are very few, if indeed there are any cases, probably, in which the proof of guilt is so clear, and perfectly conclusive, as to leave no room for doubt in the mind of any one; and yet, if any one of twelve men entertains such doubt, however slight and unfounded it may be in reality, conviction becomes impossible. Even in the case of positive testimony, setting aside all circumstantial evidence, as being still more open to objection, there will always be more or less possibility of mistake, and even of dishonesty, on the part of the witness. Circumstances are, in fact, often the best and most reliable witnesses. But neither circumstantial, nor yet positive testimony, can, in most cases, be wholly beyond doubt; and it is in the power of a skillful pleader, — more anxious to save his client than to secure the ends of justice, — by giving prominence to any slight defect in the chain of evidence, and by appealing to the conscientious scruples of the jury, and representing in the strongest light the painful responsibility they will incur, if, by any mistake, they *should* convict and condemn an innocent man, — it is in the power of a skillful advocate to so play in this manner upon the fears and the scruples of his hearers, as to secure the acquittal of those most deserving of punishment, and of whose guilt there can be really no reasonable doubt. Just in proportion as this takes place, the security of life and property, and whatever else is valuable in the community, is destroyed, and society is thrown back into a state of lawlessness and barbarism.

But, is it not better that nine guilty men should escape,

than that one innocent man should suffer? Of this I am not so sure. Better for the guilty, very possibly, it may be; whether it is better for *society*, admits of serious question. It may be better that now and then an innocent man suffer, than that the guilty should generally go unpunished. The question amounts virtually to this: whether, as respects the greatest crimes, it is better to have any law, and any penalty, or to leave society to take care of itself, in the best way it can, without any such safeguards.

6. Education. — What is the duty of the state as regards the *education* of its subjects? We have already seen that the state, as such, is directly concerned only with the civil rights and privileges of the subject, and not with his intellectual, moral, or religious character; and that it has to do with these latter only in so far as they may bear upon the former, by making the man a better citizen and a better subject. So intimate, however, and so important is this connection, that it can be by no means overlooked. It is impossible that the state should reach its highest point of prosperity, should realize the true idea of a free and noble state, without intelligence and virtue in the community. In proportion to the education and general intelligence of the people, in connection with their moral and religious culture, will be the amount of liberty enjoyed; because in this proportion will be their ability to understand, and their disposition to maintain, their rights. Neither an ignorant people, nor yet an irreligious people, are competent for self-government. Hence the importance to the state of the general diffusion of knowledge among the people, and of some system of education looking to this end. It is almost a necessity of its own existence, that some system of this kind should be in successful operation.

Hence the right and duty of the state to take measures for this purpose.

But why, it may be asked, should the state trouble itself in this matter? Why may not the business of education be safely left to the voluntary action of the people, in their several communities? This might well be, I reply, in case there were already given a people of so much education and general intelligence as to feel the importance of such action; but this is more than can, in most cases, be safely presumed. When education has already done its work in the elevation of the community, it may be safely left to such a community to provide for the intellectual culture and training of those who come after them. But it is for the state to set in operation the causes which shall produce this result; nor ought the state, under any circumstances, to relinquish all care and control of a matter so intimately connected with its own permanence, and highest prosperity.

Different Methods of Accomplishing this. — The manner in which this object can best be accomplished, will vary, doubtless, in different states, and, to some extent, in the same state, in different stages of its progress. In all cases it should be a systematic and thorough, rather than any desultory and superficial system of measures. Means should be provided for the education, and the thorough education, of all classes of the community — the poor, as well as the rich — in at least the common and most indispensable branches of learning. In addition to this, colleges, and other institutions of a higher grade, should be encouraged, and, if necessary, supported for a time, by the state.

In order to provide and put in operation such a system of general education, the state has the right to expend the public money, or to levy a direct tax for the purpose on those who are to receive the benefit, or to make it obligatory on each separate community to provide for itself the requisite means for sustaining the needed schools within its limits; and whichever mode be adopted, the public has no right to complain, or to refuse consent and hearty coöperation. The state has the right, also, to at least a general supervision and control of the whole educational movement, and of each institution or school founded under its care and patronage; it is entitled to a voice in the selection of teachers, and of books, and in the general management and course of instruction. It has also the right to require attendance upon the means provided, when, from the ignorance or prejudice of the community, or from any other cause, the advantages thus offered are not likely to be improved.

Possible Disagreement. — In thus regulating the order and course of instruction of its schools, the state may find itself sometimes in collision with individual opinions, and prejudices, in matters of religious belief. One man, of peculiar views, may object to the recognition of the Divine Being in the ordinary devotional exercises of the school, or in any of its teachings; another, to the use of the sacred Scriptures in any form; another still, to the Protestant version of the same. In the solution of all such difficulties, but one rule can be recognized. The *state*, — that is, the body of the people, — acting through its constituted authorities, has the right to decide all such matters. If the state be Infidel, it has the right to exclude all religious teachings, and all reference to the Supreme Being, from its schools; if it be Catholic, it may shape its educational system accordingly; if Jewish or Mohammedan, it has still the same right; if it be none of these, but Protestant, it has the right to use Protestant forms, and Protestant books, and inculcate, so far as it chooses, Protestant notions, in its various educational establishments. It is the duty of the individual, in such cases, to yield to the will of the majority; or if he cannot conscientiously fall in with the prescribed order, and with the customs of those around him, in such matters, he should peaceably withdraw from all participation in the system; and this he should always be allowed to do. But nothing is more absurd, or contradictory to the whole spirit and theory of civil government, than that a small minority, often a mere handful in the state, should undertake to dictate to the whole people in such matters; and no state that has a proper regard for its own dignity, or any just conception of its rights and duties, will for a moment allow any such interference with its own proper prerogative.

7. Religion. — The duty of the state with respect to the moral and religious condition of its subjects, is a matter of much moment, and of some considerable difficulty. Man is not only a political, but also a religious being; that is, he has a moral nature, as well as a social and political one; has hopes, and fears, and motives of action, drawn from this source; and these are often the strongest and most active principles of his nature. A man entirely uninfluenced by religious considerations is a man who does violence to his own nature, or else that nature is entirely and sadly perverted.

In what relation, now, shall government stand to its subjects in this matter? How shall it treat their religious convictions and beliefs? What position shall it assume with respect to the moral and religious character, the moral and religious education and training, of those who compose the state? Shall it show itself quite indifferent to the whole matter; or shall it go further, and oppose all religious institutions, and religious culture; or, knowing how intimately its own stability and prosperity depend on the religious character and culture of the people, shall it set itself directly about the business of promoting these, by establishing religious institutions, and teaching religious truths, even as it provides for the intellectual education of its subjects? These are questions of serious moment, and not altogether easy of solution.

The matter is still further complicated by the fact that there is frequently a great diversity of religious opinion and belief among the people. If there were but one prevailing religious system, and the great body of the people were united in that form or communion, it would greatly facilitate the decision of the question before us. As it is, the community — divided into many different and often rival religious sects — with which of all these, if with any, shall the state ally itself? or how can it exert that influence which it may wish to exert in religious matters? how can it, as a state, possess any religious character whatever, and not ally itself with some particular form and system, with some one church or sect?

Different Courses possible. — Evidently there are three different courses of procedure possible to the state in this matter; — that of entire indifference, or even opposition, to all religious culture; that of a fair and impartial protection of all religious sects and systems, without the adoption of any; and, finally, the selection and establishment of some one as the state religion. Each of these methods of procedure may claim some advantages; each, on the other hand, is liable to objections.

And *first*, shall the state proclaim itself *indifferent* to all religious things, systems, and sects — all effort for the moral and religious education of the people? Shall it ignore all these matters, suffering them to exist, but taking no cognizance of them — even as it knows nothing of the private and personal affairs of its citizens, their occupation and profession, their prosperity and failure in business, their social and domestic affairs, with all which, and a thousand like matters, it has, as a state, nothing whatever to do?

It is not possible, I reply, for the state to be entirely indifferent to this whole matter. It is of some consequence to it, whether its subjects have any religious belief, and religious character, or not; whether they are educated in the knowledge of the highest and most important of all truths, or are wholly ignorant of them; whether they believe in, and worship, Mohammed, Brahma, or Jehovah, or are without any belief, and any God. It cannot afford to be wholly indifferent to, and ignorant of, such matters as these. Shall it provide for the intellectual education of its people, and care nothing for their moral and religious culture? Has the latter less to do than the former with the vital prosperity of the civil institutions — with the very foundations of their permanence and their strength?

Nor can the state be itself wholly without a religion. Its own highest ends cannot be secured without direct appeal to the religious sentiment, and the moral nature of man. It must acknowledge a personal God, a future state, and retribution hereafter for the sins of this life, or it cannot even administer an oath. It must, by its public acts, recognize this God as a proper object of worship; authorize such homage as is suitable to him on special occasions; and honor, in its official capacity, the sacred days, and sacred writings. "No civil government," it has been well said, "can stand in the neglect of all religion, and no community can maintain its freedom without a government thus, in some way, acknowledging a religion."

It is of the highest consequence, moreover, that the religion which the state recognizes should be the true one; since, although a false religion may be better than none, the true one is better than either.

The state cannot, then, be indifferent to the religion of its citizens, nor wholly without a religion of its own.

The Second Method. — Shall it, then, adopt the *second* course? Placed under a necessity of recognizing some religion, and anxious that its subjects should coöperate with it, in giving to the sanctions and sentiments of a pure faith their full force on the públic mind and conscience, shall it set itself, by direct means, to propagate religious truth, by establishing, or taking under its special patronage, some one form of religious belief and worship, making that the state religion and the state church, and seeking to educate the people in it, and through it, as a means of religious culture? Such a course might seem to promise some advantages. It will give definiteness to the religious sentiment and action of the state. It will enable the state to avail itself directly of the offices of the ministers of religion, in any way that it sees fit, as important ends in accomplishing its purposes. It can shape to its own liking the moral and religious education of the people, and secure a higher degree of general religious culture. It can, in a word, control, to a greater extent than before, and that in various ways, the religious element in society.

But then, again, is there no danger from this very source? Is it safe to place in the hands of the civil authority the control of the religious element in society; thus making the church, the clergy, the system of religious education, and the public conscience, subservient to the designs of the state, — so many tools, by which it can better accomplish its purposes? Is there no danger that such power will be abused?

As a matter of fact, such an arrangement will be likely

to lead to one or the other of two results, — either the religious organization will become the dominant power in the state, and freedom will suffer; or the civil authority will predominate, and the religious element become the mere instrument of its policy. In the one case, we shall have a people subjected to priestly dictation, — the worst and most oppressive, because most bigoted, of all forms of tyranny, — in the other case, a religion subject to the state, and thereby shorn of its inherent strength and beauty. The history of religious establishments in all ages verifies this supposition. We have, on the one hand, the Romish Church, binding in chains the human conscience and the human will wherever it can obtain ascendency, and crushing all freedom of thought under the iron heel of an irresponsible hierarchy; on the other hand, the religious establishments of Europe, whether Protestant or Catholic, supported by the state, the creatures of the civil power, and losing, in proportion as they become so, their hold upon the minds and hearts of the great mass of the people.

Further Objection. — A further difficulty arises, also, from the fact that, whatever religion the state may adopt, there will always be, in the state, many who will not sympathize with that peculiar form or system, but conscientiously prefer some other, and who will therefore find themselves arrayed against the state, in the most sacred and imperative of all obligations. All, of whatever belief, and whatever organization or sect, who do not happen to belong to that one church which the state has recognized, find themselves in the position of dissenters; and these, though each sect may be small in itself, may be in the aggregate the superior number, the great body, indeed, of the people, as regards both numbers and moral wealth and force; — but whether so or not, equally entitled to their own religious convictions, and religious forms and privileges, and to the respect and support of the state in the use and enjoyment of the same, as those from whom, in these matters, they are compelled to differ. Under such circumstances, the patronage of one body by the state is injustice to all the rest.

By every such instance of honest, conscientious dissent from the established religion of the state, is the moral power of the establishment weakened. Instead of commanding the sympathy and cordial coöperation of all the religious and well-disposed members of society, in its efforts for the moral elevation of the people, and the dissemination of sacred truth, the state, however sincere and earnest in such efforts, finds itself working at an immense disadvantage, as a rival among opposing sects. And the difficulty will not be diminished, but very greatly increased, if, forgetful of its true policy, the state should seek to coërce and restrain all these dissenting bodies, or even to force them, by pains and penalties, into a tacit subjection, a formal union, with itself. This is what Romanism has ever sought to do, when it has been the acknowledged religion of the state; it is what some of the Protestant countries of Europe are still striving to accomplish; it is what Protestant England undertook, under Henry the Eighth, Elizabeth, and Charles the First.

Third Method. — The only practicable method would seem to be, then, the plan of toleration — protecting all forms of religious belief, but adopting and establishing no one of them, to the exclusion of the rest, as *the* religion, and *the* church of the state. Every man must be protected in the exercise of his religious convictions, and the enjoyment of his religious rights; every sect and denomination of religious worshippers, so long as they observe the rules of propriety and decency, may justly claim such protection at the hands of the civil power; every church or religious organization may claim it, whether Christian, Jewish, or other. The state has no right to interfere in this matter, and say to its citizens: "You must believe thus and thus — you must worship thus and thus — you must belong to this or that religious denomination, under penalty of incurring the displeasure of government, or of forfeiting such and such privileges." This does not, as some writers suppose, — Dr. Whewell among others, — imply that, in the opinion of the state, all these various churches and systems are equally false or equally true, equally advantageous or disadvantageous, to the public and the private welfare. It simply implies that all have just and equal claim to protection, and that the state has no right to interfere with a man's private religious opinions.

The rule of universal toleration, as I have already implied, is not absolutely without its limits and exceptions. Should the religious convictions and usages of any class of men lead them to outrage public sentiment, by acts indecent, or blasphemous, or shocking to the common sense and common feeling of mankind in every civilized and enlightened country, the state is under no obligation to tolerate such outrage. It is under no obligation to allow human sacrifices, or the bloody rites of paganism; the burning of widows on the funeral pile, or the barbarities of the papal Auto da Fè, and Inquisition; nor yet the immoralities and indecencies that have sometimes been practised under the plea of religion and conscience. The same rule holds here, as in regard to property. A man is to be protected in the possession and enjoyment of his own, up to the point where he begins to trespass upon the rights of others; but not a step beyond that.

So, also, if any religious sect or organization should be

found plotting against the liberties of the state, or teaching doctrines tending to sedition, and disaffection to rightful authority, or undermining the public virtue and destroying the public peace — these, as interests dear to the state, and essential to its existence, are to be defended against such encroachments, and the authors of the mischief may rightly be proceeded against, as enemies of the state.

On the other hand, the state is not to become the propagandist of what it may regard as the true faith; is not to become missionary abroad, or missionary at home; is not to plant churches, and institute theological schools for the religious education of the people. This is not its proper office. It is not for such things that it exists. The people must do this; the public authorities, as individuals, may do it if they choose; but the state, as such, exists for quite another purpose, and is out of its true province if it undertakes such matters.

This does not, however, prevent the state from having any religion of its own, or from being a truly *Christian* state. It may acknowledge the general principles of Christianity, the great truths of revelation, the existence of God, the duty of men to honor and worship him, the sacredness of the Christian Sabbath, the authority of the scriptures; it may admit the doctrine of a future state of rewards and punishments, and so the validity and significance of an oath. It may hold and maintain all these general truths of natural and revealed religion, and protect others in the belief of the same, without an *established* religion, or a state church.

Nor is there, as some have contended, danger of irreligion and atheism from this source. Facts have shown the opposite. In no country, perhaps, is the public mind more generally and more deeply imbued with the essential principles of the Christian faith, and with a regard and reverence for religious things, than in our own, where these matters are left entirely to the people; and the working of the voluntary system, thus far at least, as contrasted with the practical results of the opposite system in the state churches and established religions of the Old World, seems to point conclusively to this as the true and most effective means of maintaining the institutions, and disseminating the truths, of the Christian religion, both at home and abroad.

CHAPTER V.

DUTIES OF STATE TO STATE.

In the previous chapters our inquiries have been directed to the nature and foundation of civil government, the duties of the subject as regards the state, and of the state with reference to the subject. It is of importance to inquire further respecting the duties which one state, or organized civil community, owes to other states. And this inquiry divides itself naturally into two parts, — the ethical relations of the state to other states in general, and the ethical relations of confederate and republican states like our own, to each other in particular. These topics will be discussed in separate sections.

§ I. — The General Relations and Duties of States to each other.

States have their relations to other states, and their duties growing out of those relations, no less than to their own subjects; and these duties are as imperative and binding in the one case as in the other. The state is no more free from the law of right, in its dealings with other states, than the individual in his private dealings with other individuals. The same general principles of morality, the same obligations to truthfulness, honesty, and honor, in all engagements, apply to and bind the state, as the individual.

But, while the principles are the same, the application of them to particular circumstances may differ. The position of the state is, in many respects, a very different one from that of the individual, — it has certain rights, and duties, which do not, and cannot, belong to him. It becomes a matter of importance, then, to ascertain what are the principles of morality which apply to the intercourse of state with state, and how the relations and duties of each to each are modified by those principles.

To define specifically the rights and obligations of nations to each other, is the province of a distinct science, — that of *international law*, or, as it is sometimes called, the *laws of nations*. This science, however, has to do rather with the existing customs and usages of nations, as matters of fact, than with the strictly ethical bearings and relations of the subject, — rather with the *what is*, than the *what ought to be;* while it is rather with the latter, than the former, that Moral Philosophy concerns itself.

Our inquiries will have reference chiefly to the following points: *the rights and duties of nations as regards their general intercourse, — their mutual treaties and alliances, — their wars, — and their jurisdiction.*

1. General Intercourse. — There are two principles which should ever be recognized in the intercourse of state

with state: That each state is, in itself, sovereign and independent, and is ever to be treated as such; and also, That in all their regulations and transactions with each other, states, no less than individuals, are to be governed by the simple and unalterable principles of morality,—a strict regard to the true and the right.

The *sovereignty* of every nation — its independent right to exist for itself, and to manage its own concerns as it pleases, without restraint or constraint from abroad — is one of the fundamental principles of international justice. Any people or nation, occupying a given territory, organized for purposes of government, and actually exercising control over its own affairs, has an undoubted right to remain unmolested in that control of itself, so long as it respects the rights of other states. It may be a large or a small, a weak or a powerful state, in respect to numbers and resources; it may be a monarchy, or a republic; it may manage its affairs wisely, or foolishly; it may progress in all the arts and refinements of a high civilization, or remain stationary in the darkness and barbarism of a former age;—it matters not what may be its condition in these respects, it has still the right to be as it likes, and do as it likes, subject to no interference or dictation from states that may be older, or stronger, or wiser and more enlightened than itself. So long as it is a state at all, it is a sovereign state. It may be subdued by foreign conquest, or broken in pieces and destroyed by civil dissension; — and in that case it is no longer a state; — but, so long as it continues a distinct nationality, a separate organization, it may claim the right of absolute and independent sovereignty. England, France, the United States, have no right to dictate to China, or Japan, or any other state, however barbarous its customs, and however misguided its policy, what shall or shall not be its general management, and course of procedure, as to its own affairs.

The Second Principle. — That nations are to be governed, in all their intercourse with each other, by the simple and established principles of morality, is too plain, and too true to require discussion, though, in fact, too often overlooked. Nations have no more right than private individuals to violate the essential principles of truth and justice. They are under the same fixed and eternal laws of right — they are bound by the same obligations, that apply to individual conduct. There is an authority above them, a court of appeal to which they are amenable, and by whose ultimate decision they must abide. That public conscience, that sense of right that dwells in every bosom, and pronounces the verdict of universal approbation or condemnation on the acts of nations, and the mandates of kings, — itself but the faint echo and reproduction of that still higher and more powerful verdict of Him who sitteth on the circle of the heavens, and judgeth the actions of men, — extends its authority and jurisdiction over empires as well as individuals, and holds the mightiest nations, no less than the humblest citizen, subject to the eternal law of *right.*

There is, indeed, no code of written law, emanating from an authorized legislative body, and enforced by an authorized executive; no legal penalties awaiting transgression; no verdict of judicial tribunal arraigning the guilty nation at its bar: yet is there not the less a law and a tribunal, a verdict and a penalty. Public opinion, and the universal sense of right that holds its seat in every human bosom, and constitutes what we may call the conscience of the race, are the real judges, the real tribunal. The penalty of transgression is the public condemnation, and the public contempt, together with that self-degradation which evil-doing never fails to inflict on the transgressor of the laws of right. Nor is there wanting a still higher tribunal. The Supreme Ruler of the universe has his throne among the nations of the earth, and takes cognizance of their crimes. Individuals receive the just award of their deeds in the future; nations and states exist as such only in the present world, and receive their sentence and their punishment here. Fearful is the doom which awaits, at the hands of a righteous Providence, the nation that sets itself against the eternal laws of God.

I have said there is no written code, proceeding from an authorized legislature, and enforced with legal sanctions, by which the nations are to be governed in their intercourse with each other; for this were to suppose some positive authority, some nation, or ruler above the nations, with power to give and to punish its violation; whereas, among men, no such lawgiver and ruler of nations exists. Nevertheless, the essential principles of right are universally admitted; and by common consent, and the practice of nations, many laws and regulations have come, in process of time, to be recognized as of authority in the intercourse of nations, and have taken their place as established principles. These, whether written or unwritten, constitute what are termed the *Law of Nations, or International Law.*

Comity of Nations. — Aside from the two general principles now mentioned as regulating the intercourse of nations, namely, that each is sovereign and independent, and that each is bound by the ordinary rules and obligations of morality in all its dealings, there is to be taken into account also what we may call the *comity*, or *courtesy* of nations. The state stands on the same footing in this respect with the individual citizen. It is bound to treat all other states not merely justly and honestly, but with courtesy. It must pay due regard to the acknowledged proprieties and usages of national intercourse, as regards the forms of diplomatic reception, the honors due to the flags of other nations, and to their accredited ministers, and whatever of the like kind common courtesy and common usage require.

Any departure from these acknowledged rules of international civility, subjects a nation to the same disgrace, among nations, which attaches to the individual who is guilty of insolent or unbecoming behavior in polite society.

2. Mutual Alliances and Treaties. — It is sometimes for the advantage of nations to combine, for the accomplishment of an object of common interest to each, — as defence against the encroachments of a formidable enemy, or the prosecution of scientific research and discovery. In such cases, the parties forming alliance enter into league or covenant with each other, pledging mutual assistance for the accomplishment of the objects specified. The combination of the great powers of Europe to put down Napoleon, and the joint efforts of civilized nations for the suppression of the slave-trade, and of piracy, are instances of such alliance.

Treaties are contracts, of a more general nature, between state and state. A treaty of *alliance* is one particular kind of treaty, or contract. A great variety of specific objects may be determined by treaty between different nations, — as the regulations of commerce, settlement of boundaries, decision of vexed questions of dispute, and whatever concerns the peace and prosperity of either party.

The general principles of ethics already specified as applying to the general intercourse of state with state, apply also and equally to the matter of alliance and treaty There must be no dishonesty or fraud, no trickery and deception, no violation of truth and justice and right. Whatever treaty or alliance is based on, or involves, anything of this sort, however great may seem to be the advantage thereby accruing to either party, is a treaty or alliance which has no right to be. No state has a right to combine with other powers for the injury or oppression of any other state, or to interfere with its internal affairs and arrangements. It is the duty of every state, no less in its alliances and treaties with foreign powers, than in its single capacity, to respect the rights and recognize the sovereignty of its neighbor states.

Within the lines now specified, — that is, the lines of honesty and strict integrity, — treaties and alliances, once formed, are binding on all the parties, and have the whole force of law. It is the duty of each state scrupulously to observe all the conditions and stipulations of such a contract, even to its own detriment; and to see to it that its citizens observe the same.

3. Wars. — Nations are, unfortunately, sometimes involved in war. Is this ever justifiable, and what are the ethical principles that apply to such cases? A nation may find itself involved in conflict from either of two sources: its rights or territory may be invaded by a force from without; or, its laws may be trampled upon, with armed violence, by its own citizens. In either case there may be a necessity for a resort to arms, in order to repel the invader, or to assert the supremacy of its own statutes. The state exists for the public good, and is bound, so long as it exists, to carry out and enforce whatever measures may be deemed essential to that end. Its own laws, and its

own rights must, therefore, be maintained at all hazards, and, if need be, by force of arms, — that is, by war.

In defence of national freedom, and the public good, — in the maintenance of law and justice, — in the protection of those rights and interests which are essential to the welfare, or even the existence of the state, — this condition of war, with all its perils and inevitable miseries, becomes a matter of necessity and of duty. It is the price which must sometimes be paid for liberty, and for national existence. No state is under obligation to commit suicide, or to suffer itself to be overrun by invasion and conquest, and trampled out of existence by unscrupulous and lawless force, so long as it can resist and repel this violence. Nor is the question whether to submit, or to resist, always one of mere expediency — of profit and loss. Often it rises higher than that, and becomes a question of duty and solemn obligation. The state, existing for a given purpose, and undertaking to accomplish a given end, is under obligation to fulfill its engagement, to do what it has promised and undertaken to do; and is ethically guilty, if, having the power, it fail to protect its citizens in their just and natural rights, and guard the interests committed to its keeping. This is a duty demanded of it, not merely by a regard to its own subjects, and its own interests, but also, in many cases, by a regard to the general interests and welfare of other states and nations.

Still, war should ever be the last resort, — tried as a means of redress, only when all other means fail of accomplishing the desired end. When protests and negotiations fail, and the appeal to justice and the sense of right in the aggressor has been made in vain, and there remains no alternative but to yield or resist, — then, and not till then, may the injured state draw the sword, and appeal to the God of battles, the Eternal Justice, to decide the controversy.

According to the view now taken, it is evident that, were all nations disposed to do justly, and respect each other's rights, war would be quite unnecessary. Whenever it occurs, it always implies and involves guilt in one or both the parties. It is no slight responsibility that is thus incurred. That nation has much to answer for at the bar of justice that not only involves itself in all the miseries of war, but subjects another and a peaceable nation to the dire necessity of sacrificing its honor and its interests, or of shedding the blood of its own sons in self-defence.

Most of the wars which ravage the earth and lay desolate its fairest realms, might easily be prevented, were there but the disposition among nations to deal fairly and honorably by each other; and even when disputes arise, and questions of serious moment come up for decision, the necessity for the final resort to arms might in most cases be obviated, were the matters in dispute submitted to the judgment and arbitration of some friendly power.

Rights of War. — In ancient times, the distinction of war and peace was not very clearly defined among the nations. The condition of war was considered the natural condition of a state in relation to other and foreign states, — the general rule, to which peace was the exception; and that exception was usually the result of special convention and contract. Thus, in the Latin tongue, one and the same word denoted both a stranger and an enemy. As the distinction in question came to be more clearly defined, and war became a specific thing, in distinction from the state of universal hostility and piracy, certain rules came to be recognized, by common usage and consent, as applicable to the general conduct of nations at strife with each other; and these were designated as the *rights of war*. These rights of war, among the ancients, partook of much that was savage and barbarous in their character, in accordance with the spirit of the time. They extended to the right of enslaving, and even of putting to death, not merely all prisoners taken in war, but even all the inhabitants of a conquered country, without distinction of combatant and non-combatant. At the same time, they required the conqueror to allow the burial of the slain among the vanquished; and they attached the utmost sacredness and inviolability to the office of herald, or envoy, and scrupulously guarded the faithful observance of all truces or treaties between the belligerents.

In modern times, the rights of war have been divested of much that was savage and barbarous in their earlier form. Distinction is made between those who bear arms, and those who do not, in any community; and it is understood by all parties, that the war is not waged with women and children, and inoffensive, peaceable citizens, but only with actual combatants, — with the army and navy, or the organized fighting force of the enemy. It is the destruction of this organized force, rather than the destruction of human life, that is the object aimed at. Hence, every act of wanton cruelty and needless bloodshed is branded as worthy of reprobation; and the prisoner, once in the hands of his captors, is no longer an enemy, to be slain or enslaved at the will of the conqueror, because no longer a part of that military organization against which the war is waged. And so with the ship that has struck its flag to the enemy in naval contest. In the middle ages, it was the custom of war to spare the lives of prisoners, and set them free on payment of a ransom. Among modern nations, the vanquished soldier becomes prisoner of war merely by giving up his arms and asking quarter, and obtains his liberty by exchange with the opposite party, or, sometimes, where that cannot be effected, by *parole*, or word of honor that he will not serve again in the war.

The barbarities attending the storming and capture of a besieged town or fortress are among the most revolting and inhuman of all the manifold atrocities which stain the annals of war. Pillage, rapine, indiscriminate destruction, are but too frequently the established order of the day. To some extent, doubtless, scenes of violence are inevitable in such cases. It is impossible to protect entirely those who are non-combatants from the miseries of the siege, the famine, the assault and capture. It is the misfortune of the innocent — as too often in this world — to suffer with the guilty. To put to death, in cold blood, those who had cast themselves on the clemency or the good faith of the conqueror, would be justified, however, by no laws or usages of modern warfare. In cases of protracted resistance, measures of severity are sometimes practised, — as putting the garrison to the sword, or giving up the place to pillage, for the purpose of striking terror into other resisting and fortified places, and thus bringing the war sooner to an end. Such procedure may possibly be justified, in some extreme cases, on the ground of humanity, and the ultimate saving of life. But such acts, even if sometimes necessary, are still among the most inhuman features of war.

By the usages of modern warfare, private property is respected in an enemy's country, on the ground that it is not with the citizen, but the state, that war is waged. At sea, however, the same rule has not, as yet, been established; but the merchant's vessel is liable to be captured, and his goods seized, as not being within the territory, and on that account, in a measure, out of the protection of the state to which he belongs. It is difficult to perceive the justice and ethical ground of such a distinction.

4. INTERNATIONAL JURISDICTION. — By gradual usage and conventional agreement of nations, certain rules and maxims have come to be of acknowledged authority in respect to national territory and rights of jurisdiction. As against other states, every state has the unquestioned and exclusive right to its own territory. But it may often come in question, how far does that territory extend. Hence, it is important to settle all such questions according to some established rules. By the law of nations, the territory of any state is considered as extending to the forts, harbors, bays, and whatever parts of the sea are enclosed by headlands belonging to that state. Its jurisdiction also extends to the distance of a cannon-shot from the shore, along all its coasts. Within these lines its right of property and control is exclusive.

States have sometimes claimed still further jurisdiction over adjacent seas, as formerly Venice over the Adriatic, and, more recently, Turkey over the Euxine, Russia over the Baltic, and Denmark over the Sound. It sometimes happens that rivers run through different countries, in their course to the sea; in such cases there is at least a moral and commercial, if not an international right, of each state through whose territory it may pass, to the unobstructed right of the same, for purposes of commerce. In times of peace, this right is usually conceded, either tacitly or by convention; in case of hostilities between nations thus situated, the rights of commerce give way to the rights of war, and, by the usage of nations, the enemy's ships, as already stated, are lawful plunder. Even the goods of a neutral state are not exempt from this rule, when found in an enemy's vessel, — the maxim being that enemy's ships make enemy's goods.

The question sometimes arises, how far the jurisdiction of a state extends to its subjects when out of its territory; as, for example, in a ship on the high seas. It is generally conceded, that the vessels of any nation, at sea, and beyond the territorial limits of other states, are subject to the jurisdiction of the state to which they belong. So far as respects the violation of its own laws, that jurisdiction is exclusive. When an offence is committed against the common law of nations, it passes out of the exclusive jurisdiction of that particular state to which the vessel belongs, and may be punished by the proper tribunal of any country into whose ports the offender may be carried. This is the case with piracy, for example. Any ship suspected of being a pirate, may be searched by any stronger power, without regard to the flag under which she may choose or chance to sail; and those engaged in her navigation or defence may be tried, and, if convicted, be put to death, by the legal authorities of any other state, into whose ports they may be taken.

No reason can be shown why it should not be the same with the slave-trade. Such, however, is not the present construction of international law. The slave-trade is, indeed, condemned by the laws of all civilized nations; but it has been decided by the English courts, that it is not, in such a sense, a crime against the general law of nations, as to authorize the courts of one nation to try the loyal subjects of another, charged with this offence, except in case of special treaty to that effect.

The national jurisdiction extends, moreover, not merely

to its subjects and vessels on the high seas, but in some degree, and within certain limits, to its subjects in any foreign territory. The person of a sovereign, or an ambassador, passing into the territory of a foreign state, is not, in time of peace, considered as properly subject to its jurisdiction. The consuls, also, and other authorized agents and ministers of every state, exercise, to some extent, jurisdiction over their countrymen in foreign states where such ministers or agents may reside. Ships of war, in foreign ports, are exempt from local jurisdiction of the same; but not private vessels, unless by special agreement.

The general principles of state jurisdiction may be comprehended in the following maxims, as stated by jurists of distinction: First, That the laws of a state have force within the limits of its own government, and bind all its subjects, but have no force beyond those limits. Second, That, with the exceptions already stated, all persons found within the limits of a government, whether their residence is permanent or temporary, are to be deemed subjects of that government. And, inasmuch as men often pass from one state to another, in which the laws respecting rank, property, contracts, marriage, etc., may vary from those of the former, it has been generally conceded, as a maxim of state policy, that whatever laws respecting such matters are in force in the state from which one comes, the same shall be considered valid and binding on him in the state to which he goes, so far as they do not interfere with the established laws and rights of the latter, and of its citizens. Thus, a contract valid by the laws of the land in which it is made, is valid in all other countries.

Such are some of the general principles of international jurisprudence. For a fuller discussion of the subject, the reader is referred to the works which treat particularly of these matters; and especially to Story's Conflict of Laws, Wheaton's Elements of International Law, Manning's Commentaries on the Law of Nations, as also to the commentaries of Kent, and Blackstone.

§ II. — Ethical Relations of Republican States to Each Other.

The general principles which should regulate the intercourse of states with each other, have been pointed out in the previous sections. These principles apply, also, in the main, to the intercourse of states confederate with each other, whether as independent sovereignties, or united under one constitution as a Republic. States thus confederated, or united, sustain to each other, however, peculiar relations; and from these arise certain corresponding obligations, of a more specific nature than those already considered. I have spoken of two forms which this relation may assume — that of a simple *confederation*, and that of a *republic*.

The Confederation. — In the former case, certain states, adjacent, it may be, in territory, or drawn toward each by community of interest, for purposes of mutual benefit, or for mutual defence, form themselves into a league, and deliberate, by their representatives in council, on matters of common interest or common danger. The separate cantons of Switzerland are an example of such confederation. The different provinces of Germany were formerly, and, to some extent, are still, if I mistake not, thus united. In such cases, the several states are still independent sovereignties, maintaining each its own form of government, the authority of each absolute and exclusive within its own domains, and each separated, it may be, from its neighbors by mutual jealousies and dissensions

The congress which represents them possesses no sovereignty over any one of these states, nor over all combined; its acts are only acts of council; and any state, if dissatisfied, may at any moment withdraw from the council entirely, or refuse to execute its resolves. Such a congress may act as agent for the several states, with delegated authority, to declare and carry on war, or to make peace; to appoint ambassadors, and to conclude treaties. Such treaties and acts, however, are not binding, until they receive the assent of each sovereign state, in its separate capacity.

The Republic. — Such an arrangement as that now described is a very different matter, and involves a very different relation of the several parties, from that which is implied in a *Republic.* The union is much closer, and more perfect, in the latter case, than in the former. The several states are no longer independent and sovereign, but they compose one whole, under one national government, and to this national government is committed the sovereignty and control of the general affairs, so far as other nations are concerned, — its powers being limited and defined, however, by the constitution. Within the limits thus prescribed, its authority is complete, that is as to all things given by the states, in the first place, to its jurisdiction. All other matters remain still under the separate jurisdiction of the several states. It can raise armies, levy taxes, declare war or peace, regulate commerce, and all transactions with foreign states; in a word, may do all that any sovereign state can do, subject only to its own constitution. Our own country furnishes an example of such a Republic.

A government thus constituted derives, evidently, all its powers from the constitution. Whatever that concedes, it may do, but nothing beyond; everything else lies still in the power of the several states in their individual capacity. No one of these may interfere with the internal arrangements and affairs of any other, nor is any one responsible for what another may choose to do, or not to do.

Each state becomes a member of the republic, in the first place, only by its own consent; that is, by the adoption of the general constitution that binds together the whole. The transfer of its sovereignty to the whole must be its own free act. But that once done, and the state having once become a member of the republic, it has no longer a moral right to withdraw, or to refuse compliance with the general laws and regulations of the government, unless such condition is specially and specifically contained in the articles of primitive agreement; that is, in the original constitution.

In the forcible and just language of Dr. Hickok: "A constitution with, and one without, the rights of nullification or secession, are two very different things; and if the right is not plainly expressed, then it does not exist; and those who have adopted it, have vested rights under it which no separate state can amend or disregard." The crime of treason attaches to all deliberate and armed resistance to authority thus constituted; and the republic has the power and the right to enforce its authority against any recreant state, subject only to the limits which the constitution imposes.

PART V.

DUTIES TO GOD.

Of the general classes into which the practical duties of life were divided in our analysis, those which pertain to self, to society, or our fellow-men in general, to the family, and to the state, have already claimed our attention. It remains to consider, in the present division, those which we owe to God. In one sense, as it has been already remarked, all our duties, whether to self or to society, to the family or the state, are duties which we owe to God. He regards them as such, and will hold us responsible for their fulfillment. There is no duty in life, to whomsoever and to whatsoever it may directly pertain, the faithful performance of which he does not regard as service rendered unto him, and the neglect of which he will not count as unfaithfulness and disobedience toward himself. But, while this is true of all duties, there are some which more specially and directly pertain to God as their immediate object; and it is of these I am now to speak.

These, again, resolve themselves naturally into two classes, — those which relate to the *feelings* which we cherish, and those which relate to the *conduct* which we manifest, towards God. Among the more prominent of the former class are the duties of *Reverence* and *Love;* of the latter, the duties of *Obedience* and *Worship*. These may, perhaps, be regarded as comprehensive of all others.

Before proceeding to treat of these several duties in detail, a word ought perhaps to be said with respect to their relation and importance, as compared with other departments of duty. Of the various classes of human obligation, those which we owe to the Supreme Being are entitled to the highest rank. All other branches of duty are, in a measure, inferior and subordinate to these. These neglected, all others will be; these faithfully performed, all others will follow in their train.

This seems to have been well understood by the ancients. "It should never be thought," says Plato, "that there is any branch of human virtue of greater importance than piety towards the Deity." To the same effect, in the Memorabilia of Xenophon, Socrates speaks of the worship of the gods as a duty acknowledged everywhere, and received by all men as the first command. Cicero, likewise, in his treatise De Officiis, ranks first in order of importance those duties which we owe to the immortal gods.

CHAPTER I.

OF THE FEELINGS TOWARDS GOD.

1. Reverence. — If there is such a Being as God, the creator of all, the supreme disposer of events, the righteous ruler and judge of men, and if he is what we believe him to be, omnipotent, omniscient, omnipresent, eternal, holy, just and good, surely this great and glorious Being is worthy of the highest *reverence* of the mind. The moment

the idea of such a Being presents itself to the mind, we are instinctively impressed with the grandeur of the conception, and filled with awe, as in the presence of a superior power. That mind must be deficient in self-respect, lacking in the perception of what is seemly and proper, that does not feel and acknowledge its obligation to bow in deepest reverence before the august and glorious Being who inhabiteth eternity, and filleth immensity with his presence. That mind must be sadly disordered, and thrown from its balance, that does not instinctively yield this homage.

Even bad men may do this, and have often done it. The selfish and corrupt heart, that seeks only its own ends, and lives only for itself, may still retain with reverence and fear the thought of that infinite excellence and purity, so superior to anything of which it is itself conscious. Such a fear may indeed border on superstition, — in many cases it may be nothing more, — yet even a superstition such as this, is surely better and more reasonable than utter irreverence.

Reverence is an emotion that takes its rise in the spiritual nature of man. It is awakened in view of the spiritual, wherever manifested. The sublime aspects of nature, in so far as they express the majesty and power, and indicate the presence of the invisible One, whose breath giveth life to all creatures, and whose hand sustains the goodly fabric of creation, are fitted to awaken and call forth this emotion. The reverent mind sees God in all his works. The eternal hills are his strength; the clouds are his chariot; the lightnings are his arrows; the thunder is his voice. In the impassioned language of sacred poetry, even inanimate nature fears and adores her God. "He toucheth the hills, and they smoke." At his going forth, "the pillars of heaven tremble, and are astonished." "The deep uttereth his voice, and lifteth up his hands on high."

But it is not in the external world alone that the spiritual nature of man recognizes and reveres the Infinite Spirit. God comes yet nearer than this to the soul that he hath made in the image of his own. In all the fears and hopes that agitate that soul, as it looks forward to the future; in all its aspirations for a higher excellence than it has yet attained; in all the providences of its earthly lot; in all the utterances of the sacred oracles; in all the silent and holy communing of the soul with its Maker, — the devout mind recognizes the presence of its God, and adores with fear and trembling; and never is the soul of man more truly dignified and exalted, than when thus bowing low in deepest reverence before God.

Nor is the emotion of which I speak a painful one. In this respect it differs from *fear*, to which it is otherwise closely analogous. There is in it more of *love* than fear. The majesty and the glory, that reveal to the waiting and wondering soul the presence of the Infinite, fill that soul with *awe* indeed, but not with fear, — inspire it with a calm and holy delight. There is much, it may be, in the scene or the object contemplated, that is awful and terrible; but yet a strange and invisible attraction draws the spirit towards the object which awakens its admiring and adoring regard; and it stands in that sacred presence, as Moses before the burning bush in the desert, filled with awe, yet not choosing to turn away from a spot so holy.

The reverence of which I speak, as due to the Supreme Being, belongs also, in a degree, to all that is connected with his name and his worship, — in a word, to all sacred things. The reverent mind will never allow itself to trifle with anything that pertains to the Divine Being. His name, his word, his ordinances, his works — all are sacred, and to be revered. Whatever tends to desecrate the same, shocks the sensibility of every right mind. To take the name of God in vain, or to treat with levity anything pertaining to religion, is the height of irreverence and impiety.

2. LOVE. — It is not enough to fear God. Reverence, however becoming, and however the want of it may indicate some serious defect or degradation of character, is still not the whole, nor the chief duty of the heart towards God. The displays of his power and majesty in nature, or the simple conception of his greatness and glory, the idea of the Infinite and the Absolute, of Him who is without beginning of days, or end of years, may fill the mind that once fairly entertains so grand and sublime a thought, with a profound awe, and call forth its deepest reverence. But God is *more* than this. He is a good, as well as a great Being, and as such, deserves not merely our reverence, but our love.

Gratitude alone, if there were no higher consideration, requires this. The goodness of God is not an abstract quality, a mere conception of the mind, but a matter of personal experience, as manifested to every man in the constant and ever-varying benefits of every passing hour of life. The God whom we are to love, is the God that hath led us all our life long, and hath crowned all our days with his loving kindness. There can be no clearer evidence of the guilt, and utter ruin of the soul, than that it should find in itself, among all its varied powers, and exquisite susceptibilities of emotion, no answering chord of grateful affection for all those benefits, — that it should have a full and generous love to bestow on all inferior objects, but no love for Him who alone is worthy of supreme regard, the giver of every good and perfect gift.

All true obedience, and all true and acceptable worship, must have its seat and source in this emotion. That is an idle and a vain service, which proceeds not from true love in the heart. Indeed, as Paley has well said, "That silent piety which consists in a habit of tracing out the Creator's wisdom and goodness in the objects around us, of referring the blessings we enjoy to his bounty, and of resorting in our distresses to his succor, may possibly be more acceptable to the Deity than any visible expressions of devotion whatever."

Love to God is the spring of all true religion, and the foundation of all genuine morality. It is a duty comprehensive, in part, of all others. It is the first and great commandment, comprising within itself all minor requirements. The God who made us, and whom we serve, — in whom we live, and move, and have our being, — demands our love — will be satisfied with nothing less, deserves nothing less. Failing in this, we miss the whole duty of man.

Accordingly, God has formed us to love him, and endowed us with a nature fitted to this end. He has so constituted us, that, by the very laws of our being, whatever is beautiful and excellent naturally wins our admiration, and calls forth our love. We are not insensible to all the beauty and grandeur of his works. On every side they surprise, they delight us. But these are only a portion of his ways — the dim and faint reflection of the eternal beauty and excellence that dwells in him, their author and original. Loving and admiring these his works, he would have us, in these and above these, love and adore himself, the source of all — the Being in whom all loveliness, all beauty, dwell.

Our nature inclines us to admire, also, what is *morally* excellent, what is great and noble in character, as well as what is beautiful and lovely in the external world. There are certain attributes and qualities of mind and heart which, wherever manifested, win our admiration. We are *formed* to love and admire such qualities—it is our nature. But He who so formed us, possesses in himself, in highest perfection, these very attributes; and in so constituting us as to love what is truly great, and excellent, and worthy to be loved, he has specially formed and fitted us to love Himself, the source of all excellence.

And does he not richly deserve our love, simply for bestowing upon us a nature thus fitted for infinite enjoyment? A single sensation of happiness, it has been well remarked, though it should continue but for a moment, and terminate with that single moment, would be a cause for gratitude so long as it could be remembered. If this be so, if the enjoyment of even a single sense, for a single moment, is cause of gratitude, what shall we say of that constant enjoyment, not of one, but of all our senses; not of sense merely, but of the higher intellectual pleasures; not of intellect merely, but of heart, and soul, and all that fills the spiritual, moral nature with delight; and this not for a single moment of existence, but through life? Does not the generous donor of a happiness so varied and bountiful, and utterly undeserved, richly merit that love which he seeks to draw forth from his creatures toward himself?

CHAPTER II.

OF OBEDIENCE.

The duties of the heart, though at the foundation of all morality and all piety, do not terminate in themselves, and are not complete in themselves. Moral obligation relates to the *conduct*, no less than to the *feelings*. Reverence toward God, and love to God, lead to obedience, and terminate in that as their natural result and object. The feeling manifests itself in the conduct, insomuch that where the latter is deficient, we are warranted in concluding that the former is also lacking. There cannot be true love to God in the heart, where there is not real obedience to God in the life. The first and chief duty of all these, so far as regards the conduct of man with respect to God, is *obedience* to the divine will. "If ye love me, keep my commandments."

The obligation to obedience results both from the divine character, and from the relations we sustain to God as his creatures.

The Divine Character. — The character of God is conformable to the highest conceptions which the human mind can form of excellence and purity. In him are united all the attributes that command our admiration. To him belong not only infinite power, and matchless wisdom, but the most exalted purity, the strictest justice, the most universal benevolence. All that we see and admire in others of these virtues and perfections, is but the reflection of his own superior excellence, a feeble emanation from that Source of all beauty and splendor.

Now, it is fit that a Being of such exalted perfections should receive the homage and obedience of all hearts and all lives. His character *entitles* him to command, and obligates us to obey. There is a moral fitness and propriety that the sceptre of the universe should rest in his hands; that the Being in whom repose all wisdom, and power, and goodness, and truth, and justice, should be also the source of law, and receive the cordial obedience of the universe. For any being to refuse such obedience, is for the finite to set itself against the infinite; the feeble and imperfect to declare itself independent of the perfect; the impure and unholy to exalt itself against the holy; the creature of a day to declare itself more wise and worthy to rule than the august Being whose goings forth are from eternity. It is impossible for any candid and intelligent mind calmly to meditate upon the character and perfections of God, and not perceive in them a sufficient reason why all creatures, in all parts of his dominion, should yield him willing and earnest obedience.

Our Relations to Him. — The duty of obedience results also from the relations which we sustain to the Divine Being. He is not only in himself the source and fountain of highest excellence, but he has imparted from his own infinite resources life and happiness to all creatures. He is our *Creator.* All that we prize and value in life as such, is his gift. His breath woke us first into existence. Whatever powers of body or of mind we possess, with whatever natural attributes we are endowed, all are his, and of him. Nothing pertaining to us can we properly call our own. From the first moment of existence to the last, we exercise no faculty of thought or feeling or action, which he has not first given us, and which he does not rightly claim as belonging to himself. The very power to *disobey* is a power which he has himself conferred. In him we live, and move, and have our being; and when, in our madness and folly, we refuse him the homage and service which he justly demands, it is against him in whose hand our breath is that we vainly strike. He bears with our folly, for he knoweth our frame; he remembereth that we are dust; yet he never relinquishes his claim to our entire and hearty obedience.

The Nature of his Requirements.— A further argument and obligation to obedience is derived from the nature of the divine requirements. From such a Being, infinite in power, and all the attributes of the most perfect character, and sustaining such peculiar relations to us, as creatures, dependent on his constant protection for our continued existence, as we are on his creative power for our first origin, —from such a Being, and in such relations, any law which he might give, would carry with it the weight and binding force of a perfect moral obligation. The simple fact that he is a perfect Being, incapable of willing or commanding that which is wrong, and that he is our own Creator, and constant Benefactor, make it imperative on us to give earnest heed to the least and most trivial expression of that will which to us is law.

But, to state the matter thus, and leave it thus, would be to make but an imperfect statement of it. When we come to look at what this law is which he has given us, we find it one which, in itself, and apart from all consideration of the source from which it emanates, carries its own authority and power of obligation. It is a law not arbitrary in its mandate, and for which no reason can be assigned other than that the Maker chose to have it so; but, on the contrary, a law directly adapted to our nature and wants. It requires that which it is for our own highest good that we should do; it forbids that which it is for our own highest good to avoid. Obedience to such a law brings our whole being into harmony with itself and with the demands of its own nature; disobedience results in the disarrangement and discord of all the powers of the soul, the disorder and ultimate ruin of the physical, the mental, and the moral man. Viewed in this its true light, the Divine Will is not so much a law commanding obedience for its own sake, as a kind and faithful guide sent to direct our steps in the uncertain wilderness of life, and to point us to those paths which lead to honor and immortality and eternal life. It is that Celestial Wisdom of which Hebrew poets sang, — the merchandise of which is better than the merchandise of silver, and the gain thereof than fine gold; — more precious than rubies, and all the things thou canst desire not to be compared to her; — in her right hand, length of days; in her left hand, riches and honor; her ways, ways of pleasantness, and all her paths peace; — a tree of life to them that lay hold on her, and happy he who retaineth her.

The Dictate of Reason. — Reason, aside from the teachings of revelation, points out the duty of obedience to the divine requirements. Animals have no law but that of appetite and instinct. They have no moral nature, and are therefore not proper subjects of moral government. ɑn is a being of a higher order, endowed with powers which fit him to take rank with the noblest orders of created intelligence. To him it is given to know the right and the wrong, to look onward from the act to its consequences, to trace events to their causes; to him is given the sense of moral obligation; to him the aspirations and hopes of the future. Such is his moral nature, that he cannot be happy, cannot reach the true good of his being, his own high destiny, but by likeness to and communion with his adorable Creator. His nature demands this, is ever unsatisfied and restlessly yearning without it. His earnest soul, agitated by passions and conflicting desires, becomes as the troubled sea till it finds its rest in God — till it hears the voice of its Creator, walking upon its waves, and saying unto them, *Peace! — be still!*

Is man, then, in all his consciousness of freedom, and of power to do as he will, *without a law?* Is not this very nature of his a law unto him? This sense of right, this feeling of obligation, this consciousness of a higher end and purpose, this longing for something better, purer, than he has yet obtained — are not these all a law unto him? And shall he violate this law merely because he has the power, and can do so if he will? Is not such a course utterly irrational, and a gross abuse of the freedom with which he is endowed?

Whether we look, then, at the character and perfections of the Being who claims our homage and obedience, or at the relations which we sustain to him, or at the nature of the law he has given us, or at our own moral nature and the dictates of reason respecting the same, we find equally, and from all sources, the clearest vindication of the divine right to our service and allegiance.

As to the nature of the obedience which we owe to the Divine Will, it is sufficient to say that it must be *cordial* and *sincere*—not a matter of form merely, but a matter of the heart; otherwise it is in reality no obedience, since the very requirement that is made of us is to love the Lord our God with all our heart, and soul, and mind, and strength. It should, moreover, be a *prompt* and *ready* obedience — not reluctantly given, as that from which we would gladly be excused but for the force and pressure of circumstances, but the free, spontaneous offering of a willing mind. It should be a *decisive* obedience, comprehensive of all the powers and faculties of our being,—the obedience not of a divided and distracted kingdom, but of a heart firm in its loyalty, and true to itself and to its rightful sovereign.

CHAPTER III.

OF WORSHIP.

THE reverence and love which we owe to God, and that obedience which springs from these, and constitutes their natural and appropriate expression, have been already considered in the preceding chapters. But those affections and dispositions of heart which lead to obedience, lead also to the *worship* of God. That exalted and glorious Being who is the object of our reverence and our love, and who claims our obedience, is also the proper object of our adoration and worship. No intelligent mind can for a moment contemplate the character and attributes, the works and the ways of Jehovah, what he is, and what he does, and not feel that he is worthy of the direct adoration and homage of every created being.

The worship of the Supreme Being seems to be an instinctive principle, an impulse of our nature, a law of the soul. As such, it shows itself under all the forms and conditions of social life, in all ages, and all countries, in all the various religions of the race, whether true or false, superstitious or reasonable. Whoever builds an altar, or in the silent recesses of his heart breathes a prayer; whoever bows himself toward the rising sun, or stretches forth his hand in supplication toward the moon walking in her brightness, or the stars that gem the brow of night; whoever calls upon an unknown God, or worships the invisible spirit that filleth immensity with his presence, and is not far from every one of us, — is but acting in accordance to this impulse and instinct of his nature. He who never worships, has in reality no religion, and knows no God.

In discussing this subject two distinct topics present themselves to our attention, — the one relating to worship in itself considered, the other to the observance of sacred times and special occasions for worship — Prayer, and the Sabbath.

§ I. — Of Prayer.

Its Nature. — Prayer is not necessarily direct, or vocal; not of necessity limited to any set form, or time, or place. It is not always even the express utterance in words, or presenting in thought, of any specific petition or desire. There may be prayer without any of these conditions. The silent breathing of the heart; the silent going forth of the soul to its God in adoration and praise, or in humble penitence and contrition; the faith that rests placidly on his mercy for pardon and the forgiveness of sin; the hope that looks joyfully toward the hills from whence its help cometh; the love that finds delight in communing with so great and so glorious a friend, — these various states and exercises of the mind are all, in one sense, but so many forms and varieties of prayer. The communion and converse of the soul with God, in whatever manner or form, is in reality prayer. It is this which constitutes the prayer, when words and forms are used; and the words and forms may be dispensed with, but the prayer still go on; while, without this, the mere words and forms, however solemn and imposing, become but a vain and senseless mockery. As when one afar from home, and in some strange land, mingles with his fellow-men, the companions of his voyage, and engages, it may be, in the pursuits of business which brought him thither,—still thinking, however, of his home and friends, and longing to meet them again, and cherishing their memory and their words in his heart, while yet those thoughts find no utterance or expression before those with whom he mingles,—so is it often with the truly devout soul, cherishing its silent and sweet thoughts of God, and conversing with him in reality, while engaged in the pursuits and occupations of daily life.

I am very far, however, from implying, in what I have now said, that the true spirit of prayer does not naturally seek for itself direct and vocal utterance, and those appropriate times, and places, and forms of expression, which are suited to its wants. True, these are but the body, the other the soul; still the two are in nature conjoined. He whose prayers never take the form of direct petition, and never clothe themselves in words, nor ask for themselves any special time and place, exclusive of other things, pays questionable worship. He is like the traveller in foreign lands who contents himself with occasional thoughts of home and friends, while constantly engaged in the business or the pleasures that surround him, but takes no time for direct converse or correspondence, nor even sets apart one moment from other pursuits, as sacred to this holier occupation.

Prayer includes, not petition only, but praise and thanksgiving. It contemplates not merely our own wants, but the greatness and glory of Him whom we worship. In the adoration which is thus called forth, in the admiring wonder and delight with which the mind is thus filled, it forgets itself, often, and its little wants, and thinks only of the glorious Being in whose presence it stands, and before whose brightness it is astonished. Or it is filled with gratitude and joy, in view of all the mercies it has received at the hand of this great and glorious God, and its thankfulness finds expression in praise. In such moments its songs are prayers, and its prayers are songs.

Nor is prayer always a private matter. True, the soul naturally seeks solitude, as the condition most favorable to devotion. But not always thus. At the family altar, in the social circle, and in the more formal devotions of the solemn assembly, prayer finds its appropriate place, and its fitting utterance. Nor is the social and public worship of God less a duty, than the more private and solitary communion with him, which the devout spirit so highly prizes.

Its Source.—If we inquire whence springs this desire of the human soul to hold converse with its God,—by virtue of which not the good and devout alone, but even bad men, whose hands are stained with crime, and whose hearts, by long continuance in evil, are rendered insensible to the beauty and excellence of virtue, are nevertheless sometimes inclined to acts of devotion,—we shall find its source, if I mistake not, partly in that religious instinct, of which I have already spoken as natural to man; partly in the fears of the future, and the consciousness of ill-desert, which at times oppress and overwhelm the guilty; partly in the happiness which the pure and devout mind experiences in communing with its God. It seems to be the intention of nature that man should thus recognize his dependence on the Divine Being, and find his highest happiness in communing with him. Perhaps, also, we ought to take into account, in this connection, the *social* nature of man, as inclining him to the same result. The heart of man is ill fitted for solitude, longs for companionship, seeks to share its sorrows and its joys with some other and sympathizing heart. In man it finds not always the fellowship and sympathy it needs; in man it cannot always confide. But to its God it can come in the darkest and weariest hour of life, sure of sympathy and of relief, sure that its confidence will not be betrayed. In the just and beautiful language of Mr. Stewart: "The dejection of mind which accompanies a state of complete solitude; the disposition we have to impart to others our thoughts and feelings; the desire we have of other intelligent and moral natures to sympathize with our own,—all lead us, in the progress of reason and of moral culture, to establish gradually a mental intercourse with the Invisible Witness and Judge of our conduct. An habitual sense of the divine presence comes at last to be formed. In every object or event that we see, we trace the hand of the Almighty, and in the suggestions of reason and conscience, we listen to his inspirations. In this intercourse of the heart with God,—an intercourse which enlivens and gladdens the most desolate scenes, and which dignifies the duties of the meanest station,—the supreme felicity of our nature is to be found; and till it is firmly established, there remains a void in every breast which nothing earthly can supply."

Its Reasonableness.—In what has now been said, we find not merely an explanation, but a justification of prayer. It is eminently a reasonable and proper thing, inasmuch as it is founded in the very nature and wants of man as a dependent and social being. He is a weak and helpless creature, dependent on his God for every moment of existence, in need of a constant protection and guidance, a constant and powerful preservation. Why should he not acknowledge this dependence, by going directly to the Source of all light and life for whatever he needs? We ask for what we want, always, of our fellow-men; why should we not of our God also?

Its Efficacy.—It must be admitted, after all, that the reasonableness of prayer depends, in a measure at least, on its *efficacy*. If it were of no avail to present our petition to the throne of the Divine Majesty, little could be said in favor of such a course. That which is quite useless, and known to be so, can hardly be called a reasonable procedure. Now, it is precisely here that the gravest and weightiest objections lie against the reasonableness and duty of prayer. If it is best that we should receive that for which we ask, if this is accordant with divine wisdom and goodness, then God will certainly bestow it upon us, whether we ask it or not; but if it be not so, then he will not give it to us, even if we do ask. Of what avail, then, in either case, is our asking? I reply: this objection assumes too much. It by no means follows that whatever it is best for us to have, *in answer* to our prayers, it is best for us to have *without* the asking. The prayer may be the very condition on which the bestowal of the favor is suspended, and without which, divine wisdom would not see fit to grant it.

But it is further objected, that prayer implies a desire and request on our part that God, the infinitely wise, and just, and good, would alter the course of the world, and of his own administration, in order to suit our wishes. He has marked out a certain course of action, has established certain laws and principles, according to which the course of nature moves on from age to age. We come, in our folly and presumption, and ask him so far to alter and suspend these laws and this course of action, as to bring about some specific event, not included in the original plan, or to prevent the accomplishment of what, in the natural and established order of things, would take place. At first view, this objection appears formidable, the more so from the show of philosophy which it assumes. It is hardly necessary, as some writers have done, to bring forward an array of arguments drawn from science, in order to meet this objection. In this case, perhaps, as in many others, the best answer is the simplest and most obvious. It is this: He who lays out the plan of the universe and establishes its laws, takes into view the whole series of events; in this series of events, every prayer which we offer, every desire we breathe, has its fixed place and influence, was foreseen, and its effect determined, from the outset. We are not, therefore, in reality asking God to change the course of events, or the plan of the universe, when we offer to him our prayers, since those prayers are themselves a part of the established order. Dr. Whewell has well expressed this: "In the spiritual world, the prayers of believers are events as real as their temptations, their deliverance, their forgiveness; and the former events may very naturally be conceived to produce an effect upon the latter. There is, therefore, in such prayers, nothing inconsistent with our belief in God's goodness and wisdom." To this he adds, what is doubtless true, that when we ask for temporal blessings, as for our daily bread, our prayers are rather an expression of our dependence on God, than of a desire that he would direct the course of the world according to our wishes.

Of the real efficacy and value of prayer, we have the highest assurance, both in the encouragement to this duty which is presented in the sacred Scriptures, and also the actual experience of its benefits by believers in all ages.

Argument from Scripture. — The efficacy and duty of prayer are set forth in the Scriptures in the plainest light. "Ask and it shall be given you, seek and ye shall find," is the language and spirit of the whole Bible. What can be more explicit than this language — and the like everywhere abounds in sacred writings — as to the real efficacy and use of prayer? Besides the general instructions and precepts which enjoin the duty of prayer, there are specific directions given as to the various objects for which we may properly ask. Examples also are given of prayer for specific objects, for private and for public benefits, for the remission of sins, for deliverance from temporal evils, and for whatever the soul of man most earnestly desires. And not only have we instances of prayer in the Scriptures, but of answers to prayer, and those almost innumerable. We are not presented with precepts and examples merely, but with manifest and practical results. That God answers the prayers of his children, and has done this in manifold ways, and instances too many to be repeated and too obvious to be mistaken, is as much a matter of history as any event recorded in sacred or profane annals.

Peter prayed, and the prison doors were opened, and his chains fell off. Joshua prayed, and the sun stood still over Gibeon, and the moon over the valley of Ajalon. Elijah prayed, and the child of the Shunamite was restored to life. Moses prayed, and the Lord forgave the iniquity of Israel. Again and again, in answer to his supplications, plague, and pestilence, and the swift judgments of Heaven were stayed, and the people saved. Christ prayed, and an angel stood at his side to comfort and strengthen him.

From Christian Experience. — Nor is it from Scripture

alone that we derive evidence of the efficacy and value of prayer. The history of God's people in all ages and all times, the history of the renewed heart wherever found, is to the same effect. Whoever, in humble, earnest supplication, in a filial spirit, and with true faith, goes to God for those things which he desires, and which are proper objects of prayer, *usually*, it is not too much to say, receives that for which he asks. I do not say *always;* for it is possible that those things which we desire may not be in accordance with the divine will. Infinite Wisdom may perceive that it is not best on the whole, or best even for us, that the desire should be granted. Still the rule stands, notwithstanding all exceptions, that he who asketh anything of God, believing, shall receive.

Why Enjoined. — If we ask, now, why such a practice is enjoined in the Scriptures, why prayer is made a duty, when doubtless the same blessings might be conferred without the asking, it may be sufficient to reply, that it is *due* to the Supreme Ruler of events that we should in this manner recognize his sovereign sway, and our entire dependence on him for all the mercies of life. He will be inquired of for these things. The good and wise father may choose that his child shall *ask* for that which he is ready to bestow. It is right and fitting that the child should do so.

Such a procedure is of service also to the petitioner. It keeps alive in him the sense of his constant dependence on his God, which he might otherwise be ready to forget. It reminds him of the source whence all his blessings flow, and of his constant need of divine guidance and protection. It prepares him also to receive with grateful heart those favors which he asks, and to enjoy their reception so much the more as gifts from his Heavenly Father, in answer to his prayer.

§ II. Of the Sabbath.

If it is our duty, as we have already seen, to worship God, it would seem to be desirable and proper that there should be stated times for this worship. The observance of special days and occasions for this purpose, seems to be the dictate at once of reason and of natural religion, as indicated in the practice of all nations. Differences of opinion may exist as to the number and frequency of these occasions, and the proper method of their observance; but no nation, it may safely be affirmed, that recognizes any religion, and any Deity, fails to consecrate to its religion and its God some special time as sacred to his worship.

In treating this subject, it may be well to consider the *presumption in favor* of a Sabbath; the *authority* of the Sabbath as a positive institution; and also, very briefly, the *proper manner of observing it.*

1. Presumption in Favor of a Sabbath. — It is a strong presumption in favor of a Sabbath, that some occasion of this kind is desirable, if not absolutely necessary, as *a period of rest*, both for man and beast, from the ordinary toil of life. If this be so, then the usefulness of the occasion is certainly an argument in its favor, and goes to establish the duty of its observance. It is a well-ascertained fact, that both body and mind require intervals of relaxation from accustomed toil. Facts show that the physical system requires such rest, and that its energies are exhausted, and its vital powers impaired, when this law is disregarded. It is equally true of the mental faculties. Not only will more intellectual labor be accomplished by the faithful adherence to this law of occasional rest, but it will be accomplished with less injury to the physical and mental constitution, with less waste of vigor and of life.

These facts are so fully attested by scientific observation and general experience, and are now so generally known and admitted, that it is not necessary, in this connection, to enter into any argument to establish them.

It is not merely useful to the laborer to rest for the time being from his toil, but the prospect of a day of rest and recreation approaching, refreshes and encourages him amid the labors of the week. Nor is it the body only that feels the refreshing influence. The mind, no less than the body, requires relaxation, and that change of employment which the Sabbath brings. True, the mind is never absolutely inactive; the rest which it needs is change of occupation, and not entire cessation of thought; but this change it does need, and precisely this the Sabbath furnishes, by directing our thoughts to objects which do not so fully come before them during the labors of the week.

The influence of the Sabbath is in this way very considerable as an agent in promoting the happiness and civilization of the community. By affording intervals of rest and relief from the toils and cares of business, and the weariness of labor, it adds not merely to the physical and mental vigor, but to the sum of domestic and social enjoyment. It gives the busy laborer a day at *home* with his own family, and throws the refining and elevating influence of social intercourse over many a mind, that would be otherwise shut up to the drudgery of constant toil.

Needed for Moral and Religious Culture. — But it is chiefly as an opportunity of moral and religious culture, that the Sabbath is of advantage to man. Employed, as most men are, during the week, with active labor, whether of body or of mind, there is little leisure or inclination for religious thought, for self-culture and discipline, for progress in the knowledge of divine truth and in the way to heaven. Were there no pause in this hurried march of life, no cessation from the din and uproar of the ever-moving machinery of worldly toil, there is danger that from most minds the thoughts of a higher life, and a purer state of existence, would quite fade away, and men would become mere animals and beast of burden, intent only on the gratifications, or busied only with the drudgery, of the present hour, — knowing and caring for nothing beyond.

For all this, the periodical recurrence of the Sabbath, as a day specially devoted to moral and religious culture, and to the worship of God, affords the true, and, as I am inclined to think, the only practicable remedy. It calls the thoughts from other and merely secular employments, and invites us to the contemplation of those higher truths which concern our permanent and future well-being. As a matter of fact, it will be found that very little progress is made in religious culture, either by the individual, or by the nation, that dispenses entirely with the observance of the Sabbath as a day sacred to divine things.

Needed for Social Worship. — Such a day is needed, moreover, not only for individual improvement, but for social worship. If men are to meet together for the worship of God, and for instruction in religious truth, it is quite necessary that some set time and place should be appointed for the purpose, and that the worship should recur at regular intervals, so that all may know when and where the religious assembly is to be held, and arrange their affairs accordingly. The Sabbath provides for this. When the appointed day returns, every one knows that it is a day set apart for religious purposes; that the ordinary business of life is for the while suspended; that the occupations of the shop, the desk, the counting-room, the field, the mill, are, by general consent, laid aside; and that men will assemble on that day for religious instruction and worship. In consequence of this general understanding, men will not be seeking for us in our places of business, while we are engaged in public worship. Nor shall we, in turn, find the business of the week interrupted by the religious observances of our neighbors. If there is to be any such thing as social religious worship, it is manifestly for the convenience of all, if not an indispensable necessity, that one and the same time should be observed, so far as possible, by all persons, for this purpose. For this, also, the Sabbath provides, and it is probably not too much to say, that, were the observance of this day dispensed with, public assemblies for religious worship would not long continue to be maintained in any country. There being no special time appropriated to that purpose, any time that might be selected would be found inconvenient, and gradually the practice of coming together for the worship of God in public assembly would go out of use.

The reasons which have been mentioned are sufficient to show the use and great advantage of a Sabbath to the individual and to the community, and in this way they create a strong presumption in favor of such an institution.

Objection. — It is sometimes objected to the view now taken, that the observance of one day in seven as a period of rest, and of religious worship, is a serious loss to the community, by subtracting so much from the industry and available wealth of the nation. It is a loss of one-seventh of the time, and so of one-seventh of the resources of the laboring classes. This is entirely a mistake. It has already been stated, that both the physical and the mental constitution absolutely require rest; and that continuous labor, without interval of repose or change of occupation, wears out the system, and induces premature decay. This is true both of man and beast, both of him who works with the hands, and of him who toils with the brain. If this be so, the periodical recurrence of a day of rest, so far from being a loss, is really a gain to the laborer, and to the whole community. One might as well complain that the time devoted to sleep, or to the taking of food, are so many hours lost out of every twenty-four; that, were it not for this unfortunate and needless delay, men might work twenty hours instead of ten, and so double the amount of their present earnings. Doubtless this might be done for a time; but it would be for a *short* time, and would prove no gain in the end. Nature demands rest and refreshment; and whoever violates these fundamental laws of his constitution, and, under the pressure and excitement of business denies himself needful sleep, or needful food, or needful rest and recreation, finds himself a loser by the experiment. It is consuming the principal, for the sake of gaining higher interest; it is throwing away the sails, in order to increase the speed of the ship.

It is to be remembered, also, that even if nature could endure uninterrupted toil,—which, as at present constituted, it cannot,—the addition of an extra day of labor to the six now employed, would be quite likely to reduce the price of labor, leaving the workman no better pay at the end of the week than he has now, but obliging him to work seven days for it, instead of six. This would be all he would gain.

2. Institution and Authority of the Sabbath.—For reasons now stated, we need a Sabbath, and should be under the necessity of observing one, out of regard to our own best interests, even if none had been appointed by divine authority. It is certainly fair to presume, however, that one *has* been appointed, inasmuch as the reasons for it are so weighty. It is not probable that Divine Wis-

dom and Benevolence would overlook so important an item in the economy of human affairs,—would give man a nature requiring a Sabbath as a day of rest from toil, a day of social and domestic enjoyment, of individual moral culture, and of public worship, and not give him also the Sabbath itself. This would be much the same as if Deity were to create man with an appetite, and not supply the food adapted to its craving; or with a disposition for sleep, and make no provision for hours suitable for repose.

But, if a Sabbath has been instituted, then *when* and *where?* We find a day actually observed by all Christian nations as a Sabbath, claiming to be such an institution, and regarded, by many at least, as of divine authority. The question is, *Has* it such authority? Is the Christian Sabbath, in other words, either directly or indirectly an institution of divine appointment?

What Authority for any Day.—We shall best answer this inquiry, by first raising the previous question, What authority is there for the observance of *any* day as a Sabbath? Is there any evidence that God has ever appointed any day for this purpose, with a view to its *general* observance by the human family?

I reply: there is reason to believe that he has. There is reason to believe that at the very outset, at the creation of our world and our race, the Creator set apart one day in seven as sacred to himself, to be observed by man, in all his generations and families, as a day of worship and of rest. The sacred narrative informs us that "on the seventh day God ended his work which he had made; and he rested on the seventh day from all his work which he had made; and God blessed the seventh day and sanctified it, because that in it he had rested from all his work which God created and made." Now it must be conceded that this passage, though not in manner and form a divine command to observe every seventh day, is at least a *history* of the institution of the Sabbath, and presents, at the same time, the *reason why* the day was thus set apart. It was thus consecrated, because on that day God had rested from all his work. Now the reason, it will be observed, is of a *general* nature — applicable as much to all times and nations, as to any one. It was not a reason why the Jews should observe the day, any more than why we should observe it. The institution, as then originated, could not have been intended for the Jews especially; for the Jews, as a nation, were not in existence until some two thousand years afterwards. The fact that it was instituted at the beginning, as well as the reason assigned for its institution, both show conclusively that it was designed for all nations, and all ages of the world.

Paley's View. — I am aware that eminent authorities have taken the ground that the Sabbath was not in reality instituted at the creation, but that the passage referred to merely assigns a reason, by way of anticipation, for an institution which came into existence hundreds of years after; that is, when the Israelites were in the wilderness, on their way from Egypt to Palestine. This is the view of Dr. Paley, among others. He infers this from the silence of the sacred narrative as to any such institution or observance, through all the intervening periods of history from the creation down to the exodus of the children of Israel, — a period of some twenty-five hundred years, — during which godly men without number lived, keeping the divine precepts diligently, — and doubtless this among the rest, if any such precept or institution was in existence, — and yet not the remotest allusion do we find to any such observance during all this time. This silence he regards as unaccountable, on the supposition that all this while the Sabbath was in existence as a positive institution. Hence he infers that the transaction recorded in the sixteenth chapter of Exodus is the first actual institution of the Sabbath.

The transaction to which he refers is the gathering of the manna in the wilderness, a double quantity of which was gathered on the sixth day: "And all the rulers of the congregation came and told Moses; and he said unto them, This is that which the Lord hath said: *To-morrow is the rest of the holy Sabbath unto the Lord.*" Now, by referring to the narrative, it will be seen that there is nothing here which wears the aspect of a new institution, — no command to observe an ordinance just then for the first time promulgated, but simply a reason assigned for the circumstance that a double portion of food was provided on that day, which reason was, that "to-morrow is the Sabbath," as if the simple mention of that fact would be sufficient to explain the whole thing. This is certainly not the way in which any person at the head of government would be likely to announce a new law, or to establish a new institution. It looks rather as if the Sabbath was an institution already well known to the people, and which needed only to be mentioned, in order to be understood at once as a reason why they were not to gather manna on that as on other days.

And so unquestionably it was. The division of time into weeks of seven days, is one of the earliest monuments of antiquity of which we have any record. It was the custom of the oriental nations from the very earliest period, — a custom prevalent in India, China, Arabia, Egypt, and Assyria, — and, not improbably, derived from the Jewish patriarchs, and so to be traced back to the original institution of the Sabbath at the creation. Astronomers pronounce the week to be the most ancient monument of astronomical knowledge. It must have existed in Egypt at the time the Israelites dwelt there; and whatever may be the origin of the custom, whether derived from the Jewish patriarchs, and from the institution of the Sabbath in Eden, or not, the simple fact that it was so ancient and so universal a custom thus to divide the time into periods of seven days, and that it was a custom with which the Israelites must have become familiar during their stay in Egypt, if never before, shows that it cannot have been a new institution at the time of which we speak. The rest of the seventh day is of earlier origin than the exodus of the Israelites, and the Mosaic institution, and there is every reason to regard it as having its source in the first revelation of the divine will ever made to man.

The Jewish Sabbath. — I am far from supposing, however, that the Jewish Sabbath, *as such*, — that which was specially given to the Israelites in the wilderness, whether it was then first enacted, or only *reënacted*, and made a special ordinance, along with many others, for that people, — is an institution binding upon us. I claim for the Sabbath, as a divine institution, another and an earlier origin, a broader foundation, and a more universal design, than pertained to the Sabbath of the Mosaic institution. The Jewish, or Mosaic Sabbath, is always spoken of as a *sign* between God and the people of Israel: "Moreover, also, I gave them my Sabbath to be a sign between me and them;" which implies that it was a *peculiar* ordinance, not common to all nations, but a special institution designed for that one people. Otherwise it would have no significance as a *sign*, any more than the rising and setting of the sun, or any other well-known phenomenon common to all nations and ages of the world. Now, a Sabbath was, as I have shown, no new institution, but common to all the oriental world. It could not, therefore, as such, constitute a special sign between God and the people of Israel. That sign — the Jewish Sabbath — was not the universal Sabbath, instituted at the creation, and designed for all nations and times, but a special and peculiar institution, designed for the Jews alone — a part of their ceremonial observances, of the same general character with their other sacred days and feasts, as of unleavened bread, of pentecost, and other similar occasions prescribed in the ritual. Its duties were peculiar. It was to be observed most strictly as a day of entire rest from all physical labor. This, and not religious worship, was the *essential* and *prominent* idea of the day, although both were, of course, included in its observance. The penalties for its violation were also peculiar. The least infringement upon its sacred hours, even for the preparation of the daily food, or the making a fire, was punishable, and actually punished, with death. Now, an institution thus peculiar in its design and purpose, in its duties and its penalties, cannot well be regarded as binding on other nations and times than that to which it was specially given, and for whom it was specially intended; otherwise we should be bound to regard not only the institution, but the specific day, the specific purpose, the specific duties and manner of observance, and the peculiar penalties, as likewise in force, and binding upon us. While, therefore, I regard the Sabbath as a divine institution, designed for all nations and ages of the world, and instituted at the beginning, I cannot regard the *Jewish* Sabbath as identical with the universal and original one, but rather as a peculiar ordinance, having its specific design and its peculiar duties, and which, as such, and so far as it was *Jewish*, passed out of existence along with the whole ceremonial of which it was a part.

Authority of the Christian Sabbath. — We are ready now to inquire what authority there is for the observance of the Christian Sabbath. We have seen that both nature and revelation point to the propriety and duty of observing one day in seven as a day of rest and of worship. We must regard such observance, then, as a divine institution. But what day shall it be, and in what manner shall it be observed? As to this, we have found as yet no direction. We have no reason to suppose, as I have already shown, that the Jewish Sabbath is binding on us, either as regards the day of the week, or the duties and manner of observance. We are at liberty, then, to adopt any other. We find in the Scriptures no command on this point. We find, however, in almost universal use among Christian nations the observance of the first day of the week as a day sacred to religious purposes. We trace back this usage to the very earliest period of the Christian Church. We find traces of it among the early disciples to the Christian faith, in the first centuries of its eventful history. We find in the New Testament allusions to the custom as then existing; mention, for example, of meetings of the Christian disciples on that day, for religious worship, and that in repeated instances. We infer that the observance of that day has at least the authority of apostolic usage, if not of any more direct and positive institution. There is in this a presumption, to say the least, that it may have something more than the sanction of early and general Christian usage — that it may have, in some sense, what it is generally understood to claim, the express sanction and authority of the inspired teachers and founders of the Christian faith. Still, it must be conceded, the observance of that day, rather than any other, rests upon no positive command. The custom of Christian nations, the early and apparently apostolic usage, and the evident reasonableness of the usage, as a fit and proper tribute of respect to that great event, on which hang the hopes and destinies of the world, — the resurrection of our Lord, — constitute a sufficient basis and warrant for the observance, on our part, of the first day of the week as our Christian Sabbath. When asked, then, what is our authority for observing the first day of the week as a day of rest and of religious worship, we reply: The law of nature, and the divine sanction, both point to the duty of keeping some day, one day in seven, as sacred to religious uses; while custom, and the universal consent of Christian nations from the earliest times, as well as the great event commemorated, point to this day in particular as the one most appropriate for such observance. On these general grounds we are content to rest the matter.

3. The Proper Manner of Observing the Sabbath. — The reasons for which the Sabbath exists, and which led to its institution, are the proper guide to its right observance. We are under obligation to make such use of it as shall best conduce to those ends for which it was appointed, and thus carry out its great design. Whatever does this, is a right use of the Sabbath; whatever fails of this, however seemly and sacred in appearance, is a perversion of its true meaning and intent.

And first, the *natural*, though not of necessity the *chief* reason, for the observance of the Sabbath, must not be overlooked. Nature demands it as a day of rest. So far as possible, — so far, that is, as may consist with the necessary duties of life, and with the higher purposes of the day, — it should be observed as a day of entire cessation from the ordinary pursuits and occupations, — a day of rest both to body and to mind. Not even religious services should be so multiplied, or so conducted, as to set aside and supersede this first law of the Sabbath. If in any manner, or by any mode of observance, the day becomes as laborious and exhausting to the powers of body and mind as other days of the week, it is no longer, in the proper sense, a Sabbath, whatever else it may be.

But it is certainly not the *whole* design of the Sabbath that it should be a period of rest. It is a day given for *individual moral and religious culture;* given for this purpose to every man, as individually responsible for his own moral improvement, and as needing for this purpose time for religious meditation, and for direct intercourse with the Divine Being. To this end the day is given, — a day of which the special and proper business is that now indicated; given to every man as his sacred right, which no man may take from him, and which he has no right to take from himself, by any occupation inconsistent with the purpose of the day. Not even public religious observances should be allowed to deprive us of this individual use and benefit of the Sabbath, as a means of personal religious culture.

We are not, however, to overlook the *public worship of God* in the solemn assembly. This is *one*, and one of the most obvious and important, of the appropriate duties of the Sabbath. It should have its place, but it should not be allowed to usurp the time which belongs to other and equally important duties.

In a word, the Sabbath is a day of sacred rest, and of religious worship; and whoever thus employs it, employs it aright.

CONFLICT OF DUTIES.

In the preceding pages on Practical Ethics, we have discussed the duties which pertain more directly to self, to society, to the family, to the state, and to God. It may sometimes happen that, of these several classes, some one may present claims apparently in conflict with those of another. How shall these conflicting claims be reconciled? Which shall we obey? This is a question of some moment in practical ethics, and its brief consideration may fitly conclude our discussion of this department of the science.

Strictly speaking, there can be no such thing as a *conflict* of *duties*. Duties are never in collision; obligations never clash. There is one, and but one, right thing to be done; one, and but one, right course to pursue, all things considered; and whatever is in conflict with this, is not, and cannot be, a duty, whatever may seem to be its claims. The will of God, which is the rule of duty to man, whether as given in nature and the constitution of things, or in revelation, is always consistent with itself. Hence, to one and the same person, at one and the same moment, the path of duty never lies in opposite directions.

Cases of apparent Conflict. — It is often difficult, nevertheless, to determine what is the path of duty. Opposite courses, which bear at least the semblance of obligation, present their claims; and these claims are often in conflict with each other. It is, for example, my duty as a good citizen to respect and honor the state. But, suppose the state is not a proper object of respect,—its laws unjust, its policy dishonorable, its whole character discreditable,—am I still to honor and respect it?

It is my duty as a citizen to support the government of my country by my influence, and, if necessary, by my personal service. But, suppose it is engaged in an unjust and iniquitous war, or in measures revolting to sentiments of honor and justice, and the claims of humanity—am I still to maintain and defend it, on the principle, "My country—right or wrong?"

In like manner, the duties of a parent to his family may seem to be inconsistent with those services which are due to society and the state, or with those which he owes to himself. He is under obligation to provide for his own household. To do this effectually, may at times, and under the pressure of peculiar circumstances, require an amount of exertion inconsistent with a due regard to the laws of life and health. Shall he disregard the latter, in his anxiety to secure the former?

It is the duty of the child to honor and obey the parent. But, suppose the parent to be a wretched victim of intemperance and vice—how can the child honor and respect such a parent? Or, suppose the commands of the parent to run counter to those of God—is the child, in such a case, absolved from the obligation of filial obedience? or is he to obey, whatever the command may be? In general, suppose the laws of the family, or of the state, to conflict with the dictates of conscience and the laws of God, which shall be obeyed—God or man?

A General Rule.—These are cases not unlikely to

occur, and which, in fact, frequently do occur, in the course of events. They are questions of practical moment. It is difficult to lay down rules that shall meet all such cases. Without attempting to do this, it may, I think, be taken as a general rule, applicable to all such matters, that where there are conflicting claims, the preference is to be given to those which are in themselves the higher and the more important, which proceed from and rest upon the highest authority. Thus, the interests of society are wider, and its welfare of more consequence, than those of self. So, also, with the interests of the family; they are more and higher than those of the individual. The authority of the state is superior to the authority of the parent, and, other things being equal, is entitled, in consequence, to superior regard. It is an authority *comprehensive*, in a measure, of the other. On the same principle, and *a fortiori*, the claims and authority of God are comprehensive of and superior to all others; and where they come in conflict with the claims and authority of man, whether in society, in the family, or in the state, all such claims and obligations become null and void, and the law of God alone is binding.

On no other principle can we justify any instance of disobedience to unjust and wicked legislation; as, for example, the refusal of Daniel to comply with the edict which forbade, for a given time, the worship of any God; the refusal of the three Jewish governors to fall down and worship the golden image that Nebuchadnezzar had set up on the plain of Dura; the refusal of the apostles to preach no more in the name of Christ, as ordered by the magistrates; the refusal of the early Christians to abjure faith in Christ, and burn incense to heathen gods. The whole history of the Christian Church, of sacrifice and suffering and death for the faith and the truth, is a practical recognition of this great principle. There had been no martyrs but for this higher law.

It is important to be borne in mind, however, in all such cases of opposing and contradictory claims, that we are justified in refusing obedience to the plain and positive commands of those in authority, whether parents or rulers, only when such commands are plainly and unquestionably in conflict with the divine precepts. The case should be a plain one. If it be not so, — if there be room for reasonable doubt whether, after all, there is any real discrepancy between the two authorities, the divine and the human, — we are not, as it seems to me, merely on the strength of that doubt and uncertainty, to set aside the direct and positive demands of human legislation. Much less are we to set up our own notions as law, and slide into the belief that, because a given course is highly pleasing or displeasing to us, it is equally so to the divine mind. Our inclinations and prejudices may, or may not, be coincident with truth, and the divine will. At all events, they are not our guide.

AUTHORITIES.

THE following works may be consulted with profit by the critical reader, who wishes to acquaint himself with the literature of the department.

ENGLISH AUTHORS.

Paley. — Moral Philosophy.
Whewell. — Elements of Morality.
Cudworth. — Eternal and Immutable Morality.
Stewart. — Active and Moral Powers.
Reid. — Essays on the Active Powers.
Cogan. — Ethical Treatise.
" Ethical Questions.
Smith, Adam. — Theory of Moral Sentiments.
Cudworth. — Intellectual System.
Price (Dr. R.). — Review of Morals.
" " Dissertations.
Hutcheson. — Inquiry into the Ideas of Beauty and Virtue.
Taylor (Dr. J.). — Examination of do.
" " Sketch of Moral Philosophy.
Ferguson (Dr. A.). — Institutes of Moral Philosophy.
Campbell (Dr. Arch.). — Inquiry into the Original of Moral Virtue

Hume (David). — Treatise of Human Nature.
" " Inquiry concerning the Principles of Morality.
Butler. — Sermons on Human Nature.
Abercrombie (J.). — Philosophy of the Moral Feelings.
Hampden (R.). — Lectures on Moral Philosophy.
M'Cosh. — Divine Government.
Shaftesbury. — Inquiry Concerning Virtue.
Warburton. — Divine Legation.
Clark, Samuel. — Evidence of Natural and Revealed Religion.
Hobbes. — Leviathan.
Bentham. — Principles of Morals and Legislation.
" Deontology.
Taylor, Jeremy. — Rule of Conscience.
More, Henry. — Euchiridion Ethicum.

AMERICAN AUTHORS.

Wayland. — Elements of Moral Science.
Hickok. — System of Moral Science.
Winslow. — Elements of Moral Philosophy.
Alexander. — Moral Philosophy.
Bowen (Fr.). — Metaphysics and Ethics.
Mahan. — Moral Philosophy.
Edwards (President). — The Nature of True Virtue.

GREEK AUTHORS.

Plato. — Opera (Ed. Stallbaum), especially Crito, Phædo, Republic, and Gorgias ; Œuvres, Traduites par Cousin ; also, English editions by Cary and by Taylor.

Aristotle. — Ethicorum and Nicomachum libri. Ethics and Politics, translated by Gillies. Also, Ethics, translated by Browne, and do. by Taylor.

LATIN AUTHORS.

Cicero. — De Officiis.
" Tusculanæ Disputationes.
" De Legibus.

FRENCH AUTHORS.

Cousin. — Œuvres complètes.
" Fragmens Philosophiques.
" Psychology (Tr. Henry).
" The True, the Beautiful, and the Good.
Damiron. — Cours de Philosophie — Morale.
Descartes. — Œuvres Complètes (Cousin), especially,
" Meditations — Discours de la Mèthode.
Jouffroy. — Noveaux Melanges Philosophiques.
" Introduction to Ethics (Tr. Channing).
Malebranche. — Rechèrche de la Vérité.
" Traité de Morale.
Amédée Jacques. — Man. de Phil. a l'usage des coll.
Dictionnaire des Sciences Philosophiques — art. Morale.

GERMAN AUTHORS.

Kant. — Werke (Herausg. von Rosenkrantz).
" Critik der Urtheilskraft.
" Metaphysik der sitten; also,
" Metaphysics of Ethics (transl. Semple).
" Rechtslehre.
Jacobi. — Werke.
Rosenkrantz. — Psychologie, oder die Wissench. von subj. Geist.
Hegel. — Werke, vollständige Ausgabe.
" Encyclopädie der Wissenchaften.
Schelling. — Philosophische Schriften.
Leibnitz. — Werke.
" Noveaux Essais.

On Civil Government, and Duties to the State, the following works may be consulted:

Plato. — Republic and Laws. Crito.
Aristotle. — Politics.
Cicero. — De Repub.
Montesquieu. — Spirit of Laws.
Burlamaqui. — Principles of Natural and Political Law
Puffendorf. — Law of Nature and Nations.
Gognet. — Origin of Laws.
Blackstone. — Commentaries, Book I.
Locke. — Civil Government.
Wines. — Commentary on Hebrew Laws — Introductory Essay.
Constitution of the United States, and of the several States.

On the History of Ethical Opinions, the following are the principal authorities:

Cousin. — Lectures on History of Philosophy.
Ritter. — History of Ancient Philosophy.
Schwegler. — (Seelye Translat.) History of Philosophy.
Tennemann. — (Johnson Trans.) Manual of History of Philosophy.
Mackintosh, Sir J. — Ethical Philosophy.
Stewart, Dugald. — Dissertations on History of Philosophy.
Whewell. — History of Moral Philosophy in England.
Morell. — History of Philosophy.

www.ingramcontent.com/pod-product-compliance
Lightning Source LLC
LaVergne TN
LVHW010147110826
845151LV00002B/451